MIRACLE
ON THE HUDSON

BALLANTINE BOOKS / NEW YORK

MIRACLE
ON THE HUDSON

**The Survivors of
Flight 1549 Tell Their
Extraordinary Stories
of Courage, Faith,
and Determination**

with
WILLIAM PROCHNAU
and
LAURA PARKER

Published in the United States by Ballantine Books, an imprint of
The Random House Publishing Group, a division of Random House, Inc.,
New York.

BALLANTINE and colophon are registered trademarks of Random House, Inc.

Library of Congress Cataloging-in-Publication Data

Prochnau, William W.
Miracle on the Hudson : the survivors of flight 1549 tell their extraordinary stories
of courage, faith, and determination / with Bill Prochnau and Laura Parker.
          p.   cm.
Includes bibliographical references.
ISBN 978-0-345-51994-8 (hardcover : alk. paper)
1. Airplanes—Ditching—Hudson River (N.Y. and N.J.)   2. US Airways
Flight 1549 Crash landing, 2009.   3. Aircraft accidents—New York
(State)—New York.   4. Aircraft bird strikes—New York (State)—
New York.   I. Parker, Laura.   II. Title.
TL711.D5P76 2009
363.12'4097471—dc22
2009035947

Printed in the United States of America on acid-free paper

www.ballantinebooks.com

2 4 6 8 9 7 5 3 1

First Edition

Book design by Susan Turner

Dedicated to our families for their love and ongoing support.
We love you.
—Passengers of Flight 1549

You don't choose your family.
They are God's gift to you, as you are to them.
—DESMOND TUTU

———

To Monica, Anna, and Jenny;
and to Bruce and Shirley
—William Prochnau and Laura Parker

Contents

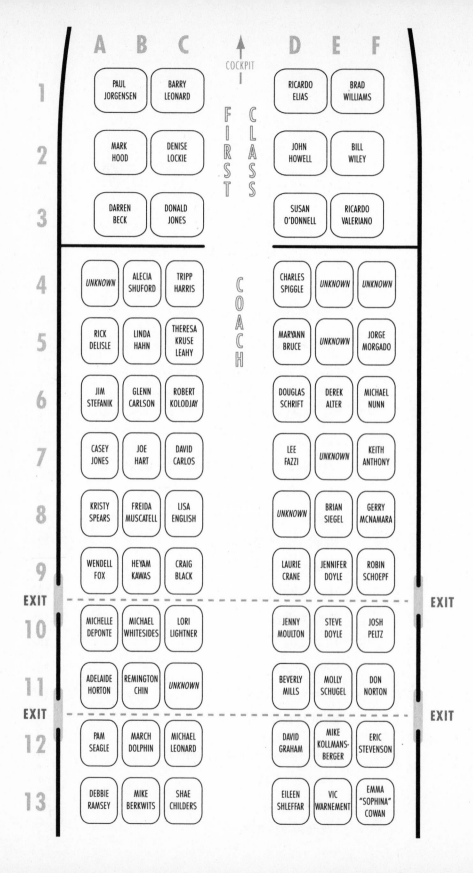

	A	B	C		D	E	F
14	JAY MCDONALD	MARY BERKWITS	AMY JOLLY		STEPHEN LIS	STEPHANIE KING	ANDREW GRAY
15	DAVE SANDERSON	CHRIS COBB	STEVE O'BRIEN		CLAY PRESLEY	DAN VINTON	LARRY SNODGRASS
16	FRED BERRETTA	CARL BAZARIAN	VINCE SPERA		STEWART WALLACE	WARREN HOLLAND	ALBERTO PANERO
17	ALEX MAGNESS	NICK GAMACHE	SUSAN WITTMANN		LAURA ZYCH	DIANE HIGGINS	LUCILLE PALMER
18	SHERI NEJMAN	BILL ELKIN	JERRY SHANKO		CHRIS ROONEY	KARIN HILL	DICK RICHARDSON
19	*UNKNOWN*	*UNKNOWN*	SCOTT SHARKEY		HIROKI TAKIGAWA	TESS SOSA, holding DAMIAN	JIM WHITAKER
20	BEN BOSTIC	BRENT CIMINO	BETH MCHUGH		ALYSON BELL	BALAJI GANESAN	AMBER WELLS
21	*UNKNOWN*	*UNKNOWN*	BRAD WENTZELL		*UNKNOWN*	BEVERLY WATERS	JAMES CLARK
22	JEFF KOLODJAY	CHRIS RINI	JOSEPH HALL		CLAUDETTE MASON	NICO ILIEV	*UNKNOWN*
23	SOFIA SOSA	MARTIN SOSA	KEITH ANTON		LUTHER LOCKHART	BILL ZUHOWSKI	DAVID SONTAG
24	MATT KANE	FRANK SCUDERE	JIM HANKS, JR.		MICHELE DAVIS	REENEE WILLIAMS	RAYMOND MANDRELL
25	BILLY CAMPBELL	BILL NIX	KANAU DEGUCHI		IAN WELLS	ANDREW JAMISON	LAUREL HUBBARD
26	IRINA LEVSHINA	TRACEY ALLEN-WOLSKO	VICKI BARNHARDT		VALLIE COLLINS	*EMPTY*	BRIAN MOSS

A B C COACH D E F

REAR GALLEY ↓

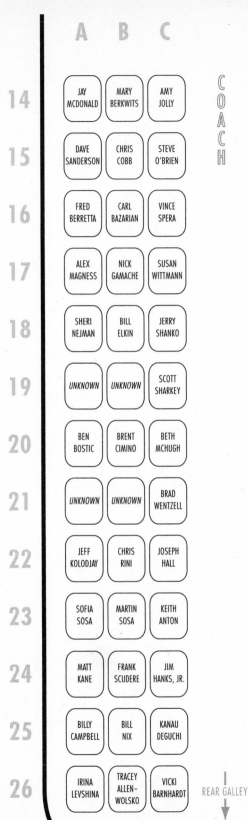

Seventy-five Tons over the Bronx

THE FIRST 9-1-1 CALL CAME AT 3:29 P.M. A RATTLED VOICE, CHAFED BY A
strong Bronx rasp, overwhelmed the operator with a burst of words:

"Yeah, I'm witnessing an airplane that is going down. . . . It's on
fire. . . ."

"Where are you, sir?"

". . . Oh my God . . ."

"Where are you? . . ."

". . . I don't know where he's going to fall. It's gone now. Oh my
God . . ."

"Where are you? . . ."

"In the Bronx. Oh my God. I heard a big boom and he came
straight over us. Oh my God . . . Wow."

The unidentified man, standing at an obscure tenement street corner, caught only the briefest glimpse of the aircraft before it disappeared behind the buildings, but he got a good look: "It looked like an Airbus plane, a big plane. . . . Oh my God . . . Wow . . ."

Eight blocks away, at Middle School 45, vice principal Joy Smith-Jones heard the same explosion and looked up to see the seventy-five-ton aircraft passing above the nearby Bronx Zoo and still heading north.

Moments later, a New Yorker near the George Washington Bridge saw a plane now heading south and "flying really, really low." His first thought was "not again." Michael Sklar, commuting to his home in Fort Lee, New Jersey, just across the river, thought he was hallucinating when he "saw a jet so low over the bridge." He "waited in dread to hear a boom and see a fireball" after the plane disappeared out of his sight.

Twenty-five miles away in Westbury, Long Island, at the control center that handles New York's major airports, flight-controller Patrick Harten had cleared the runways for an emergency landing of the troubled craft at either LaGuardia Airport or the smaller Teterboro Airport, a few miles west into New Jersey. Then came the last communication from the cockpit: "We can't do it. We're gonna be in the Hudson." Harten, a ten-year veteran, was sure he had heard a death sentence. The controller quickly lost radio and radar contact with the plane as it disappeared below the tops of Manhattan's skyscrapers and one thought riveted into his mind: He would be "the last person to talk to anyone on that plane."

In this day and age, the first sign that an airliner might be descending toward any major American city—but New York City, of all places—flashes instantly through secret government channels around the country, alerting authorities to activate a range of contingency plans. On this January day, word moved immediately to the

Transportation Security Administration's fifth-floor security center in Northern Virginia, where officials were going over plans to prevent air or rocket attacks on President-Elect Obama's inauguration, just five days away. It sped simultaneously to the FBI, the Homeland Security Department, a dozen other agencies, and cross-country to the North American Aerospace Defense Command headquarters in Colorado Springs. The thirty people in the duty room fell dead silent, listening intently to the loudspeaker updates about the plane's behavior. Early reports said that a light plane was in trouble; then, that birds had struck one engine, then both, of a commercial carrier shortly after takeoff from LaGuardia.

Briefly, according to the *New York Times,* officials considered one of those post-9/11 contingency plans—the launch of supersonic fighter-interceptors to shoot down the plane, though that thought was quickly discarded: With the plane already well below the profile of New York's choicest skyscraper targets, it was far too late.

More important, and far more quickly than the government could have reacted, it became preeminently clear that the pilot was maneuvering for an attempted water landing in the Hudson River. The mere attempt at a water landing could save hundreds or more lives on the ground of the most densely populated island in the world. It would also give the 155 terrified occupants of the fatally crippled aircraft—now descending at more than three times the normal sink rate—a dice roll's chance of coming out alive.

In the next ten seconds the shimmering white US Airways Airbus A320, Flight 1549, bound until minutes earlier from New York's LaGuardia Airport to Charlotte, North Carolina—now an unlikely glider—continued toward its lumbering collision with the Hudson. Thousands of New Yorkers watched from their high skyscraper windows in Manhattan and riverside condos in New Jersey. Within moments television mesmerized millions around the nation, then billions around the world, as what seemed certain to be a most awful catastrophe in a string of calamities become a different story altogether—one with a sorely needed happy ending.

Few remembered the most deadly crash in one of the rivers that encircled their island. Almost fifty years to the day, in February 1959, an American Airlines Lockheed Electra prop jet (an airplane built in the transitional era between propeller flights and commercial jets) plowed into the East River while trying to land at LaGuardia. Of the seventy-three people aboard, sixty-five were killed. Given the national mind-set in January 2009, if people had known of that disaster, few would have imagined the possibility of a less catastrophic outcome.

The America of mid-January 2009 was not a happy place. In the previous several months, one disaster after another had battered folks around the country until many were downright scared. Jobs were shed, pensions and savings gone. The bottom had fallen out of housing prices, taking with it the security blankets of most Americans' largest "savings accounts." The stock market had lost almost half its value. The bulwark of the traditional American way of life—that solid, sturdy, conservative bank on Main Street—had gone to Las Vegas with the people's money and lost big. The country was still fighting two wars. For most Americans, the national mood was as bleak as it had ever been at any time in their lives.

If ever the country—and the world—was ready for a feel-good story, it was ready on January 15.

Then Flight 1549 hydroplaned into the icy gray river somewhere around Fiftieth Street, a few blocks beyond the southern end of Manhattan's Central Park, disappeared briefly in its own spray, and magically bobbed back into view seemingly intact. The river quickly ate up the speed of the aircraft's 150-mile-an-hour crash landing, ripped off its left engine, and gracefully turned it almost 45 degrees, pointing its nose at midtown Manhattan. Poetically, the plane seemed to be taking a slight bow to its stunned audience—the city that makes legends, New York.

The first words and pictures went out within minutes by way of the new technological and sociological phenomenon, Twitter. But the plane also was positioned in such a way so that the first passenger out the door and onto the wing could have waved to the old-line media giants of the world—the newspapers and the television networks—already bustling into gear for the story they yearned for as much as the public.

One of the people inside the plane, a man who seconds earlier was absolutely certain he would soon be dead, described the pure perfection of that moment: "This happened within sight of where nine-eleven occurred," William Wiley, a computer specialist from Johnson City, Tennessee, said. "And it was such a message of hope."

A previously unknown fifty-seven-year-old pilot, Chesley B. Sullenberger, became an overnight hero for so deftly putting a Hollywood ending on one of the shortest but most remarkable flights in aviation history. Rescue teams from both sides of the river, the nobles of the 9/11 tragedy, quickly began plucking the passengers of Flight 1549 out of the icy water.

As televisions all over the world flickered to the compelling scene, unseen dramas still played out.

With the first passengers emerging—jumping into the water, clambering onto the wings and into rafts—a sixty-five-year-old Baltimore lawyer stood in the far rear of the plane in icy water up to the top of his necktie. Stunned that he had survived the crash, he now felt certain he would drown as the aircraft sank tail first.

His was just one of the 155 stories this remarkable day.

MIRACLE
ON THE HUDSON

1

Come Fly with Me

NEW YORK AWOKE THAT THURSDAY MORNING IN JANUARY TO A STORY-book scene—Manhattan in a snowstorm; the flakes whipping almost sideways through the skyscraper canyons and a bright coat of white blotting out all of mankind's gray. Storybook, that is, if you were hunkered down and had no intention of flying.

Arctic air had also brought in the winter's coldest day, with early-morning temperatures in the low teens and single-digit wind chills. Ice formed around the edges of the Hudson and floes halted ferry traffic in the northern suburbs upstream.

Along the Avenue of the Americas, Tripp Harris bent into the wind as he bucked his way to get his morning coffee at Starbucks. The one-block walk seemed like a mile. A technological adviser to

banks, he had flown up the night before from Charlotte, North Carolina—"Wall Street South," as his hometown, a burgeoning banking
center, had become known. For the past four months, the banking
calamity had helped keep US Airways, which had a financial calamity
of its own, flying almost at full capacity on its premier north-south
runs.

Harris, one of the modern "road warriors" who racked up miles
with back-to-back business flights, had scheduled a single morning
meeting at Citibank. He would make the turnaround in twenty-four
hours, less if he was lucky. Knowing the kind of mess the snow would
make of LaGuardia, New York's ancient but conveniently located airport, Harris had booked the five o'clock on US Air. With a little luck
and the hole card of his frequent-flier status, he'd push for an earlier
one—Flight 1549, a two-hour, home-for-dinner flight to Douglas
International.

Not far away, a few blocks east of the Waldorf, in a window seat
at the Café Basil on Third Avenue, Beverly Waters, another Southerner, born and raised just south of Charlotte, drank in the scene
with pure joy. She *loved* the snow, "the flakes were big and
Christmas-y," and she thrived on watching the sidewalk drama, too.
With their long, rapid strides, the native New Yorkers moved through
the storm as if it didn't exist, and nothing else did, either. Beverly had
had a successful business trip but she was ready for home and her
family. She was a nervous flier, but she hadn't joined the Xanax set
yet. Her boarding pass—seat 21E, Flight 1549—sat snugly in her
purse.

All around the metropolitan area that morning, others were making the choices that would place them on the flight of the decade.

In the historic little town of Goshen, New York, an hour and a
half north of the city, the woman who would be Flight 1549's most
senior citizen, eighty-five-year-old Lucille Palmer, took a midmorn-

ing call from her son: "Why are you going down there today? The weather is terrible," he had said. Her great-grandson was down there and it was his first birthday, that's why. And though she couldn't get around very well without her walker, she'd have her daughter, Diane Higgins, with her. In any case, a little thing like turbulence at thirty thousand feet didn't bother her a whit. Neither did snow. She was Brooklyn born, and Brooklyn tough.

Bill Zuhowski left Mattituck, Long Island, just before 7:00 a.m. with six inches of snow on the ground, no match for his '03 Chevy Silverado. His flying plans didn't include Charlotte, though. He was headed for an 11:30 Spirit Airways flight to Myrtle Beach, where he planned to celebrate a buddy's birthday. Zuhowski didn't fly much, sticking close to his job at a Long Island swimming-pool company. But he intended to drive the sixty-five miles down the Long Island Expressway to the Manhasset Station, ride the train the last fifteen miles to LaGuardia, and be wearing his shorts in Myrtle Beach by mid-afternoon. Best-laid plans . . .

The snow turned the LIE into a mire of fender benders. By the time Zuhowski parked the Silverado, his train had left. Grabbing a cab, he made it halfway to the airport before he discovered that his ticket was still in the truck. When he finally showed up, his flight had not left; it had been canceled. But the snow had let up and his dreams of a warm weekend in Myrtle Beach remained alive when his pal promised to pick him up in Charlotte. Zuhowski booked a rear seat on US Airways Flight 1549, which still showed on the reader boards as a 2:45 p.m. departure, although not many LaGuardia veterans thought that meant much.

LaGuardia is an urban airport, *not* one of the modern exurban jetports with long, multiple runways and a lot of give and take. It has two stubby crisscross runways, seven thousand feet each, with three of the endings over water. Despite its limitations, LaGuardia remains a favorite for New Yorkers and visitors alike. The airport was born in good New York fashion, and that is why, with luck, you can take a cab to midtown Manhattan and get there in twenty minutes. Back in the 1930s, the city's legendary mayor, Fiorello LaGuardia, flew home one day with a ticket marked: Destination New York. The plane, as usual, put down in New Jersey. Enough is enough, stormed the mayor of the greatest city in the world, and by 1939, New York had not only its World's Fair but its own modern airport, then considered the greatest advancement in aviation design and eventually named in honor of the hell-raising mayor.

Seventy years later LaGuardia has become the most congested airport in the country, a takeoff or landing occurring every forty-seven seconds. It also has the most flight delays. Add a snowstorm and not only do New York skies close down but most of the Northeast corridor goes with it. The delays on the morning of January 15, 2009, averaged two hours and fifty-eight minutes until the sun broke through around noon. Then flights began to open up, though they were still running late. Early birds and latecomers leapt at the chance for a spot on US Airways Flight 1549, the beleaguered, twice-bankrupt airline's mid-afternoon mainstay to one of its hub cities, Charlotte.

The group joining Harris and Waters and Palmer and Zuhowski at LaGuardia was as great a cross section of modern America as New York could produce. It was also a group of people weighed down by all the woes of a world teetering on the edge of economic collapse. Twenty passengers were from the Charlotte-based Bank of America, just a small contingent of the company's weekly commuters to New York, there to work on the government-driven merger with failing Merrill Lynch, which had gone through four months to the day earlier. "The merger from hell," they called it in Charlotte, forcing a square peg into a round hole.

Some, out of date and out of tune, thought of a flight from New

York to Charlotte as Babylon to the Bible Belt. In 2009, you couldn't get much further from reality. Charlotte had long since become the second largest financial center in the country. Its skyscrapers didn't stretch as high as those in New York, but sixty stories can scrape some blue and, in good times, a little green. At the start of the financial crisis, the city's banks counted their assets in the trillions, not billions, although some of the zeroes had started peeling off, along with the hopes and futures of many of the people flying that day. More than one of the bankers on board was carrying his résumé—out of self-defense. The layoffs in Charlotte had been extensive. House prices were plunging, pensions disappearing, worries soaring higher than bank stocks had ever gone. On January 15, BoA shares dropped to a midday low of $7.35, heading to half that price a month later and down from their onetime high of near $55.

The circumstances at Charlotte's other major bank, Wachovia, which had just been bought out of certain bankruptcy by Wells Fargo, were even more tenuous for the flying merger transition teams. Three Wachovia executives were returning on the flight after another round of trying to mesh the inner wheels of their bank with the mysterious turns of Wells Fargo's.

Charles Spiggle, an executive in leveraged buyouts and acquisitions, was heading home. Spiggle was a top dog at Wachovia. But, like millions of Americans at that time, he and his wife had already had their family meeting, cut their discretionary spending, and tried to imagine what their alternatives might be.

"Yes, we were worried," Spiggle said. "Not petrified. But we didn't know then what was coming. We had had eighteen months of a credit-market meltdown."

But the people coming together at LaGuardia were a cross section in many other ways, too.

A who's who of Flight 1549 ranged all over the map:

A gangsta rap, hip-hop music producer from Miami, Raymond Mandrell

A Jordanian Arabic-language specialist from the United Nations, Heyam Kawas

Salespeople of everything from patio doors to newly organized financial plans to intricately sophisticated software

Department-store buyers picking over a shattered New York apparel market after a disastrous Christmas season

One of the country's leading professional drag racers, Chris Rini

A dreaming young singer from Australia, Emma Cowan

Young lovers, one a veteran of twenty-seven months in Afghanistan

A Charlotte bride-to-be thirty days away from her wedding

Two copilots from other airlines deadheading to their own next stations, Derek Alter of Colgan Air and Susan O'Donnell of American Airlines

Several students, including a med student researching hospital jobs in the big town, Alberto Panero

A NASCAR executive, Amber Wells

A television executive whose network had filmed the story of September 11's United Flight 93, the hijacked airliner brought down in a fiery nosedive by passengers who fought back, Billy Campbell

Two New York–based Japanese traders, Hiroki Takigawa and Kanau Deguchi

A computer specialist born in India's Silicon Valley, Balaji Ganesan

Add in three small children—one a nine-month-old lap passenger— a personal trainer, a Feldenkrais practitioner, a nurse, a teacher, a cartographer, a waitress, lawyers, students, retirees

The passengers of Flight 1549 would be anybody and everybody.

• • •

THREE HAD SAT in on the taping of the David Letterman show the previous night, when the sardonic late-night comedian made two airplane-crash jokes before turning serious to reveal that the day marked the ninth anniversary of the quintuple-bypass surgery that gave him what he called the "gift of life." In granting him the miracle of the extra years, he said, the gift also gave the world his five-year-old son, Harry. None of the three passengers would remember the airplane jokes. They would remember the "gift of life."

No group in the crowded US Airways terminal bounced around more happily than six golfing buddies, including a father and son. They all hailed from the little New England crossroads town of Chicopee, Massachusetts. Heading for a long-awaited vacation in Myrtle Beach, the same Spirit Airways cancellation that sent Bill Zuhowski to US Air brought them over, too. They wrestled a bargain price out of the airline by using Flight 1549 to Charlotte as a connection. To celebrate, they headed for the bar. There, over the first drinks of the vacation, they worked out teams and settled the courses they would play, all the things weekend golfers do. Before leaving, Jeff Kolodjay, the de facto leader and son in the father-son team, phoned his wife and told her he had just finished the best ten-dollar beer he'd ever had.

Another group that drew attention in the crowded waiting room was a gang that came to be known later as the "Belk Six." Named after the "Oceanic Six" who went down in a plane crash in ABC's hit series *Lost,* the five women and one man were buyers scouting out junior miss clothes for Charlotte's Belk Department Store, a home-owned enterprise that had grown to include three hundred stores throughout the South. The women were dressed as if they were about to enter a stretch limo for a Manhattan party instead of the coach section of an Airbus to North Carolina. The group would stand out anywhere. They worked a-mile-a-minute, high-pressure Manhattan-style jobs, cracked wise and sharp-tongued as they went.

One of their managers, thirty-five-year-old Lori Lightner, statuesque at six foot one, stood with her long black hair coming down over a full-length black down coat and fashionable black boots. The only Belk man, thirty-seven-year-old Michael Leonard, seemed a little pudgy for the group—five foot ten and about two hundred pounds—but he stood out in one other distinct way. "I am about as politically incorrect as you can get," Leonard said. "I think I am the only straight-male buyer in junior misses in the entire country. That must mean I'm good."

Laura Zych, a comely five-foot-ten new arrival to the group from Fargo, North Dakota, did not look like anyone from the Fargo we know and love. Just before boarding, she sat alone eating lunch at a table next to the golfers. When they got up to leave, one of them stopped at her table and wondered if he could ask her a question.

"Of course," she replied.

"We have a bet at our table," Rob Kolodjay, Jeff's father, explained. "Are you a model?"

Zych smiled, even blushed a little, and then said, "Thanks, but I'm not. I work in the apparel/fashion industry." Flattered, she giggled to herself all the way back to Gate 21, where boarding was beginning almost forty-five minutes late—not bad for a snowy day at LaGuardia.

Brian Moss, a thirty-five-year-old business analyst for Bank of America, remembered he had to call his ex-wife about their daughter. With all the merger travel, they had made a deal that he would try to get home in time to pick up their six-year-old from after-school care. He called to tell her that the snow had cleared and flights were taking off, adding one of those lines you wish you'd never said: "If you don't hear from me by five o'clock, that means the plane went down."

Moss shrugged about it later. So it goes. "I thought it was pretty witty at the time," he said.

At the entrance to the jetway, US Airways made the usual last call for a handful of standby seats yielded by no-shows. Brian Siegel, a BoA executive who runs their golf sponsorships, arrived too late to join the standby list. No chance. But as he was making a phone call nearby, he heard names being called for the last seat. "Mary Jones, please step to the ticket counter." No one showed. "William Smith. . . ." No one showed.

Finally, Siegel walked over and interceded in the reading of the names.

"Sounds like you've got a seat," he said.

"Aren't you lucky?" the ticket agent replied. "One left."

Siegel could feel the heat of glaring eyes near him. But no one embarrassed him out of it.

"I really hate to say it because it sounds like such a cliché," Siegel said later. "I travel so much, but there's always that thing about the last seat. There's always the thought. . . . But I decided long ago I wouldn't play that game. If I don't take it, something will happen on the next flight."

Meanwhile, a day that had started bad was turning worse for Martin Sosa, a Greenwich Village architect, and his wife, Tess, who were headed to Charlotte because of a family emergency. They had just suffered the indignity of security officials insisting on checking their nine-month-old infant's baby food, jar by jar. Sosa couldn't believe it. "Do you want to go into a private room for the inspection?" the inspectors had asked. *Private room?* thought Sosa, thoroughly annoyed. *It's just baby food!*

Sosa's muttering did not speed up the process. Fifteen minutes later the family moved on with growing anxiety.

The delay made them—father, mother, nine-month-old Damian, and four-year-old Sofia—still later for a flight on which they weren't even seated together. With luck they would find passengers who would switch with them once they boarded.

On the tarmac outside Gate 21 stood the Airbus, tail number

N106US, gleaming in the winter sun with its classic US Airways colors—snow white with a touch-up of red and blue. The plane had been flying for ten years and was about to make its 16,300th takeoff.

The European A320 was a handsome and symbolic airliner, built by a consortium of nations that effectively ended America's and Boeing's domination of the worldwide commercial aircraft industry.

As the passengers entered the cabin, turned right and headed toward their seats, most had no sense of a tattered airline or a tattered airline industry, although both were true. The coach passengers jockeyed their way down a single aisle of cleanly upholstered deep-blue leatherette seats, three on each side. In first class, the seats—heavily sought after by the road warriors—were arranged two on each side for a total of twelve seats in three rows. The Airbus was a flying cigar canister, no place for a claustrophobe, but it did its job well and looked pleasant enough.

In the aisle, Martin and Tess Sosa worked the crowd hard for a seat switch but were only partly successful. Bill Zuhowski, the young man who made the long drive from Mattituck in his Silverado eight hours earlier, yielded his seat to the father so he could be next to Sofia. But Tess Sosa couldn't get anybody to budge. Later, other passengers said they had never seen so many heavily traveled men bury their faces in their newspapers as she approached. Her anxiety rose and both she and Martin implored the flight attendants to do something.

"I can't order passengers to change their seats," flight attendant Doreen Welsh said evenly.

Even so, tempers flared briefly.

Michael Leonard remembered watching the scene unfold and telling Lori Lightner just before he buckled in two rows behind her: "Whenever I fly with my two girls, I can be a real jerk with the airline people."

"You can be a real jerk any time," Lightner replied, cracking wise in the Belk Six way.

Then all were buckled in and the passengers could feel the tug of the pushback from the gate. Suddenly, Tess Sosa unbuckled and started into the aisle, as if she wanted one more chance. This time Welsh spoke sternly: "Sit back down."

The plane began the slow maneuver toward the runway.

The happiest members in the Sosa family were the children. Damian began nursing. Sofia pulled at her father's arm.

"Are we flying yet, Daddy?" she asked. "Are we flying yet?"

"Not yet," her father said. "Not yet, Sofia."

Flight 1549 moved into eleventh place in line for takeoff.

2

"One Thousand One, One Thousand Two, One Thousand Three"

MINUTES LATER, FLIGHT 1549 NEARED THE TURN ONTO RUNWAY 4-22, Air Traffic Control allowed one last Northwest Airways jet to squeeze in front, and then Chesley Sullenberger, with his co-pilot, Jeffrey Skiles at the controls, finally had his aircraft on the runway and rolling. The time was 3:25 p.m. and thirty-three seconds. The pilot radioed a terse "Good day" to Air Traffic Control and then, seven seconds later, "Cactus fifteen forty-nine, seven hundred feet climbing to five thousand."

Passengers sitting on the left side of the plane had two quick passing views. None recognized the first, and few the other. The first was the amorphous patch of the East River where the Lockheed Electra had gone in disastrously fifty years earlier. The second was Rikers

Island, the largest penal colony in the world and holder of fourteen thousand New York City prisoners. Rikers was also home to several thousand Canada geese who had adapted to civilization better than their neighbors—so well that these birds had altered their intrinsic nature. They no longer migrated but found life on Rikers plentiful and easy enough to stay year-round. Some had grown as heavy as twelve pounds. It was nice to be a homebody. Their migrating cousins could grow to that weight, too, and with their powerful six-foot wingspans fly more than a thousand miles a day.

According to a Gallup poll, one in five Americans has a fear of flying, and almost half are at least somewhat uncomfortable with it despite the irrefutable evidence that it is about one hundred times safer than driving a car. With Charlotte a little under two hours away, those who were and those who weren't nervous settled into their differing routines.

Just behind Tess Sosa, in the window seat 20F, Amber Wells had never thought of herself as one of the twenty percent who were afraid. Intimately involved with the opening of the NASCAR Hall of Fame in 2010, she flew often; "nervous flier" didn't fit the NASCAR image. A deeply religious, thirty-four-year-old, five foot six blonde—and a Southerner in every way—she had long ago set a routine for all her airplane flights: She always picked up a quick-read gossip magazine to lull her into catch-up sleep. But first she had one other resolute flying habit. Having heard that the first two minutes are the most dangerous moments, she began each trip by silently counting off the time and she did it again now:

One thousand one, one thousand two, one thousand three. . . .

One row ahead, sitting in the aisle next to Tess Sosa, Hiroki Takigawa, a Japanese trader based in New York, was a step ahead of Amber. He is one of those fliers—"I love flying," he says—so comfortable, he nods off immediately. He attributes this tendency to the

motion, the droning of the engines, the escape from the endless de-
mands of the office, and mostly, to the slight drop in his blood pressure as the plane begins to pressurize.

Farther up front, Joe Hart was fuming, rather than sleeping. A
self-described "sarcastic salesman" with a temper that flared and de-
flated almost as quickly, Hart was going through one of his furious
moments. He traveled so much that, even after the debacle just
ahead, he would fly thirty-six flight segments with US Airways in the
next three months alone. He had Chairman's Preferred status in US
Airways's mileage club and free miles stacked as high as an A320.
That, Hart thought, should have given him an upgrade to first class.
Instead, he was stuck in economy—in a middle seat, at that!—and
found himself staring straight ahead from 7B, past the bulkhead, into
first class, where a uniformed American Airlines first officer, Susan
O'Donnell, was deadheading in "Hart's" first-class seat, 3D. *God-
damn! All the money I spend on this bozo airline and a non-revenue
has my seat?! I'm gonna write a letter!* Then he took a deep breath,
said *Screw it* to himself, and looked past the shoulders of his seatmate, Casey Jones of Bank of America, out the window into the pale
winter-blue sky. *What a great day for flying,* he thought. Hart had a
short string but he also loved to be in the clouds.

In the first-class cabin Denise Lockie sat in 2C next to Mark
Hood, a tall and personable ex-Marine who had fought in Desert
Storm. Both executives for high-powered companies, their jobs
made both of them workhorse fliers who logged more than 100,000
miles a year. Lockie had sat down chattering excitedly about the
events coming up in Washington—five days till Barack Obama's inauguration! But Hood had failed to share her enthusiasm. "What's
he ever accomplished?" he had countered. *Whoops,* Lockie told
herself, *politics and religion. . . .* She changed the subject and the
two row mates began a friendly conversation. They had even bet

on how long the takeoff would be delayed. Hood won with thirty minutes.

Back in coach Martin Sosa, still upset and never at ease in airplanes—"Man was not meant to fly," he'd say—had fought to wedge his six foot one, 250-pound frame into the tiny middle seat 23B. Sitting space shrinks to near misery level in the back of planes that are owned by thread-poor airlines, few more so than the fleet of US Airways, which advertised itself as an "à la carte" company that charged for coffee and Cokes and had announced plans to begin charging for blankets and pillows packaged in a seven-dollar "Power-Nap Sack." A free soda and a pillow wouldn't have comforted Sosa, anyway. But his daughter, in the window seat beside him, bubbled with a child's untainted joy at the roaring climb into the sky. Sosa put on all the cover a father could manage. "Now we're flying, Sofia," he said and hugged her. "We're up in the air." Then he glanced forward toward Tess and Damian. Maybe when the plane leveled out, someone besides the young man would understand.

Wells counted on.

. . . . one thousand twenty-seven, one thousand twenty-eight, one thousand twenty-nine. . . .

Commercial flying is not a social event, unless you are the golfers or the Belk Six or the handful of couples on the plane. Some of the Charlotte-bound passengers knew one another but were scattered throughout the cabin, and even many of the squadron of Bank of America merger workers were strangers to one another. The road warriors, buried in their laptops, can fly a million miles without remembering a single fellow passenger's face. More laid-back travelers stuff wires in their ears and zone out with music. Normally, the passengers on a flight like 1549 would walk into Douglas International about 5:30 in the afternoon and never think of their fellow fliers again.

There are a couple of places on an aircraft where this isn't true. One is the cabin's dreaded last row—number twenty-six on that Airbus A320. When the computers dump you in the sardine row, it can seem like the curse of Icarus as you are trapped between the bulkhead in back of you and the seat backs of row twenty-five that invariably land in your lap.

Vallie Collins, a cheerful twice-a-month business flier from Knoxville, didn't really deserve 26D. But the computer spat it out as the last aisle seat on the plane. She had front-of-the-cabin elite status for all her miles on her regular airlines, Delta and Northwest. But her favorites wanted $800 more for a ticket than did "à la carte" US Air. *Hey, we're in a recession,* she thought, and settled for the back of the bus.

When Collins had reached the back row of the rapidly filling aircraft, she glanced past the empty middle seat to the man at the window, Brian Moss of Bank of America. In the way of all airline passengers in these pack-the-plane days, they rolled their eyes at the unlikelihood that their happy situation of a missing third traveler would hold. But when the doors closed and Flight 1549 began its pushback, the middle seat remained empty. Collins grinned from ear to ear. "This must be our lucky day." She noticed Moss was reading a gliding book. "Are you into gliding?" she asked. "My husband went gliding just a few months ago."

"Nope," Moss said. "Never been. Hang gliding is my hobby."

They chatted briefly. Then they were back inside themselves, Collins pulling out a *USA Today* and taking a bite out of her Power Bar, not thinking any more about gliding, as fifty thousand pounds of thrust from two roaring turbofan jet engines easily lifted them in a steep climb over Hunts Point and the Bronx, and toward home.

• • •

ACROSS THE AISLE, three women, all in their late thirties and all regular fliers, but of quite different moods about it, had squeezed themselves into seats A, B, and C.

Irina Levshina, a Russian-born cartographer for The Nature Conservancy in New York, had the window seat. She loved the over-the-horizon views, perhaps because she had come over the horizon from her youth. Shortly after arriving in the United States for graduate school thirteen years earlier, she met the man who would become her husband. Now she was flying beyond Charlotte to Las Vegas to meet him after a business conference. But that morning she had almost canceled the trip. She didn't consider herself superstitious but something had told her not to fly that day. She couldn't put her finger on it. The feeling was powerful: Don't go. In the end, she decided she was just being silly. Her husband would be so disappointed. . . .

Next to her, Tracey Allen-Wolsko, also from Bank of America, had wedged herself into 26B, already having prepped herself with "my friend, Mr. Xanax" and made sure her flying medal—St. Patrick on one side, "Protect This Plane" on the other—was stored safely in her purse.

Wolsko is a thoroughly modern, professional woman. But flying terrifies her. Years earlier she had had a hair-raising moment on a small commuter plane that got caught in the wash of a large jet near Atlanta. Her plane pitched to the left and dropped suddenly. The pilot overcompensated, causing the craft to pitch right and farther down before pulling out. Not a word emerged from the cockpit, but after a hard landing in Atlanta, the passengers were met by a troop of concerned airline officials. Younger then, she continued on the second leg to New Orleans after getting herself "dead drunk," as she put it. She tried twice more to fly after that, and then quit her job and took a five-year hiatus from airplanes.

Now Wolsko was trying again. But she made no pretenses that she was any less uncomfortable: Flying still scared the dickens out of her. When she had come aboard Flight 1549, she had turned to Levshina and asked if she minded pulling down the window shade. "I hate to fly," she explained. "I don't like watching takeoffs."

She thought Levshina looked at her strangely. But Levshina shrugged and told herself, *I see New York often enough,* and she would have plenty of time for the views later.

Right about then, Doreen Welsh, the flight attendant, came by and Wolsko flagged her. "Is this your first flight today?. . . How are the skies? . . . Are they bumpy?" Then she added sheepishly, "Just a heads-up. I don't like to fly. I'm a little nervous."

Welsh, a veteran of multiple millions of miles in thirty-nine years as a flight attendant, smiled at one more nervous passenger and said, "Don't worry, flying makes me nervous, too."

Vicki Barnhardt, a traveling mom whose young daughter was eagerly awaiting her return, arrived last to take the aisle seat, 26C. Her business associate, Dick Richardson, now seated ahead of her in 18F, had wanted to stay over because of the snow. But she won, or maybe it was eight-year-old Samantha, back in Charlotte, who won.

Moments later, as the plane continued its climb, Wolsko sat, elbows tight to her sides and eyes closed, silently repeating what she calls her takeoff meditation—an *ommm* that lulls her through repetition, *It will be okay, it will be okay, it will be okay.*

. . . . one thousand forty-three, one thousand forty-four, one thousand forty-five. . . .

Scattered among the rows of deep-blue seats of the Airbus were far more than one jittery passenger, more than one with stranger premonitions than Levshina's, more than one with nightmares that carried into the takeoff, and at least one with a previous flight experience that would have grounded many travelers.

Pam Seagle, a level-headed forty-two-year-old marketer for BoA, virtually had to talk herself into making another air commute to New York. Seagle has had only two air-crash dreams in her life. The first came in 1996, when her subconscious vividly saw a rising commercial jet explode in midair, its red tail plummeting into the sea in flames. The next morning she told her husband, who worked for US Airways at the time. Red tail? That's TWA, and they have a terrific safety record, he said, trying to mollify her. Two nights later, TWA Flight 800 blew up off Long Island, its bright red tail section falling into the sea. It was one of the most spectacular and long-investigated catastrophes in aviation history. The Sunday night before this Thursday in January, Seagle had her second dream—so clear and terrifying that she had to turn around and walk away from the check-in counter for a flight to Atlanta she had set for the next day. Then the bank wanted her to go to New York, so by Tuesday she had steeled herself, and as she gazed out the window on this routine takeoff, she felt as if she had inoculated herself against her nightmare—one safe trip up, one to go.

Tess Sosa had had her dreadful dream in the hospital after little Damian was born, nine and a half months earlier. He was a little older in the dream, and the airplane they were flying in crashed horribly into the sea. Sosa had never been an anxious flier. But the hubbub over the seats, the silliness of the baby food investigation, the crowds, the separation of her family, all combined to make Tess Sosa one nervous flier indeed.

Others had had bad days, too. Alecia Shuford, another BoA commuter, made her usual takeoff call to her husband. It somehow seemed more important this time. She had spent an inexplicably bizarre morning in New York, one she still doesn't understand. She woke up early, filled with unidentifiably ominous feelings, enduring them all day and acting on many. At 6:30 a.m., she began taking cellphone pictures of herself and sending them home, something she had never done before. She took one in the hotel bathroom and framed it in funereal black. "It's the eeriest picture I ever sent to anyone." Her husband told her later that it looked like an obituary and it "creeped him out." She made preflight calls to her two children and told them to listen to their Daddy, that he did a good job while she was away. "It was a really weird day," she recalled later.

The man seated directly over the right engine of Flight 1549, Eric Stevenson, had as much reason as anyone to feel a few twitchy nerves. Twenty-two years earlier, Stevenson had been in a takeoff climb much as now, but over the Pacific Ocean leaving Los Angeles, when the pilot of the Boeing 767 mistakenly turned off the engines. The plane nosed into a harrowing plunge for more than a minute before the pilots were able to relight the engines five hundred feet above the water. Eric was twenty-three at the time and remembers looking into the eyes of the man next to him, thinking *This is the last person I'll ever see.* The returned look had the same terror in it. Now, though, no thought was farther from his mind as Flight 1549 bulled higher over the Bronx.

. . . . *one thousand fifty-seven, one thousand fifty-eight, one thousand fifty-nine.* . . .

By mid-January of 2009, the United States had passed through almost twenty-nine months without a death in a commercial aviation accident, a record run. Still, with thirty thousand commercial take-offs a day, one has to wonder if any of those flights leaves without its share of passengers harboring premonitions and frightening dreams and those Rx standbys of modern flying, Xanax and Ambien, to quell anxiety and lull them to sleep. Even rationally putting aside unlikely outcomes, as Brian Siegel did when he took the last standby ticket, how many people don't *at least* entertain a doubt about coincidence and fate when taking the last seat on a flight they weren't scheduled to be aboard? After all, many of us still walk around ladders, avoid black cats, and routinely ride elevators that pass nonexistent thirteenth floors.

The overwhelming majority of passengers on Flight 1549 were headed to Charlotte with only the concerns of the day on their minds: Will I have a job next month? Where did my retirement plan go? Is my house worth the mortgage I still owe on it? How will I get my children through college?

It was a normal turn-of-the-year planeload; the road warriors heading home for a weekend with the kids, a few visiting ailing relatives, and many looking far past a deeply troubled world to personal concerns and hopeful futures.

Near the back of the plane, Raymond Mandrell, thirty, a hip-hop promoter and recorder from Miami, and Reenee Williams, a twenty-four-year-old publicist from Tallahassee, fought back the revenge of a long night on the town. But they felt pretty good anyway. Despite their day-after discomforts, things had gone well for them. It had been Mandrell's first trip to the big city, and he and Williams had successfully extended contracts for their mutual client, Tallahassee hip-hop artist Mr. Bones. It was a big score for Mandrell's Double Action Entertainment, just as it was for Williams's 360 Music Studio. This had been the first time they had worked together and, in their game, it seemed like a perfect business fit. "He does the streets down South," Williams said. "I know the business end." So they had done the town till almost dawn, getting just one hour of sleep. In the baggage compartment, their luggage overflowed with the music they were taking away from New York's top recording companies. Mr. Bones got what he wanted. So did they. Life was good.

For the six New England golfers, heading for at least eighteen holes and a few libations a day at Myrtle Beach, life looked pretty good, too. It was too bad that they weren't sitting together, but they had been lucky to get this flight at all. In the circumstances, Jeff Kolodjay, a thirty-one-year-old pharmaceutical marketer sitting just in front of Martin Sosa, figured that he had done pretty well by his dad, a retired postal worker, and his four buddies. He had been calling all the airlines for replacement tickets and each had demanded much costlier fares than Spirit's. Finally, he just stood in line at the US Airways counter at LaGuardia, while working the cell phone with other airlines. When he reached the front, Kolodjay had US Airways on the phone and a smiling US Air ticket agent right in front of him. He explained his plight to both. The phone voice, from God knows where, said six seats at a thousand dollars each. The smiling voice behind the counter said six seats at $221 each. "But they won't be together, sir. Will that do?" Kolodjay closed his cell phone and quickly accepted the offer. Now, from seat 22A, he gazed out at the blue sky. Sunshine!

    . . . . one thousand sixty-six . . . one thousand sixty-seven . . . one thousand sixty-eight. . . .

Next to the left-side emergency exit door in seat 10A, which she always tried to get, thirty-year-old Michelle DePonte of Charlotte rasped with bronchitis but was flying higher than the Airbus. She'd been in New York less than twenty-four hours but, wearing the nine-hundred-dollar Christian Louboutin shoes from Barney's, had finished the final fitting for her wedding dress. The dress, not quite ready for the flight, was coming later by Federal Express. The shoes were tucked into her bag in the overhead bin. The wedding, in Maui, was exactly one month away.

A few rows back, twenty-eight-year-old Andrew Gray stared out the right side of the plane as the whitened megalopolis of New York shrank beneath him. It was such a different view from what he'd recently known. Louisiana-born, he had done what he promised he would do—serve his country for twenty-seven months as an officer in the 173rd Airborne Brigade in Afghanistan. In the first year he led a rifle platoon of forty-one men on mounted patrols in the mountainous terrain of Paktika Province bordering Pakistan. As an army officer, he counted as his greatest accomplishment the fact that, while he had made use of medevacs because of the IED-infested roads they patrolled, he had brought all forty-one of his men through the year without, as they say in the army, "loss of life, limb, or eyesight." But the best result of those years was the woman sitting next to him, Stephanie King. They had met on eHarmony, a computer dating service and, to Stephanie, a lawyer from West Bend, Wisconsin, their whole story was still a bit of a wonder.

Andrew was between tours of Afghanistan and stationed in Italy when they began their online relationship. The first real news he had for his newfound friend came as a shocker: He had been transferred back to Afghanistan for a second twelve-month tour that later turned into fifteen months when the army stop-lossed him.

The next months remained technologically based and cautious but increasingly inquisitive. "We never said 'I love you' in an email," Stephanie says. "We never said 'I love you' in a telephone call. We got to know each other." They first met face-to-face after five months, when Andrew came home for two weeks of R&R. They still didn't rush, but they did spend every hour together and, as Stephanie said, they "clicked." The click held for the next year—through the distance and a war—and two months before this flight, Andrew proposed. Now they were headed for Charlotte for a connection to Las Vegas to see Stephanie's mother, who taught there, and to shop for a dress for a summer wedding. Staring out the window at the snow, it occurred to Andrew that they were on the wrong side of the plane to have a final view of Manhattan's skyline. But then, if he turned his head left, he'd be looking at Stephanie and she was the better of the views anyway.

. . . . *One thousand sixty-nine, one thousand seventy, one thousand seventy-one.* . . .

Next to Pam Seagle, March Dolphin, a fifty-seven-year-old Feldenkrais therapist from Brooklyn, finally began to relax after a day of frustration. She and four siblings from around the country were meeting in Las Vegas for the next day's surprise eightieth birthday party for their mother. The snowy morning had meant canceled flights, long lines, and harried people. But now a spot on Flight 1549 had saved the surprise. Dolphin took a deep breath. It would be a long flight, but she would get there for her mom.

. . . . *One thousand seventy-four, one thousand seventy-five.* . . .

In the cockpit, Sullenberger exulted at the change in the weather. "What a beautiful view of the Hudson," he said to his flight officer, Jeffrey Skiles.

. . . . *One thousand eighty-one, one thousand eighty-two.* . . .

In row eighteen, the son of a Hawaiian Airlines pilot and a recent engineering graduate from Colorado, Chris Rooney, twenty-four, had just finished explaining the basic dynamics of flight to his girlfriend, Karin Hill, also twenty-four. The geometrics of the wings and the passage of air over and under them, the manipulative effect of the flaps, the combination of engine thrust, speed, and weight that mesh for takeoff speed, the aviation point known as V_2. . . . The information—the science of it all—calmed her, and they were quiet now as the Airbus nosed above the Bronx Zoo.

. . . . *One thousand eighty-five, one thousand eighty-six.* . . .

Ricardo Valeriano, a thirty-eight-year-old money raiser for solar-energy projects, gazed out the window from his first-class seat, 3F, and was mildly surprised to see what he believed to be a tight formation of military fighter aircraft in the distance at a roughly corresponding altitude.

. . . . *One thousand eighty-seven.* . . .

Bill Wiley, a computer software expert one seat ahead of Valeriano, recalls seeing nothing specific at the time, but now looks back on that moment with vivid recollection. "I remember seeing the sun glitter off windows in the Bronx, and the last thought I had was, *Boy, they've taken all the drama out of commercial flight. Nothing ever happens anymore.*"

. . . . one thousand eighty-eight. . . .

On the other side of the aisle at the window of 2A, Mark Hood and Denise Lockie were chatting when Hood, from the corner of his eye, saw "this gray blob just shoot by."

. . . . One thousand eighty-nine. . . .

Amber Wells's count reached exactly one thousand ninety seconds after takeoff—when just in front of her the right engine blew and the big aircraft shuddered. Wells remembers her reaction with great precision.

"My exact words were, 'You've got to be fucking kidding.' I said it aloud."

3

The Flight from Labrador

A SINGLE, PIERCING SCREAM ECHOED THROUGH THE CABIN.

Eileen Shleffar, a fifty-six-year-old merchandise manager for Belk, had let out a full-throated screech. Intently preoccupied with counting down the seconds the same way Amber Wells had been, Shleffar is such a nervous flier—"I am hypersensitive to every bump, move, hit, air pocket, wing noise, wheels up, the whole thing"—that "the scream just escaped from my mouth. Just a very loud, brief, short scream."

Shleffar was embarrassed—"I felt like such a dork; no one else screamed"—but she has a remarkable sense of quick-line humor. She keeps the buyers in stitches on these trips with a nonstop series of fearful-flier one-liners like, "I get jet lag for two days after the two-hour flight to Charlotte." Embarrassed briefly perhaps, but later several passengers told her that she was the only one in the bunch who was smart enough to scream.

At least three passengers immediately thought terrorism. Even though he saw a blur fly by his window, Warren Holland, a forty-year-old bond trader for BoA seated in 16E, said, "My first thought was a bomb in the cockpit or luggage compartment. I knew it was catastrophic."

Larry Snodgrass, fifty-nine, who flies weekly out of Charlotte, flashed on the image of terrorists, too, then thought that the engine had exploded. "But never did I think it was a bird strike," he said.

Stephen Lis, a forty-two-year-old business executive from Philadelphia, immediately thought: *Did someone just hit the left side of the plane with a missile?*

The combination of the noise and the shudder caused Brian Siegel, one of the BoA bankers, to think briefly of a midair collision with another airplane, but he kept his suspicion to himself. It is remarkable how little conversation takes place in an airplane even in a situation like this. Airliners are flying tubes, filled with strangers. Still, most of the passengers knew fairly quickly that they had hit birds because so many had seen them.

At least a dozen passengers said they saw birds or dark objects fly by or get sucked into the engines. Everyone heard the collision, not just the bang—which they described in greatly varying intensity—but also the grinding shrapnel sound inside the engines. Many also heard the thud of birds colliding with the wings, the fuselage, and the radome at the nose of the plane.

The descriptions of the noise range from an explosion to a pop, depending on where passengers were sitting, their fear levels, or both. From his first-class seat 1C, Barry Leonard, a successful businessman who can talk as descriptively as a novelist, was taken more by the engine sound after the bang—"tennis shoes rolling around in a dryer . . . *bump-bump, bump-bump*"—as the birds scrambled the metal innards of the engine, and the engine, in turn, liquefied the birds. In the last rows, however, most passengers said the collision sounded more like a pop.

On the left side, where the damage seemed worse—although that would prove to be entirely inconsequential to the catastrophe itself—Michelle DePonte, the bride-to-be, seated in an exit row almost directly over the wing, saw "a bunch of black balls fly straight into the engine." Michael Whitesides, a thirty-seven-year-old Charlotte sales representative, sitting next to her in the middle seat, saw a "very large bird" swallowed up, and other birds go by.

Billy Campbell, the television executive, immediately looked at the left engine and saw "a bonfire." A regular flier, seated in window seat 25A, Campbell had a clean look at the engine; he had seen small fires and spitting sparks on flights before—but nothing like this.

On the right side, where most of the flock flew, Brian Moss, in the last row, didn't see the birds enter the engine but did see it flash. He also caught a brief glimpse of a large flock off to the side of the plane, much as Ricardo Valeriano, in first-class, had seen the optical illusion of a distant fighter squadron. Eric Stevenson of Paris, seated just behind the exit row in seat 12F, was looking out the window at the Bronx and suddenly saw "a brown mass" disappear into the right engine with a series of thuds.

In seat 1F, Brad Williams, one of the bankers, saw a single bird flash by toward the engine. John Howell, an executive for the international accounting firm, KPMG, in aisle seat 2D, heard the thuds and saw several geese bouncing along the side of the plane after they had presumably hit the nose and the forward fuselage. One picture freeze-framed in his mind: a large goose, its body pointing forward but its neck twisted back. Bill Wiley, sitting next to him, looked out a split second later and saw nothing. As he peered directly into the right engine behind him, he was surprised by what he found. "It was pristine," he said. "Not a dent to the cowling. No bent blades. But you could tell it was winding down."

The reaction throughout the cabin after Shleffar's scream can best be described as a short, collective gasp, as passengers with various degrees of knowledge and with myriad temperaments tried to evaluate this sudden arrow shot into their lives.

Many people just zoned out, or numbed inward on their fears. Amber Wells, who'd seen a fireball and black smoke coming from the right engine, closed her eyes, leaned back against the headrest, and began saying "The Lord's Prayer," over and over. She felt the plane bank left and thought they were going back to the airport but otherwise had "no clue what was going on." She didn't particularly want one. "Ignorance was bliss. I was not scared like some. I didn't think we were going to die. I had no concept of death that day."

Others immediately concluded that the situation was deadly. Vallie Collins's mind rewound to a moment long ago when she'd ridden next to a pilot during heavy turbulence. "Don't worry," he had assured her. "In the cockpit, all we worry about is birds and fire." That assurance had been a balm to her for almost ten years. Not now. The left engine was on fire and her seatmate, Moss, although quite calm, had seen the birds.

Some thought little of it. Laurie Crane, fifty-eight, one of the Belk Six, heard "a major thump." But half-asleep, her mink draped over her legs, the sound didn't alarm her.

At first, many of the old-time fliers, knowing that the plane could fly safely on one engine, felt more inconvenienced than worried. The second deadheading pilot on the flight, Derek Alter, prominent in his Colgan Air[1] uniform, suddenly felt bombarded with questions from

---

[1] Less than a month later, a Colgan Air flight would crash nose-first on approach to the Buffalo airport, killing all forty-nine people aboard and one man on the ground, ending the long period of fatality-free U.S. commercial flying. The crash would also have a profoundly strong psychological effect on the passengers aboard Flight 1549.

the passengers near his seat in the front of the plane. Alter had dozed off, but when someone told him they had hit birds, he awoke and said, "Oh, in that case, we are turning back. This happens all the time." Alter had no idea that both engines had been taken out. "It just doesn't happen."

Few in the cabin thought of that dire possibility in those first seconds after the bird strike, either, even though the airplane had taken on the silence of a tomb. The aisle down the middle of the plane seemed to become a wall. For a long while, no one on the right side talked to anyone on the left side and vice versa. Although a long while was not very long on Flight 1549. They had about three minutes to go.

THE ONLY PEOPLE aboard Flight 1549 who understood the situation were sitting ahead of the locked door of the cockpit, and it did not look good.

First Officer Jeffrey Skiles, who was flying the plane on takeoff, had seen them first—a huge flock of geese flying in perfect V formation—approaching from the right, at an angle to the Airbus. As a flier, Skiles had a flickering sense of awe at the perfectly disciplined "V" formation of the birds, and, with the plane climbing, he briefly thought they might miss each other. But those thoughts lasted microseconds. Almost instantly, Sullenberger saw them, too—"large, massive, big birds" with huge wingspans that filled his windscreen. He had never seen anything like it before. His first inclination, which he subdued, was to duck. In his memory he still sees them in silhouette, as in a black-and-white photo, with large bodies and wide wingspans.

The flight paths, synchronized by nature and computers to an identical altitude, intersected before men or geese could react. It was a broadside at about 300 miles an hour—250 by the climbing plane, 50 by the cruising birds.

The cockpit voice recorder documented the fate of both in 4.6 seconds—from 3:27 and 10.4 seconds, to 3:27 and 15 seconds.

SULLENBERGER: "Birds."

SKILES: "Whoa."

RECORDED UNSPOKEN SOUND: *Thump/thud* followed by aircraft shuddering.

SKILES: "Oh, shit."

SULLENBERGER: "Oh, yeah."

RECORDED UNSPOKEN SOUND: Decrease in engine noise/frequency.

SKILES: "Uh-oh."

SULLENBERGER: "We got one roll . . . both of 'em rolling back."

At that moment, the flight to Charlotte effectively ended. "My airplane," Sullenberger said as he took the controls back from Skiles, and the two men put their minds on a kind of computerized human autopilot. Their training, their discipline, their self-confidence, and, not to be underestimated in the least, their highly honed instincts would settle the fate of the 155 persons briefly stranded in the sky over New York City. There was no playbook for this one. There was not enough time to finish an engine restart checklist although Skiles started through one; not enough time for the slightest change of mind. Decide. Commit. Go.

AIRCRAFT HAVE BEEN hitting birds since they first ventured into avian territory. Orville Wright hit the first—a red-winged blackbird—on a flight in 1905.

Since then airplanes have struck almost everything that flies. Even the space shuttle hit a vulture, and a goose broke through the canopy of a T-38 trainer, killing an early astronaut, Theodore Freeman, on a training flight in 1964. More than one commercial airline pilot has been able to land after birds had penetrated the cockpit, their broken bodies spraying the pilots and their instruments.

At least 229 persons have died from bird strikes (or occasional runway collisions with land animals) in the past thirty years, according to the National Transportation Safety Board. The strikes have destroyed 194 aircraft, including 26 large commercial planes, and regularly cost U.S. carriers approximately $265 million a year. That said, the statistics that exist on the actual number of bird strikes are limp, as the Federal Aviation Administration estimates that only one in five is reported. The FAA's count for 2007 is 7,666 reports, which means that the true number could be almost 40,000 bird strikes a year in the United States, or more than 100 a day.

Just two months before US Airways Flight 1549, a similar bird strike went almost unnoticed by the world. Ireland's Ryanair, one of Europe's most successful regional airlines, lost both engines of a Boeing 737 to swarms of starlings on approach to Rome's Ciampino Airport. That pilot's skill in getting the craft down with no deaths or serious injuries ranked with the acumen that Sullenberger was about to display to the world.

Modern aircraft have been struck, and occasionally taken down, by eagles, turkey vultures, cranes, swans, pelicans, buzzards, geese, ducks, wild turkeys, great blue herons, swarms of starlings (those tiny urban pests), and almost every imaginable kind of small bird. On Flight 1549, Smithsonian scientists concluded that the bird parts, known as snarge, removed from the engines, wings, and fuselage came overwhelmingly from Canada geese but also from ducks, doves, and various songbirds.

Because of the bird's size and flocking patterns, and the tremendous growth of its population (as more and more animal protection programs have been implemented), no bird is a larger threat to aircraft than the Canada goose (*Branta canadensis*). Almost extinct a century ago, the North American population was well over 5.6 million birds in 2007. Some, like those Sullenberger and Skiles met face-to-face, migrate long distances. Most don't, a major change in the past thirty years. With six-foot wingspans, they are one of nature's largest birds, the males averaging eight pounds but some as heavy as fourteen. The engines of an Airbus, for one example, are certified to withstand the intake of a four-pound bird. In ground tests, the manufacturers rocket dead four-pounders at the engines to prove it—but they don't rocket eight-pounders because there isn't any point. The engines can't take them.

Through DNA testing, scientists can identify a bird species from snarge, and in the case of geese, down to one of twenty-nine subspecies. Other tests can determine almost exactly where they came from by identifying the food they ate before they molted, which occurs before migration from their northern home. The geese that collided with Flight 1549 were eating food found in Labrador—not other parts of Newfoundland or Quebec, but Labrador.

The science is incredibly precise, but then, so are migrating geese. They are not considered a particularly intelligent bird, but year after year, generation after generation, they return to the same summer and winter homes, and like many other migrating species are even thought to use the stars for navigation.

That leaves one unresolved mystery about this particular flock. Why were Labrador geese migrating in the dead of winter? Almost certainly they left Labrador far earlier, probably in October. Canada geese, in their remarkably efficient V formations, are quite capable of traveling up to 1,500 miles a day from Labrador straight over New

York to inviting grounds around Chesapeake Bay or the Delmarva Peninsula. So scientists believe that this wasn't a Labrador-Chesapeake nonstop. Rather, they think the northeastern cold snap that fouled up other flying schedules that day forced the birds up again from their normal winter home north of the city in search of more hospitable grounds to the south.

Some casual observers, including a few passengers on the plane, were surprised that geese flew so high. But migrating Canada geese can travel at eight thousand feet, and their average migratory altitude is right where they were that day, around three thousand.

The many species of geese produce remarkable nature stories. Asia's isolated bar-headed variety (*Anser indicus*) migrate over the Himalayas between far western China and the Tibetan Highlands to India and Pakistan, often catching 200-mile-an-hour jet streams to make their 1,000-mile journeys in one nonstop flight. They have been seen as high as 33,000 feet flying over Mount Everest. The bar heads made front-page news a few years ago when flocks became sick and died in China just before their migration, worrying epidemiologists that they might be spreading the deadly bird-flu virus, H5N1, to the subcontinent.

The worst known crash caused by Canada geese received minimal publicity because it involved a military plane full of secret equipment. In 1995, an Air Force AWACS (Airborne Warning and Control System) plane—a reconfigured Boeing 707 used as an aerial surveillance station—crashed after colliding with a flock shortly after takeoff from Elmendorf Air Force Base in Alaska. All twenty-four people aboard were killed in the ensuing explosion. Some other military collisions are just as gruesome: An Air Force supersonic F-16 went down after a turkey vulture smashed through its canopy, decapitating the pilot and blinding the copilot with snarge.

Vultures are unusually threatening because they fly effortlessly for hours at about 2,500 feet, looking for prey. Birds with predators try to take evasive action; vultures don't even waver. Geese don't often break ranks either. Following their leader in that beautifully efficient V allows them to use 70 percent less energy. It is such a part of their nature that, when something disorients the lead goose, flocks have been known to follow him in perfect formation directly into the ground.

The speed of sound makes it difficult to hear a jet coming and quieter and quieter jet engines also have given geese and other birds less time to react. Whether this flock even had time for evasion or a break in ranks with an Airbus racing at them is a moot question. Flight 1549 hit their formation broadside. Goose parts were found all over the aircraft even after it lay in the Hudson for days.

The odds against this flock of birds crossing the path of this particular Airbus were extremely long. But the odds are usually long when accidents happen—the kind in which you can say, "If only we were twelfth in line for takeoff instead of eleventh . . . " "If we hadn't changed gates . . . " "If . . . If . . . If . . . "

IMMEDIATELY AFTER THE strike, the cabin filled with a slight haze of smoke and a smell that gave almost everyone the shivers. The odor was described in many ways, none pleasantly. Alex Magness, a New Yorker in seat 17A, summed it up as well as any. "It was putrid and instantaneous, burning flesh or fuel or whatever combination. It was unique, a terrible smell." Ricardo Valeriano described it as "a distinct smell of jet fuel, burning hair, and burning flesh. It's a concoction you never want to smell in your life, especially when you're in an airplane."

In the rear cabin someone shouted "Fire!" though it's not clear if this was a response to the fire in the engines or the haze with its sickening smell. But it caused an immediate commotion. At the time, Doreen Welsh was checking overheads and making sure nothing had come loose in the cabin. Vallie Collins, her nerves already frayed, unbuckled from her back-row seat and moved into the aisle: "Do you want me to call for help?" she asked, meaning did she want her to hit the attendant call button? Welsh was not looking for assistance from passengers and asked Collins to sit back down but to take the middle seat, next to Brian Moss, so she could use the aisle seat, if necessary.

After the ohmygods and other gasps settled down, you could hear conversations up and down the aisle in a way that you never do in an airplane. Quiet prayers began—prayers to many visions of God. Christians, a Hindu, Jews, and a Muslim were all on the plane.

Cell phones popped out everywhere but, despite their pervasiveness in modern life, many went unused. Some people started, and on second thought, stopped calling or texting because of the impact it might have on their loved ones. A few passengers were disapproving, believing that a clutter of cell traffic would interfere with the pilots' communications and instrumentation at a life-and-death time (it had no impact). Others just didn't want to listen to fellow passengers' calls, given how quiet the plane had become. They all had their own thoughts and fears racing through their heads.

Several passengers immediately experienced the same kind of stomach-dropping feeling of "not again" that had hit Eric Stevenson, the survivor of the flight that plunged toward the Pacific. Jay McDonald, a thirty-nine-year-old software salesman from Charlotte, had lived through surgery for a benign brain tumor two years earlier. "One of the millions of thoughts going through my head was, *How can this possibly be happening again?*" he said. *"Why did I survive that to go down in a plane crash two years later? It didn't make any sense. I'll always be asking why."*

When the birds hit, McDonald, seated in 14A just behind the

left engine, had been enjoying the perfect view downward at the Yankee Stadiums, old and new. He immediately averted his eyes from the window. He knew the left engine was out. But afterward he had no memory of looking at it again or of watching the raging bonfire that others saw spewing out the back. He couldn't believe, or didn't accept, that the right engine was gone, too, although he is an observant man. Instead, he acutely noticed the lights flickering, smelled the ugly odor, and felt the immediate loss of the plane's momentum.

This is not a normal abnormality, he thought. "So I'm frozen in my seat, looking ahead, listening to people, and conversations are going on everywhere, slightly louder than normal. Nobody seemed hysterical. It was just a lot of rhetorical questions to the world: What's happening? Are we going to blow up? Are we going to crash? Why isn't the captain telling us? I just remember the questions. I don't remember any answers, if there were any."

McDonald started reliving some airplane-crash dreams he had had. But he just stuffed those away. It wasn't *that* bad. He wasn't having the easiest time convincing himself. He wondered if he should call his wife.

"I remember seeing a woman with a phone to her ear and I thought, *Does that work? What the hell would you want to be saying to anyone right now?* I wouldn't want my wife to know I suffered at the end. I'd rather she thought we didn't know what hit us. I just wasn't going to hit her with it, email her or text her."

Apparently, the woman on the phone was Eileen Shleffar, the woman who had let out the scream. A self-proclaimed "phonaholic," Shleffar had just begun a truly remarkable cellular conversation.

"I looked around and I knew," Shleffar said. "I just knew. I could see the flashes from my window. I reached down into my handbag and picked up my phone, thinking to myself it will never come on before we crash. Kudos to Verizon. They were right there. I pushed send to my husband's number and he picked up. He said, 'What's going on. Is your plane late?' I said, 'No, we've hit something.' Then the call dropped."

That began a virtually nonstop dialogue, interspersed with a couple of short service drops, between Shleffar and her husband, David, all the way down and out into the Hudson River. For a good part of that time, David, who knows his wife is a nervous flier, didn't have the remotest idea what his wife was talking about.

Eileen described their conversation, "I looked and the screen was back. I pushed the button [again]. David said, 'What's going on now? Are you okay?'

" 'I don't know what's going on. Something is burning badly.'

"He said, 'Are you at the airport? What are they saying as an announcement?'

"And I said, 'Ohmygod, it's so quiet in here.'

"It seemed so long, like we'd been up fifteen minutes or an hour. Or a lifetime. And I just kept thinking any minute we would be, poof, gone. Like in a fireball. We would just explode.

"He says, 'What do you mean? Are you at the airport?'

"I was not hysterical. I wasn't crying. He said later I was deadly calm. It was clear he couldn't absorb what I was saying. But it didn't really matter. He is my rock. Talking to him gave me strength."

David Shleffar was not in the best setting to absorb such a call— if there ever is a good setting. He surely could be excused for not tracking for the first minute or so. Eileen explains:

"As it turns out, he was at the car wash and they were in there detailing his car. When he understood me, as a reflex reaction, he said to the attendants 'Get out, get out, get out!' There were rags flying and people jumping out of the car and he just kept yelling, 'Get out, get out!' He threw the tip money at them and jumped in the car and took off. He drove home like a madman. The call dropped out again for a few seconds."

Throughout the airplane localized minidramas continued.

In the back row on the left, where the nervous flier Tracey Wolsko had taken the middle seat and asked the New Yorker Irina Levshina to please close the window shade for takeoff, Wolsko now became the rock. Both Levshina and Vicki Barnhardt, in the aisle seat, reached for their cell phones. Wolsko reached out to both and, taking their hands, said, "Girls, put down those cell phones. Just pray. It's going to be all right." Levshina reports that the descent was almost an out-of-body experience: "Like a movie or something," she said. "It can't be happening to me. It's not my life. It was weird." But she found Wolsko's gesture calming, and this American success story, born in the USSR, clasped hands and began praying with the two Floridians—one Presbyterian, one Jewish—both almost precisely her age. Silently, Levshina prayed in Russian.

In row nineteen what had already been a terrible day now turned into a true nightmare for Tess Sosa, the Greenwich Village mother who had been nursing her nine-month-old son during the takeoff. Four rows back, her four-year-old daughter, Sofia, sat with her father, Martin. Tess hollered back, "Everything's going to be okay, Sofia. Please listen to Daddy." She recalls that she was trying "to stay calm because I am holding a baby and I do not want to incite any anxiety and agony on Damian." But it was difficult. She had not been able to settle down after the turmoil over the seating, and what she considered unacceptable behavior by the airline and some of the passengers who wouldn't help accommodate her family.

Next to her on the aisle side sat Hiroki Takigawa, the Japanese trader stationed in New York who loves to fly but falls asleep immediately. He remembers Sosa saying on takeoff, "This is so eerie, this is so eerie," as he drifted off. The bird strike awakened him, and he found Sosa highly distressed. But, Takigawa thought, she was most fortunate to have the man in the window seat sitting next to her.

Jim Whitaker, a forty-four-year-old Roman Catholic who flies well over 100,000 miles a year, is the quintessential road warrior. A hard-charging man who calls himself a "recovering architect and thankful for it," Whitaker works in construction—large projects, one of which is the 2010 home of the New York Giants and Jets, the New Meadowlands just across the river in New Jersey. He soon would be able to see his prized job from an altitude that would shake him. A father of five with close-cropped graying hair, Whitaker instantly took to little Damian and understood the fears of the mother.

"What's happening?" she asked him urgently after the bird strike. "Are we going to be okay?"

Whitaker looked out the window at the dead engine and turned back calmly. "Oh, an engine problem," he said. "I've had this happen before. No worries."

"He was very composed about it," Sosa remembers. "I said, 'How do you know?' He said, 'I just know.' "

Whitaker would continue to reassure her, and do more, throughout the rest of the short flight.

"I was pathologically lying the whole time," he said later.

4

The Bridge

THE POWER OF ITS TAKEOFF THRUST CAUSED THE AIRBUS, NOW AN almost-dead hulk of seventy-five tons of man's best technology, to lug a few hundred feet higher. It reached its maximum altitude at just over three thousand feet above the Bronx Zoo. This increase quickly cost it speed. It felt, one of the passengers said, like taking the foot off the gas at seventy miles an hour. To Susan Wittmann, a fifty-seven-year-old Charlotte banker, it seemed "almost like the plane stopped in midair for a nanosecond." To avoid a stall and to take a look at the playing field that he now needed, Sullenberger banked the plane into a steep left turn back toward Manhattan. This would cost him almost half the altitude but allow him to regain speed and give him some control of the Airbus as well as a sense of how far the huge glider would still take him.

Off to the right beckoned New Jersey's Teterboro Airport, a reliever airport for general aviation in New York's crowded airspace, and to the left, the airport he had just departed, LaGuardia. Both stretched out distantly, at least marginally possible to reach. But in a metropolitan area of high-rises and dense population, "marginally" was a recipe for a huge disaster.

At times, a human mind can work almost as quickly as a computer, and with a greater assurance that all the right data have been pumped in. This was one of those times. Despite questions to Ground Control, and clearance requests for runways, Sullenberger came to his conclusions rapidly.

Inside the plane a numbed lack of recognition, mixed with a healthy dose of fear, pervaded the cabin. It was not terror yet. "But it was a moment of building tension, chirps and gasps and sighs and ohmygods," Whitaker said. You could hear people weeping quietly, not wails or shrieks but quiet sobs. Many of the passengers had gone completely within themselves and had not spoken even to their seatmates. Many would not look out the window all the way down.

IT IS NEARLY impossible to fathom the incredibly short periods of time involved and how many spiraling thoughts spun disconnected through the passengers' minds in those moments. Later, it would often take passengers hours to explain what had happened in those three minutes. In good Hollywood fashion, whole lives *did* flash through some minds—a guy's first girlfriend, Little League baseball games, weddings, births of children, births of grandchildren. But that Hollywood version didn't happen as commonly as one might imagine. Just as often, lost futures flashed by, kaleidoscopes of sadness— a young son's high-school basketball games unseen, a young daughter's wedding with a missing father, grandchildren who aren't born yet, never going fishing with kids as they grow up, the great, grieving sadness of leaving behind a three-year-old who won't remember you. The essential collided with the unimportant—beds left unmade, dishes left in the sink, garbage not taken out, a forgotten kiss good-bye.

TWENTY OR THIRTY seconds now since the bird strike . . .

Stephanie King, the lawyer and bride-to-be from Wisconsin, started crying and couldn't stop. She wasn't moved by fear as much as by horrible disbelief: That all the happiness, and even the unlikelihood, of the romance and the nearing wedding with the man trying to comfort her could possibly end this way. From West Bend, Wisconsin, to Monroe, Louisiana, via Afghanistan and eHarmony, and she loved him so much. How could it end this way now? Gray tried to comfort her, but he felt a yawning chasm of helplessness. He could lead forty-one men through Afghan war zones safely, but he couldn't protect this wonderful woman next to him on a routine connecting flight. "I was pretty naïve to the problem with the airplane at first," Gray said, concluding in retrospect that he just disconnected because he couldn't accept it. "I couldn't believe it was that bad. To me, it smelled very electrical, like when you are overseas and you plug a 110-volt appliance into a 220 plug. 'Don't worry, don't worry,' I told her. 'We just blew a fuse.' "

The other young lovers, Chris Rooney and Karin Hill from Colorado Springs, struggled through the first moments, too. Hill also broke into tears, and Rooney, the son of a pilot, the engineer who had just explained the mechanics of air travel to calm her on takeoff, could only say now, "Don't worry. We're going back." Deep down, he thought they were going in the water. He couldn't tell her that.

They prayed.

The large banking turn, although it was steep—not quite a dive, more reminiscent of a theme-park ride than a commercial airplane flight—affected passengers in different ways. Casey Jones, a senior vice president at BoA, wondered briefly if they were headed into a spiral-down crash. For others, it was evidence of a one-engine turn back to LaGuardia.

The two deadheading commercial pilots aboard assured their seatmates that the latter was the case. Derek Alter remained certain that the Airbus still had one engine. "We practice this all the time," he told people nearby. "Line up over the Hudson, hit the Statue of Liberty, cut left, and you're lined up with Runway 4."

In first class, Valeriano asked Susan O'Donnell of American Airlines: "Is everything going to be okay?"

"Yes," she replied, "we are going back to LaGuardia."

They were in a most peculiar circumstance—as if the more they knew, the more psychically numbed they were to the dead silence telling them loud and clear that both engines were gone. Two engines are *never* gone.

Not all were lost to what was happening, of course. The sharp, almost 180-degree turn accompanied by the rapid descent alerted many to their plight. In the middle of the turn, one of the golfers, Jeff Kolodjay, looked out his left-hand window at the engine and saw the flames blowing toward the fuselage. *Wow, there's no fireman coming to put this engine out,* he thought. "The buildings were getting closer. I thought, *He's not going to put people on the ground in danger by hitting a building. Wow, we're going to land in the water, and that's not how you're supposed to write up a safe landing.*"

The turn also changed the view outside for everyone. Those on the right-hand side now saw New Jersey and the river. Those on the left-hand side could see LaGuardia and Manhattan. As they had arced through the air, the left-hand side had been temporarily given a panoramic view of the southern part of the metropolitan area and both sides of the river. Alex Magness, the New Yorker in seat 17A on the left side, was one of the minority who had already concluded that both engines were gone. "The plane was as quiet as a bedroom at night," he said.

Looking out his window, "It became very clear to me that the Hudson was becoming our runway. I said to my seatmate [Nick Gamache of Raleigh, North Carolina], 'I think we are going in the water.' Someone behind me said, 'No, we're going to New Jersey.' Everyone wanted to believe we were going back to an airport." For Magness, the peril still did not reach a level that surpassed an earlier moment of horror in his life. On September 11, 2001, he had emerged from the subway at 9:00 a.m. on his way to work at One Liberty Plaza, the skyscraper office building next to the World Trade Center. As he reached the street, flames had begun spewing out, and people soon were jumping from high up in the North Tower. His instinct was to get away from the sheer awfulness and be among friends. That emotional need placed him—minutes later—in an elevator to his twentieth-floor office when "the scream of engines in flight and an explosion" (from the second strike, to the South Tower across the street) jammed him between floors. The rest of his morning became an escape, along with thousands of other New Yorkers, from the terror and danger of that day. Even in the deadly situation he found himself now, he could not feel as horrified or imperiled as he had felt in September 2001.

The about-face gave Adelaide Horton, a fifty-eight-year-old ad executive from North Carolina, her first good look back at La-Guardia. "I knew immediately we couldn't make it back. I was hoping we wouldn't try. It would be bad enough if we all crashed and burned, but it would be horrible if we killed other people around us. I instinctively knew he wouldn't do that and we were going in the river."

Seated behind Horton, Pam Seagle had already noted the steep loss of altitude. Now the lack of engine sound penetrated her consciousness. She looked at the grand panorama of Manhattan. *Oh my, they must think this a terrorist act,* she said to herself. Then she returned to her own situation: *No engine sound, no announcement, and losing altitude,* Seagle thought. She knew they were going down—and not at an airport.

Fred Berretta, a private pilot and BoA bond salesman in Charlotte, became one of the first to penetrate the "great wall" in the aisle. "It just hit me," Berretta said. "There was no engine noise from the left engine and all I could hear was the wind going by. I called out to a passenger on the right side and he said he didn't hear any noise from the right, either. I had this huge rush of adrenaline and I knew this was very serious indeed."

Between Berretta and Seagle, Mike and Mary Berkwits sat in middle seats, one row apart, in 13B and 14B. Married for thirty years, they call North Carolina home but they are New Yorkers through and through. They own a boat and often take it up the Hudson. Call Central Casting for a pair of New Yorkers and they would send you Mike, fifty-five, and Mary, fifty-two. They talk it, they act it, and now both were at their best. She is a steadfast Roman Catholic, he a steadfast agnostic.

Almost as quickly as it hit Berretta, the dead silence told Mike Berkwits that both engines were out. But the New Yorker in him—extremely proud of the heroics on 9/11—knew that New York would save them. "New Yorkers know how to handle disasters," he said. "They just show up. I thought we were going to hit the water, the doors would open up, I'd step onto a boat, they'd take me to shore, and then"—like any New Yorker who has tried to catch a cab during rush hour—"we'd have to figure out how to get home." Only later, at one of the many television appearances he made in the aftermath, did he realize how dangerous it had been. "The angst hit me and hit me again. How could I have been so oblivious to the danger?" He still is troubled about how he could have blanked so much out.

But on the plane, Berkwits's strange imperviousness, as well as his wife's calm, helped three nervous seatmates get through. On one side of him sat Debbie Ramsey, a forty-nine-year-old buyer for a store called New York New York in an outlet mall in Pigeon Forge, Tennessee. On the other sat Shae Childers, thirty-eight, a buyer for a family clothing store in Gaffney, South Carolina. Childers's friend and a buyer for the same store, Amy Jolly, twenty-nine, sat just behind her, next to Mary.

The group sat almost alongside the engine. When it blew, they all jumped out of their skins. Ramsey, very alarmed, put her hand on Mike's leg and asked: "Are we going to be okay?"

"Don't worry," he replied. "We lost an engine and we're going back."

Then she was embarrassed about her hand on his leg.

"Now, don't you worry about that," Berkwits said. "My wife's got her hand on my head."

For the rest of the flight the Berkwitses did not exchange a word with each other—only the hand touches over the seat. They both busily tried to preoccupy their seatmates.

"I tried not to let my mind go to dying," Jolly said. "But several times I asked Mary, 'Are we going to die? Is it going to be quick or is it going to hurt?' Every time, Mary would reply, 'I'm a stomach-cancer survivor. I don't plan to die from this. I have a niece your age. You're way too young to die. We will be okay.' "

Mike took on the unusual self-appointed role as a tour guide of the New York sights rushing up toward them. When Ramsey started panicking, Berkwits started in: "Look, there's Yankee Stadium, the old one and the new one right next to each other. Won't get a better view. There's Grant's Tomb."

"I knew he was trying to calm me down," Ramsey said. "I was praying: 'Please, God, don't take me today.' I had my phone in my pocket and I took it out and turned it on to call my husband and the man—Mr. Berkwits, I found out later—was trying to calm me down and something told me, *Don't call home. You don't want to worry him.*"

The rapid descent was worrying to Childers. She had no fear of flying, but the rapid loss of altitude frightened her and, a Baptist, she began to pray. She kept her tight grip on the hand of her friend and workmate, Amy Jolly, in the seat behind her. She had found the Berkwitses' remarkable nonchalance reassuring, too. Mike Berkwits recalls telling her to look at the George Washington Bridge as they approached it. But Childers doesn't remember that—or even seeing it. For a start, she was in an aisle seat and on the wrong side of the plane to get a view. Passengers in aisle seats were at a disadvantage—or maybe, it was an advantage—because they couldn't see much.

Not seeing the bridge probably proved a blessing for most. As the plane silently sank over the great span, it was one of the least reassuring sights of the descent. If you were on the right side of the plane, and you had a view of just how close the bridge was, it would have taken a stunning amount of disassociation to continue blanking out the fear.

Seventeen bridges carry traffic in and out of Manhattan but only one crosses the Hudson to New Jersey. Twice as large as any suspension bridge in the world when it was completed at the beginning of the Depression in 1931, the George Washington Bridge remains a breathtaking span crossing almost a mile of river, with fourteen lanes of traffic on two levels. During afternoon rush hour, all lanes are jammed.

But the bridge's most imposing structures are the huge rectangular towers at each end, built as broad, jutting rectangles with perpendicular exposed-steel girders reinforced by a cross-thatch of open steel beams. They rise 635 feet above the river. Flight 1549, having lost 1,800 feet of altitude, now swept just outside the Manhattan tower at an altitude of 1,245 feet—a mere 600 feet above its apex. If the people on the right-hand side of the plane were looking—and many weren't, and didn't want to—they could clearly see the towers and the bridge. Some could even see the cars—and they saw the river, broad and up close. On the left-hand side the passengers could see the plane's level in proportion to Manhattan's skyline. It flew at the height of the observation tower of the Empire State Building and more than one hundred feet lower than what had been the top of the World Trade Center's Twin Towers.

Suddenly, someone yelled, "When is someone going to tell us something?"

At about the same time, Bill Zuhowski, the occasional flier from Mattituck, Long Island, got a jolting awakening from the man seated next to him. Up till then, Zuhowski had little concept of what was happening. He hadn't yet ruled out the possibility that the plane would recover and continue on to Charlotte, and crashing had not seriously penetrated his thoughts. Then his seatmate, Luther Lockhart, a personal trainer from the Bronx, locked arms with him and announced, "It's nice to know you're going to die ahead of time."

"It was very alarming," Zuhowski said. "But then a moment later the man had his head down and he asked me, 'Are we back at the airport yet?' " The strange incident shook Zuhowski but it also forced him to recognize that it was time to face reality. The problem became, as it did for everyone: How do I process any of this information? What do I *do* with it? "Obviously I got fearful," Zuhowski said. "But you can be as scared and panicky as you can be and there's nothing you can do. You're strapped into your seat and that's it."

Lockhart said later that his mind was seesawing all over the place. "I wasn't, like, frantic," he said. "I kept telling myself, *Man, I'm gonna die.* But it was more like I was feeling, *Wow, I'm gonna die. Shit, I'm gonna die.* It was like an event. I was very much at peace with dying."

Wendell Fox, a retired Charlotte policeman and BoA fraud investigator, saw the top of the bridge, looked at the plane starting to line up with the river, and "figured I was gonna die. I just assumed the plane would break apart and it was loaded with fuel and we would probably die a violent death. But it would be quick."

Brad Wentzell, a traveling patio-door wholesaler from Charlotte, thought at first that they might hit the bridge. "When we made it over," he said, "I realized we were not going to any airport. There was no way. I could feel us floating. I said two 'Our Fathers.' I said, 'Lord, I have not lived a perfect life. Please forgive me for my sins. Take care of my wife and daughter. Take me to the Gates of Heaven.' "

Ian Wells, a twenty-one-year-old college student from Rye, New York, had been thinking of his family in what seemed like long, intimate memories. "It felt like a million years since we hit the birds. Time moved very slowly." In fact ninety-eight seconds had passed from the time of the bird strike until the plane reached the bridge. "We had done the hard left turn, almost like the wing is perpendicular, and then leveled out lower and lower and slower. I know the area. I could see the cliffs of New Jersey. As we went over the GW Bridge, I looked at the river and knew right then we weren't going back to any airport. We were going into the river. This is going to be very bad."

Michelle DePonte, the imminent bride, saw the river and "knew we would die on impact. Instantly." She found the thought beyond imagining. "I sat there in a daze, to be honest," she said. "A month before my wedding day. In my own mind, I kept thinking: *Is this re-*

ally happening? I've been with this guy for ten years and I'm going to crash a month to the day before we were going to get married?"

Josh Peltz, a thirty-nine-year-old software sales executive from Charlotte, watched from his Jersey-side window in row ten. "When we went over the bridge, I knew there was no airport for us. We were going into the river." Peltz has a wry side to him, which in less than a minute would show itself to everyone, not all of whom would be ready for it. "I had hoped that we were going to land on the Hudson Parkway or on one of the roads on the other side of the shore, but then quickly realized no pilot would do that. You couldn't redirect traffic that quickly," he said. Then the wry side comes out: "Although," he quipped, "a big plane coming toward you might redirect it pretty quick."

Beth McHugh, sixty-four, watching from seat 20C on the Manhattan side, had come to a much earlier, but private, conclusion that both engines were gone. She accepted it. But after that, the flight became very disorienting. "I looked out the window and saw the George Washington Bridge, just the towers of it, and it was so close," she said. Now she watched "and we were going down fairly fast and I had been assuming we were still over the buildings of Manhattan. On the aisle, I couldn't see that much. I was sure we were going to die. I was sure it was going to be really, really bad."

Jim Whitaker had begun the process of dealing with his death. A staunch Roman Catholic, he was not as fearful as some. "I was sure of what would happen afterward," he said. "I knew with certainty the Moment After. I did think about my family and what they would have to endure. I expected to die. But dying is not the worst thing that can happen to you. There is an endless series of worst things that come before dying." Whitaker had lost a child to Sudden Infant Death Syndrome (SIDS). That was a worst thing.

Meanwhile, Whitaker continued to try to reassure Tess Sosa as best he could. She remembers him saying at about that time, "It's all okay. I have five children of my own and I expect to see them again."

Martin Sosa was having a far worse time. Like a large number of people aboard the plane, he had a morbid fear of drowning. In fact, he said, "My two biggest fears throughout my life have been of falling out of the sky or drowning." Now he faced both and it was terrifying. He looked back over what had been mere seconds of his life.

"I knew right away something had gone terribly wrong," he said. "I could see the engine was on fire. Okay, this isn't good. Then we heard the other go out. Complete silence. Someone yelling 'fire, fire.' Then I saw the flight attendant in the back with an extinguisher. Okay. That's definitely not good.

"You're going through these thoughts. Sofia is freaking out. 'Daddy, what's that smell?' It's going to be okay. Don't worry. Don't worry. I'm going, 'Oh my God.' At that moment the plane banks sharply to the left. I said to myself it doesn't look like we are going to the airport. I saw us going to the GW Bridge. I realized then that we were going into the water. I watched as we descended quickly below on the skyline of Manhattan on my left. I was angry. I was cursing. A lot of people went into prayer. I was cursing expletives."

At who?

"I was just angry. Fuck, fuck. You couldn't believe this is happening to you. This was like the end of your life. You're going to just die. How is this going to play out? Is the plane going to disintegrate? How am I going to grab Sofia? What if I fall unconscious? You just don't know what's going to happen."

At that point, most people aboard still hadn't connected with the reality of this moment in the flight. They just didn't see it. Many had their eyes closed in prayer or averted from the outside. Others simply remained psychologically blind to it all, although that would become much more difficult in a few seconds.

"I could look right out the window and I remained in some kind of denial till almost the end," said Brian Moss, who continued to try to help Vallie Collins with her fears in the aircraft's back row. On the other side of that aisle, Irina Levshina, who loved window seats so she could look at the views, had not raised the window shade. She was praying—and completely in the dark.

Another BoA banker, Jerry Shanko, said he thought he was paying attention, but "I was in denial of what was happening. Planes don't crash. This isn't a normal circumstance. We didn't blow up, so I figured we were going to be okay. When I look back, I'm cued in that there was an eerie silence in the cabin. There was no engine noise. But my mind refused to pick up on it."

Months afterward, Douglas Schrift, a thirty-six-year-old Charlotte construction industry executive, said one of the lessons he took away from the flight was that people in the same situation do not necessarily see things with the same eyes. That surely was the case now and through the few remaining seconds of the flight.

The drag racer, Chris Rini, of Holmes, New York, heading south to talk to his engine maker as a new season approached, stared down at the bridge as they passed over. "I could see in the cars," he told *Racin' Today,* a motor sports online magazine. "I'm sure those people were a little nervous, too." He was not that afraid yet. He always assumed if he were going to die in a crash, it would be a car crash, not a plane crash. A world-class driver, Rini had taken his souped-up Dodge Strata to speeds that had approached the plane's as it was gliding now.

Eric Stevenson might have been more alarmed: Flight 1549 had descended farther and faster than the near-death experience he had survived over the Pacific twenty-two years earlier. But the plane was still twice as high as the Boeing 767 had been before pulling out of its dive. Stevenson hung on tenaciously to the thought that 1549 was headed for Newark.

This flight just seemed different to him.

In the 1987 near-crash, "The crew had come on and said, 'Prepare for a water landing,'" he recalled. "People had pulled out their life preservers and put them on. For me that was totally the end. Now I was thinking this plane has got to be able to land. I couldn't imagine this was going to be that devastating an incident."

All throughout the plane, the 150 passengers of Flight 1549 were living in different realms of the mind. Some were watching what was going on as if it were a movie. "I felt like I was watching myself from a distance," said Kanau Deguchi, one of the Japanese traders. A few were watching like it was a rare experience, like Mike Berkwits. To a few it was actually an adventure, a basically unfrightening opportunity to watch the final act in their lives.

Little Damian lay sound asleep.

Many were praying—all those faiths, all those visions of God and the route to His Place:

Balaji Ganesan, a Hindu, looking at the river from seat 20E, sat next to Amber Wells, a Methodist deep in her prayer.

Heyam Kawas, a Muslim, was hunched over in prayer to a different God—different, perhaps, only because men had made him so.

A silent Russian prayer next to a silent Jewish prayer, the believers holding hands.

There were Roman Catholics, Armenian Orthodox, and all the various Christian faiths that had set their own paths. Christmas and Easter churchgoers. Agnostics and nonbelievers. Men and women who had no idea they were religious until this moment, converts in a kind of flying foxhole.

Takigawa was the plane's lone Buddhist, a religion in which prayers are inward meditations rather than outward conversations with a Higher Being. Takigawa would say later that, amidst all the praying, he felt isolated and lonely, sometimes a little lost, left out of the group.

Flight 1549 was gliding now at just over two hundred miles an hour, slightly over one thousand feet above the New Jersey side of the Hudson and descending at a high sink rate. On one side, the pricey condos of Jersey's Hudson Cove beckoned; on the other sat New York's West 155th Street—the north border of Harlem and once the proud site of the Big Apple's Polo Grounds.

At that moment, Chesley Sullenberger's voice entered the cabin for the first time since takeoff almost four minutes earlier.

"This is your captain," he said. "Brace for impact."

5

"Brace! Brace! Heads Down! Stay Down!"

"WHEN YOU HEAR THOSE WORDS—'BRACE FOR IMPACT'—ON AN AIR-plane flight," Douglas Schrift said later, "you don't think you heard them right. I looked around and I heard a couple of people say, 'Did he say, *"brace for impact*?"' Then the flight attendants started chant-ing. Kind of a creepy chant. Like a horror movie. *'Brace! Brace! Heads down! Stay down!'* Over and over. It was very creepy chanting."

Trying to explain how the mind works at such a moment, Schrift said, is almost impossible. Others described their minds as though they were in a Chinese Ping-Pong match, but with players using all four sides of the table. "Should you pray? Should you call your wife? You try to reconcile your reactions to your emotions," Schrift ex-plained. "At the same time, you are aware of some of what is going on around you. Some sobbing. Gasps. One man asked me in a monotone voice, 'How close are we?' Another responded, 'We are on the water.' Which meant we are about to hit the water."

Jim Whitaker said he absorbed those words with only a small wince because he knew they were coming. "But it was the trigger moment that released the emotional chaos inside the plane," he said. "Adrenaline and fear went into overdrive. People were crying, yelling, praying, holding hands. Ohmygods. The takeaway memory for me is looking at people near me and seeing that visceral reaction and gen-uine fear for one's life in their eyes." Others called the moment sur-real and some described having out-of-body experiences. "No, not to me," Whitaker said. "This did not seem to be any of those things. This was very real. Very tactile. Very in your face. Gut-wrenching. It was as real as living gets."

Some went inward and stayed there. Heyam Kawas, a five-foot-three Jordanian and an Arabic-language specialist at the United Na-tions since 1992, had kept her head down in prayer since the collision with the birds. She didn't understand the pilot's words, so she lifted her head and asked the man next to her. "Brace for land-ing," he said kindly and showed her how to do it. Kawas was terri-fied. But looking back, to her it is as if she slept the rest of the way. She remembers nothing. "I kept my head down till I woke up with the man nudging me and saying, 'Go now,'" she said.

"The blood just flowed out of my body with the thought that my life is now going to go away," said Jeff Kolodjay, the team leader of the golfers whose father and buddies were scattered about ahead of him in the plane. "I thought to myself, *Wow, I'm thirty-one years old. I'm a healthy guy. Why is this happening? What can I do to make sure I get through this?* I slowly realized there was nothing.

"It's amazing how time can just stand still. I swear I had no fewer than fifty thousand thoughts in the next few seconds. It was a crazy, crazy mental process. I don't know if this is a good thing to say but some people have the opportunity to prepare to die, whether it be old age or a terminal disease. But going from such jubilation, from such a wonderful high of going on this trip with my dad and friends, to all of a sudden this sheer panic of, Oh my God . . .

"Selfishly I said to myself, *Make this painless.* I envisioned my body being ripped apart and metal being torn through it. Really vivid thoughts. I looked at the back of the seat in front of me and saw the two handles of the tray table. Are these going to go through me?

"I looked out the window. We were getting closer to the water, and I said to myself, *Hey, look, we're going to be fifty feet under water in a few seconds. Take the biggest breath you can possibly take. If you have the chance, take it.* I took the deepest breath I could. I wanted to scream at my dad, 'I love you!' but the last thing he wants to hear is the voice of his son before he crashes in an airplane."

In exit row ten, two highly driven professional women, Lori Lightner and Michelle DePonte, were seated in seats A and C, with Michael Whitesides, a deeply religious sales manager for a Japanese firm, between them. Lightner, the fashionable six-foot-one merchandise manager for Belk, burst out with an immediate response to the disconnected PA voice of Sullenberger: "Oh, crap, we're crashing!"

Like everyone in the Belk group, Lightner worked eighty hours a week in a high-wire, high-tension job trying to know, or determine for them, what junior misses would be wearing in Charlotte six months from now. With a life so fast-paced, combined with a distinct fear of flying, she liked to remove the real world from her mind by diving into books when on airplane flights. She became so detached, she had recently flown across the country sitting next to Hilary Duff without realizing it.

Now she dropped her book and grabbed her cell to call her husband. "I'm crashing and I'm dying and I want to tell him I love him," she said later. But her hand was shaking so much, she couldn't get the phone to function. Then Whitesides, who had been mostly silent, suddenly locked arms with both women and began to pray intensely.

"The praying seemed more important," Lightner said in a rapid-fire staccato that matches her work life. "I prayed for my family and my husband and helping them deal with it, the finances and all. I hoped Eric, my husband, understood he should get double on my life insurance because I was on a work trip. Maybe it's a strange thing to do, thinking about your insurance when you are dying, but I'm a practical person. But my first prayer was a quick 'Forgive me for everything I've done wrong. I don't have time to go through it all because I'm going to die.'"

At the window, Michelle DePonte had already gone into the death transition when she saw the George Washington Bridge. She, like Lightner, started dwelling on an accidental life insurance policy that she had just bought. She hadn't been sure about it. Now she was. "I figured I would never get benefits from it," she said. *Now, I will,* she thought.

Tripp Harris found his mind moving in the opposite direction of where novelists and moviemakers said it would go.

"They tell you your life is supposed to flash in front your eyes," Harris said. "For me it was totally opposite. It went to the things I had planned to do, that I was looking forward to doing. Like throwing a baseball with my son. He is two and a half years old. Of getting to see him grow up."

In traumatic situations, many people enter what psychiatrists call a dissociated state of mind, thinking incredibly rapidly—kaleido-scopically—but not necessarily in any coherent pattern. It's a hyp-notic state common to soldiers in combat—or more often *after* mind-numbing combat. The same thing happens to survivors of ter-rible accidents and victims of violent crimes; mind-numbing protec-tion against a reality the mind can't face.

The strange, rhythmic, slightly shrill chanting of the flight atten-dants—*Brace! Brace!*—didn't get through to Michelle DePonte. "I was imagining one of those airplane movies where the plane hits the water, does a spiral kind of move, a cartwheel, and there wasn't one ounce of 'I'm going to live' after that. I don't know how many people thought they were going to live, but that was it for me. It's my worst fear, crashing in an airplane, and it's happening and no one ever survives."

Sitting next to an emergency exit, staring over at the doorway in the side of the plane, DePonte's thoughts might have unnerved some of her fellow passengers. "I always get a window emergency exit row," she said. "For leg room and escape potential, never thinking the latter would be useful. I've never paid attention to the woman who asks if you can handle the door. Now I'm thinking this is really happening. Can you get out? No.[1] My last thought was that I was going to crash and it would be instantaneous and I wouldn't feel anything because I would die automatically."

Anyone who flies regularly knows that most passengers ignore safety instructions. Later, in the investigation of Flight 1549's crash, the National Transportation Safety Board determined that only twenty-five passengers had watched the demonstration, and just twelve had read the pre-flight instructions. Surprisingly, after the "Brace for impact" announcement, only two donned the life jackets beneath their seats before the plane crashed. Some did not know what "Brace for impact" meant, and a large number did not understand the proper position.

"How the heck do you brace?" asked Amber Wells, who had counted down the takeoff. "I looked around at others because I didn't have any idea."

Despite much evidence to the contrary, many fliers, like De-Ponte, equate crashing with dying—there seem to be few alterna-

---

[1] DePonte explained later that she did not mean she couldn't open the door, which she and Whitesides did together efficiently. She thought that she and everyone would be dead and the door irrelevant.

tives. Also, bracing positions have evolved over the years, and it is difficult to imagine, for example, a truly protective position for a six-foot-four man in one of the sardine seats in the back of the economy section. Further, unknown to the passengers, Sullenberger had come on a full ninety seconds before impact—perhaps a prescribed time, but an eon on this flight that would last, in total, only three hundred seconds.

Fidgety and scared, some passengers simply couldn't stay in the brace position that long. Many decided to gawk, or just to peek, during the final seconds. (This would contribute to more than thirty people injuring their heads on impact, albeit in mostly minor ways.)

"To me, it was just an eternity," said Beverly Waters, a forty-eight-year-old marketer from Gastonia, North Carolina. "My heart's about to come out of my chest. I'm nervous, scared. Are we going to crash into buildings? A field? What did it mean? And the flight attendants. 'Brace-brace-heads-down-stay-down,' over and over."

Laura Zych, the thirty-year-old Belk buyer who had just moved to Charlotte from Fargo, had staved off her loneliness by rambunctiously multiplying her wardrobe with recession-priced clothes in New York. Now she found something quite different calming her. For moments at a time the attendants' chant would seem to fade and the plane would go silent for Zych. "All you could hear was the baby crying. It was very surreal," Zych said. "You know how it is when you get on a plane and that annoying child is crying and it just won't stop? It wasn't that way. It was like, at least when you hear that sound, it means we're all still alive."

Little Sofia Sosa, the four-year-old, was doing the crying. To protect her, Sofia's father, Martin, had winched her seat belt in so tightly that it hurt. Hearing the sobs a few rows ahead, Tess turned around to try to comfort her daughter.

But Tess Sosa—Greek-born with the full name of Anastasia Tess

Gianiks, and small but tough at five foot four and 115 pounds—had a greater problem. How could she brace and protect the fragile nine-month-old child in her lap?

She looked once again at Whitaker. "Oh, we're approaching a runway," she said.

"Yeah," Whitaker said.

She looked Whitaker in the eye. "He's looking, like, Yeah. But he knew. And I think I knew by then, too. I decided to lean over him and look out the window, and he pulled back and gestured for me to look. I saw water and I knew we were landing in water," she said, and found the water somewhat comforting.

As for Whitaker, Sosa said: "I felt like he was someone there telling me things were taking their course and I just believed him. He asked to brace my son in a very matter-of-fact way. I was at the same time devastated and relieved. I had no idea how I could do it. I am pretty small. Damian is fairly large. The stewardesses said, 'Heads down! Stay down!' But then I heard a lot of strong male voices saying, 'Duck and cover. Duck and cover.' That is what I remember more. I was, like, thinking, *Is this a war zone?* When he asked if he could brace my son, it was like he was there to eliminate a lot of agony in my head."

Whitaker, who is six foot one and 180 pounds, remembers it this way: "Even before takeoff, when it was clear that she was very distressed, I told her about my own children. I was trying not to be a frightening seatmate, some strange businessman you don't know, and allow her to be less anxious about the ride.

"Now the crew was giving instructions to lean forward and prepare for impact. And of course that's when my seatmate and I—only a few minutes into our new intimate relationship in life—had to do something. She wasn't going to be able to lean forward with a child in her arms. So I asked Tess if I could hold her son while everyone got into a brace position. The anxiety level was heading off the charts. Crew yelling instructions. The anxiety was exponentially increasing.

"She looked at me in an incredibly distraught and human moment and said something to the effect, 'Are you sure?' And I said, 'Absolutely,' and held out my arms. And she handed her son to me.

"He was small enough that he could be held across my chest like a football, but I knew if I could put both arms around him in the long direction of his body, I'd have the best chance to hold on to him, depending on how rough the impact was. He was quiet as a church mouse. I was still fearful I could crush him. So I put one knee on the back of the seat in front of me and pushed back in my seat as hard as I could."

ALL THE OTHER dramas intensified, row by row.

Mike Leonard turned to a seatmate he had never seen before and probably would never see again.

"Looks like we're goin' in the drink," he said.

"Yup," responded March Dolphin, the Brooklyn physical therapist who so desperately wanted to get to her mother's eightieth birthday party.

Pam Seagle, the BoA marketing expert sitting on the window side of Dolphin, finally broke out of the reverie she had been in since the bird strike. Her palms had turned sweaty then, and she had fallen totally silent and even worried about the poor New Yorkers below watching another plane coming down toward them. Suddenly, she opened up. She asked about the nearest emergency exit, which she thought was a couple of rows away. Leonard told her it was right in front of her, one row up. Seagle pulled out of her acceptance mode and moved into an aggressive one: *I'm too young. My kids need me.*

They are teenagers. This isn't how I want to die. I moved quickly into *Uh-uh, no, I'm getting myself out of here. I can get out if we go in the river.*"

In seat 13D, Eileen Shleffar continued to chronicle the news to her husband, David, in Charlotte. "The call had dropped. I pushed the button again. 'We're going down,' I said when he came on. 'I love you. I love Samantha. Take good care of everyone. I hope I get to talk to everyone again. I will call if I can.'"

The phone call seemed endless, but the elapsed time had been less than two minutes. David was still confused.

"What is happening?" he asked.

"The captain just said, 'Brace for impact,'" she replied. "All I see is buildings on the left and buildings on the right and I think we're going to crash," she said.

"What do you mean, crash?"

"He knows I'm a bad flier," Shleffar explained. "Then, suddenly, I realized I didn't know how to brace and I looked around to see what everyone else was doing."

Later, Shleffar was asked if she realized how odd it was to talk on a cell phone all the way through the crash. "It was very odd. I know that. But it kept me in focus. It gave me strength. David is my rock."

In the last row, Vallie Collins leaned over and grabbed under her knees "and said good-bye to this earthly life." Then she added, half to herself, half in prayer, "And, okay, I haven't done as well as I could have but I've done well enough to get into Heaven."

For Andrew Gray, U.S. Army captain, retired as of December, "This was the moment that I realized we were in a shit sandwich." He was heartbroken and disappointed in himself. "That hum the engines make," he said, "it's always there. It fades into the background on flights. But I could almost hear the wind go by. We're just gliding. And I knew. Holy crap, everything I had told Stephanie was a lie, was false. Things were not going to be okay."

Stephanie heard "a lady shrieking, a gasp. I looked at Andrew. I immediately felt a sinking feeling. I thought we were going to crash into the buildings. You don't know how long you have to live."

In the retelling, Gray winces at Stephanie's words. "Oh, that would have been harder if I had known," Gray said. "I looked out and saw water." Like Tess Sosa, but unlike so many others, the water gave him a ray of hope. In his mind, moving at miles a second now, he began playing out survival possibilities and thought of swimming out. His heart sank again. A military plane, maybe. A chopper. But with 150 people? Could he get Stephanie out of this? *What if I'm unconscious or she's unconscious,* he worried.

"So then you accept that you are probably going to die. In many ways we were very fortunate. We were with someone we loved. About to get married. Life partners. I became calm. I was going to die, but I was going to die with somebody I loved."

Stephanie King remembered: "We were holding hands. Andrew looked at me and said, 'Babe, I love you.' I'm like, 'I love you, too.' We gave each other a kiss. We were still holding hands. We have to brace. . . ."

They blocked out all the other anxiety and prayers and moaning and cell phones around them and prayed.

King: "Please, God, help us through this."

Gray: "Lord, please deliver us and get us out of this mess somehow."

The other young lovers, Chris Rooney and Karin Hill, went through a similar moment: "We looked at each other and kissed and said we loved each other and held on to each other," Rooney said. "Karin huddled into my lap and I huddled over her—not the proper brace but that was our brace position all the way down. And we prayed."

Balaji Ganesan, a thirty-year-old information-technology expert born in Bangalore—the Silicon Valley of India—was heading home to his wife and eighteen-month-old daughter in Fremont, California. Sitting behind Tess Sosa, he had been charmed by Damian—"a jolly good fellow." Now he thought: *You got on a plane to go to a meeting, you are going on with your life, and this could be it.* "I'm staring into the seat in front of mine. This is the last time seeing things, thinking things. I am gone. I remembered my family and said good-bye to them. That's it."

Lucille Palmer, the tough but now frail Brooklyn-born eighty-five-year-old great-grandmother, ignored her window, her mind in a daze. "I didn't look out. I don't know what was going on in my mind. I wasn't even afraid. I was a blank," she said. When Sullenberger's terse words flashed through the cabin, she turned to her daughter, a fifty-eight-year-old public-health nurse, Diane Higgins.

"What'd he say?" Lucille asked her daughter, adding: "We're going down?"

"No, Ma," Higgins answered. But her mind was a ragged mess: The plane seemed so stable, it almost felt as if they were arriving at an airport. But there was no airport. From the middle seat, Higgins looked out. "All I could see was buildings. I thought we would crash into a neighborhood. I thought we were going to die. We grabbed each other as tight as we could and leaned forward."

In the first-class window seat 2A, Mark Hood, the ex-Marine who had served in Desert Storm in 1991 and then gone into the chaos of Monrovia to rescue noncombatants, talked to Denise Lockie next to him, and prayed most of the way down.

Lockie had just turned across the aisle to the American Airlines pilot, Susan O'Donnell, and asked if they were going down.

"She said, 'Yes,' and added a one-word expletive," Lockie said. Not very religious herself, she continued to pray with Hood. But from that point on, thoughts and prayers collided in anarchy inside her head. Single and without children, she thought about her sister and how this would devastate her. "But silly things intruded like not making my bed before the trip and who is going to come into my house and clean things up?"

Hood's prayers had turned to his eighteen-year-old son who was about the same age he had been when he lost his brother. "I prayed that my son would handle this better than I did, and I asked God's help for him." But Hood also looked out the window and his thoughts of very likely death shifted a bit. "I started to get this suspicion that this didn't feel like we were going to die. Things, the plane, seem to feel awfully in line."

Brian Siegel, one of the Charlotte bankers, conceded that he was in denial all the way down and did not think about dying. The captain's announcement made no sense. "I can't believe I'm on a plane and this guy just said *impact,*" Siegel recalled. It didn't get through to him as a fatal moment. "We were never out of control," he recalls. "Something in me said he's going to put this down in the river. I thought about the crash into the Potomac years ago—not a great thought—but I just thought, *Wow, this water is going to be cold.*"

The chanting continued; to many, it was a morbid sound track. . . . *Brace! Brace! Heads down! Stay down! Brace! Brace! Heads down! Stay down!* . . .

Memories of past crashes and video images of recent crashes, often into water, flashed through many minds, and they brought no comfort. The visions that invaded the passengers' minds had much to do with their age and background, and their television viewing habits.

Being Japanese, Hiroki Takigawa, found his mind stuck on a crash that had traumatized Japan and the world when he was a young man. At the height of the tourist season in August 1985, Japan Air Lines Flight 123, a Boeing 747 with 524 persons aboard, flew erratically for thirty-two minutes after a rear bulkhead rupture disabled the hydraulics, before crashing into the side of a mountain seventy miles northwest of Tokyo. The worst single-plane accident in history, all but four passengers were killed, and the bodies of the dead were badly mutilated. The epic thirty-two minutes that the pilots remained in radio contact and the passengers flew with the near-certainty of the outcome added immensely to the horror. Letters to family members were found blowing about near the wreckage. The entire Japanese nation mourned.

Takigawa was nineteen at the time. Now, married with an eleven-year-old son, a single thought refused to budge from his mind: "I just hoped that even if I die, my body would be in good shape to show my family. That's what I hoped at the very, very last moment."

But it was another scene that replayed in most minds, leading those who remembered it to the conclusion that water landings or ditchings were almost hopelessly deadly. It has become the Hope Diamond of airplane-disaster video clips and provides a strong insight into the power—not to mention limitations—of our visual age.

The video in question shows the hijacked Ethiopian Airlines Flight 961, a Boeing 767 wide body, attempting a water landing just off Grand Comoro Island, near the east coast of Africa. The crash occurred in front of a posh resort hotel jammed with tourists.

The video, taken by one of the vacationers, is an imagery-age icon, a must-have clip in every producer's library, a latter-day Zapruder film. Now thirteen years old, it has been replayed thousands upon thousands of times on every cable disaster show and repeatedly in the mainstream media in the aftermath of similar accidents.

In the video, the gleaming wide-body jet skirts over the ocean just beyond the surf line. The left wing tips slightly toward the water and makes contact first. The jet cartwheels spectacularly and breaks into pieces.

The less memorable commentary that sometimes accompanies the video raises some of the mitigating circumstances that plagued the flight—the most significant being that hijackers were wrestling with the pilots at the final moment. But many elements either go unsaid or slip under the mind's carpet forever.

The pictures do not tell the full story. The wing, for instance, did touch first, predictably a disastrous event. But, unseen, the left engine also caught on a coral reef and the plane's landing speed was two hundred miles per hour. Either or both could have started the cartwheel. Rarely remembered, too, is that 50 of the 175 occupants survived. As many as fifty other passengers lived through the crash only to drown most horribly. Their bodies were found inside the wreckage in relatively shallow water, with their inflated life vests trapping them against the ceiling even as scores of rescuers, many of them vacationing scuba divers, raced toward the wreckage.

But the image remains immensely powerful. And it stuck, like a childhood nightmare, in many minds aboard Flight 1549 as Sullenberger's ninety-second warning ticked away.

Joe Hart, fifty, a Cornelius, North Carolina, investment sales executive, insisted, "Nobody survives a plane crash in the water. We've all seen the video clips of the one off East Africa that did the cartwheel."

"If you've seen the tape of the plane that went down off the coast of Africa," Dick Richardson, a fifty-six-year-old Charlotte executive agreed, "that's the story of planes trying to land in water. That thing just cartwheeled. I thought I would die."

Even experienced fliers riveted on the cartwheel image. "I have a few flying hours," said Billy Wiley, fifty-two, a computer expert from Johnson City, Tennessee. "I had some conception of how risky this was going to be. I was thinking about the Ethiopian crash. I was sure that I was about to die."

Meanwhile, for most, time seemed to expand not contract. Frazzled minds fought with frazzled bodies in awkward bracing positions.

And it was so, so quiet. Heads began to pop up again, eyes began darting around at other passengers, out the windows. Except for the hushed whispers of prayers—*"Our Father who art in Heaven," "Now I lay me down to sleep," "Hail Mary, full of grace"*—only the chant pervaded the cabin, unrelenting. Then another voice came on like a PA announcement in the middle of the plane. A window passenger began counting down the distance to the water out loud.

  . . . Fifty feet, forty feet, thirty-five feet. . .

6

The Last Moments of Flight 1549

ON A CLOUDY DAY IN 1963, OVER A CITY THEN KNOWN AS LENINGRAD, A young Russian pilot named Victor Mostovoy circled his Aeroflot Tupolev-124 to deplete it of fuel before attempting a belly landing with a broken landing gear. He circled the great city, historically known as St. Petersburg, one time too many. Suddenly out of fuel, his engines went silent at 1,650 feet. Only twenty-seven years old, he held fifty-two lives and the pride of the Soviet Union in his hands.

Like another pilot forty-six years later, Mostovoy surveyed the scene beneath him—the city where the czars had built their palaces now had become a crowded Soviet metropolis. Pulkovo Airport, thirteen miles away, had prepared its dirt runway for a rough wheels-up landing, but it was now out of range. Mostovoy saw only one option. His eyes glued to the Neva River, a busy, serpentine waterway of drawbridges and regular boat traffic that wound through the city.

At three hundred feet he glided over one bridge, at one hundred feet over the next, and almost left paint on a third before landing in the river, just missing a tugboat. The plane remained afloat and the tug then towed it to shore. No one was injured.

Mostovoy's triumph came at the height of the Cold War and long before the age of never-ending news. Very little was heard about it—in fact, it has been in the news far more since Flight 1549's short journey than in the previous forty-six years.

Water landings, ditchings, and crashes have been a mix of catastrophic transoceanic plummets from high altitudes, jets plunging just short or just past a runway with all lives lost, terrorist bombings, and military shoot downs—and some success stories.

Perhaps the water event that aviation buffs bandy about most is the Japan Air Lines flight from Tokyo in 1968, which made a three-point landing in the fog—2½ miles short of the runway in San Francisco Bay. All 107 survived and the plane even went on to fly again. When asked what went wrong, the pilot, Kohei Asoh, answered: "As you Americans say, I fucked up."

But there have been other successful ditchings as well. On the eve of mass commercial jet flight in 1956, two Boeing Stratocruisers ditched with reasonably successful outcomes. In April of that year a Northwest Airlines flight went down in the cold waters of Puget Sound, a near-perfect ditching. Boats and planes hurried to the scene, but the thirty-eight passengers, including two children, felt the wings and then the fuselage sink below their feet before rescuers arrived, a full six minutes after the plane went under. Five of the thirty-eight, including one of the children, died from drowning.

Six months later, Pan American Flight 006, an around-the-world flight making the last leg from Honolulu to San Francisco, lost one engine at a point too far out from Hawaii to return and not far enough along to reach California. By radio, the airplane located a coast guard weather ship in the area, flew to it, and orbited the ship several hours till dawn. Then it ditched in fifteen-foot waves that broke the fuselage in half. The plane sank in seventeen minutes, but the thirty-eight passengers and crew all made it into rafts and were rescued by the coast guard. The successful ditching became a "media sensation," with full-page photos in *Life* magazine.

But an "unplanned water landing," as the National Transportation Safety Board defined the event in the Hudson on January 15, 2009 (taking it out of the category of a ditching), was about as rare then as it had been when Comrade Captain Mostovoy looked out over Leningrad and made the correct, snap decision to head for the Neva. And if a "miracle on the Hudson" was about to occur, it would require a sequence of "miracles" to enable it. One Safety Board official close to the investigation counted as many as eight "miracle requirements," starting with the cockpit crew's experience and innate abilities to make almost instant decisions to deny the temptation of the airports and go instead for the Hudson, then do what they never could have been trained to do. The official went on to list the weather, a calm river clear of traffic, trained rescuers ready at the snap of one's fingers, the structural strength of the airplane, senior flight attendants, and, not least, passengers who, despite natural and dreadful fears that would not end when the plane hit the water, did indeed scramble, and occasionally lose it, but got it back fast and did not panic.

"This is not like seeing God's image in a piece of French toast," the official said, "but sometimes miracles do occur."

• • •

JOSH PELTZ STARTED the countdown to the water for two reasons that he can recall. The flight attendants' *brace-brace* chant seemed to speed up and rise an octave the longer they continued, perhaps as their own anxiety rose. "It was driving me crazy," Peltz said. He looked across his row to a woman on the aisle, Jenny Moulton of Charlotte, whom he had met in the terminal. *The same anxiety must be rising in her, too,* he thought. And, being in the center of the aircraft, Moulton must be unable to see anything—she was flying blind. By that time everyone had strange looks in their eyes, and the look in Moulton's told him he should do something. So he did.

With 150 widely different personalities sitting in the increasingly claustrophobic tightness of the silent aircraft, amid a sea of blue upholstery—blue, a downer color, according to psychologists—it was unrealistic to think that everyone wanted this added service. Fred Berretta, a Charlotte banker sitting six rows behind Peltz, remembers one woman yelling: "Please stop! You're terrifying all of us." Peltz didn't hear her. Berretta actually liked the count, noting that by the end, Peltz's read on the moment of impact was pretty close to perfect.

Peltz also shared a feeling with most of the others: a total loss of control over his destiny, a feeling of helplessness, which probably was tougher on the hard-driving professionals—their confidence in their ability to control fate had, after all, contributed greatly to their materialistic success—than on some of the others. That said, there were no predictable or average psyches aboard Flight 1549. Some accepted; some fought; some hid. And some who had opened their arms once before, now opened their arms to the next logical step.

Peltz, like many aboard, was hardly average or predictable. He had already gone through the acceptance of his own death. "Everything will be okay, no matter what happens," he had concluded. "I made peace with my world, if that makes sense. It's a horrible feeling but also a release. Then, as soon as that sensation came over me, that sense of letting go, I realized I didn't want to go. This pilot is doing everything he can to land this plane safely. I need to do what I need to be doing."

That meant getting the exit door open if he got the chance. That's when he discovered that his mind was not functioning on all cylinders—or perhaps the cylinders were spinning too quickly and in too many competing directions. Others near the exit doors had similar experiences: the most routine act, especially for a disciplined mind, becoming almost hopelessly complex and befuddling at a time of incredibly elevated stress. The procedure was quite simple; in fact, the instructions may have been more complicated than the actual workings of the door. "At least, in my mind's state, they didn't seem simple—six pages of instructions, I recall. I'd go through the steps and then I'd say to myself, *What was step three again?* I do move toward humor in stressful situations. I actually started laughing to myself. I felt like I was cramming for midterms in my school days. At a rather accelerated pace."

Sitting just behind Peltz in seat 11F, at the other right-side emergency door, Don Norton, who lives in the Charlotte suburbs, had the same experience. "I must have read them for twenty seconds," he said. "I didn't comprehend a word that I saw."[1]

Except for the endless chant and the Peltz countdown, the plane grew increasingly silent. "The anxiety was palpable," said Carl Bazarian, a sixty-two-year-old investment banker from Amelia Island, Florida. Oddly, Bazarian had lived much of his life with a recurring dream about an airplane "taking off, banking to the left toward a bridge, and the plane has no propulsion." The dream always ended

---

[1] Still, the two men, as well as the other passengers next to the exit doors, Adelaide Horton and Michelle DePonte, would be remarkably efficient in working those escape routes. When the time came, the doors virtually burst out of the plane within seconds of each other.

inconclusively, but he recognized the scenario immediately. An Armenian Orthodox Christian, he now said the "Lord's Prayer" in Armenian. But his mind competed with itself, as if it were at war, all the way down. "I went from white-knuckle panic—I mean white knuckle—to my mind actually extricating itself from my body and looking back. I knew we were going to die. I didn't want to suffer the trauma. But that experience lasted only a few seconds." Then he went back into meditation and prayer. "I guess it was a long two minutes."

Minds flitted at astonishing speeds in almost every direction. Steve O'Brien, a New Yorker who had moved to Charlotte, skittered from the important to the melancholy. "I thought how ironic it was that I was going to die in the Hudson," he said. "Three of my four grandparents came in from Ireland at Ellis Island, and now I was going out that way. Full circle." Ellis Island lay dead ahead, five miles downstream where the river empties into New York Harbor.

Tracey Wolsko, who'd tried to blot out her fear of flying by bringing down the window shade on takeoff, now focused powerfully on survival: "I can do it. I can do it. It's not going to be pretty. I'm going to be hurt, but I've got to keep focused. I know my game plan. I know how to exit. There's gonna be blood. I'm gonna have broken bones. I remember, God, please not my face. Anything but my face." Wolsko placed her pillow between her arms and her face and thought: *I'm not ready to make my husband a wealthy widower. I do not want my mom to bury a child.*

Thoughts turned invariably to family and children, none more poignantly than those of Brad Wentzell, a thirty-one-year-old salesman from Charlotte via Boston who thought he would never see his three-year-old daughter again: "I could smell her. That was a very real feeling. Every dad knows the smell of their daughter, their child. It's a warm, sweaty, sweet smell mixed with a little bit of diapers and mischief, and I could smell her." He pondered Heaven, and the belief that you don't miss people and earthly matters there. "I don't know if I would want to miss that."

AT LEAST TWO passengers carried life stories with them that added almost unimaginably to the complexity of their emotions.

John Howell, flying first class in seat 2D, stared probingly into the eyes of Flight Attendant Sheila Dail, looking for some kind of indication of what was really happening. Dail did well, he thought, gesturing and making the kind of eye contact that said they would be fine. But he could see out the windows "and I knew we weren't going to be fine."

Howell, a client adviser for the high-powered international tax and accounting company, KPMG, seemed to spend his life in the air, and usually with New York at one end. Now he tried to think of all the bracing options and finally cinched his seat belt very tightly, almost as if to punish himself, and grabbed his ankles. "But it seemed half-hearted," he said. "I didn't think there was much chance at all. So I'm holding my ankles, expecting the worst, and suddenly I just grew livid about it all. I couldn't believe that I was going to do this to everyone. I was thinking of my parents and the rest of my family. I was not frightened. I was just overwhelmingly annoyed with myself. This was too much of a burden for them. And since I saw the geese, it seemed even more ridiculous."

But there was something else. Howell's brother, George DiPasquale, a New York City firefighter, had died a hero seven years earlier in the rubble of the World Trade Center, his body never found. A towering man at six foot five, DiPasquale had been a powerful person in many lives. An elder in the Jehovah's Witnesses, his fellow firefighters at the station in Hell's Kitchen called him "Holy Man." He'd been singled out so often as a special person among the 343 fire-fighters who gave their lives that day that his widow finally asked the media to stop writing stories about him.

"My parents suffered so badly. Many people suffered for so many years after that," Howell said. "Now I'm going to cause it to happen all over again. And it was a question of choice. I didn't *have* to have this job. I didn't *have* to be going down in an airplane in New York. It seemed selfish. New York. *Again*."

Howell berated himself all the way down to the Hudson.

Eric Stevenson had finally concluded it was happening to him again—déjà vu with an exclamation point. But it wasn't until the plane sank down to four or five hundred feet—the lowest level that his dead-engine Boeing 767 reached—that it hit him with full force that the hauntingly similar flights would not end the same way. No engine would relight this time. No Newark, as he had thought just moments ago. Unlike the flight twenty-two years earlier, when he sat in the middle of the wide-body jet and could see nothing, this time he had a perfect window view. He didn't think a landing would have been survivable the first time around; he didn't think it would this time, either. "I thought we would break up," he recalled, feeling what could only be described as "utter disbelief." It all seemed so wildly against all odds.

Oh my God, it was only supposed to be a once-in-a-lifetime event and here it is happening all over again, he thought. "I could not believe it. I can't believe I am on another plane that's going down. It's just not real."

He flashed back to 1987 over the Pacific in that big jet with two-five-two seating: him sitting there, wedged blindly in among the five as flight attendants gave more detailed instructions about life jackets and other details of landing, ditching, crashing, whatever, in the water. He remembered that people didn't really "hear" them over the

Pacific, either. All around him he could hear the *psssht, psssht, psssht* of life jackets inflating and flight attendants shouting, "Don't inflate the life jackets in the aircraft! Don't inflate the life jackets in the aircraft!" *Psssht, psssht, psssht* . . .

Stevenson concluded later that the shock of it all might have been greater for him because he held on to the dream of a Newark Airport landing so long before the reality of Flight 1549's final destination broke through. "When I passed through that threshold," he said, "it was stunning: *Oh my God, we are going to crash.*" He hurriedly wrote a note to his mother and sister and placed it in his shirt pocket as he had twenty-two years ago in hopes that they would find it afterward. Then he put his arms on the seat ahead, placed his head on them, and turned his neck to look out at the water quickly rising toward him. It was not a good brace position. But many of the passengers did not have good brace positions. That is part of the miracle on the Hudson.

At six foot five, Alex Magness is a big man in every way—thirty-eight years old and fast-track successful as a New York sales director for Hewlett Packard. Seated in the tightest of seats, a rear-coach window, 17A, the head-on-knees brace position was impossible for him. He couldn't even wedge his knees straight against the seat ahead. Next to him, Nick Gamache, a software sales engineer from Raleigh, North Carolina, tried to help by moving slightly to the left so Magness could angle his knees away from the seat back. He became a six-foot-five-inch pretzel. "In the coming impact," he said "my choice was to break my neck by hitting the ceiling or break my neck by hitting the seat back." He found himself checking the distance to the ceiling. "The main thing I thought about was whether I'm going to go flying all over this cabin." His mind shot back to September 11 and emerging from the subway to see people leaping out of the flaming World Trade Center tower. He wasn't at all sure that, personally, this was worse than that. Lifting his head briefly, he saw the skyline of Manhattan racing by. The pilot had kept the wings straight, almost as if he were making an airport landing. Like many, Magness surely had not given up.

Another determined watcher was Billy Campbell in window seat 25A in the back. He saw boats in the river "very close to us." Campbell continued to glance out the window occasionally all the way down.

In Charlotte, Eileen Shleffar's husband was racing home from the carwash as the plane neared the river, so their phone call was temporarily interrupted again. "I was still hopeful," she said, "but I realized I do not know what the brace position is and this is not a good time to wonder about that. There was so much room in the aisle I turned my legs out into it and I hugged my legs. When I looked up and down the aisle, I saw no one else was doing that. When I looked left and right, all I could see were buildings and I thought, *So what does this matter?*" Eventually, she moved back into a more conventional position.

Most passengers got themselves into one of the two recommended brace positions: either placing their head down and grabbing their ankles, or arranging their arms on the back of the seat in front of them and resting their head on their arms. But many peeked, many rose up from time to time, and many found themselves suffering feelings of fatalism.

Bill Zuhowski braced, but in doing so, he asked himself: "*How do you brace for death? What difference will it make if my head is up or down? This is going to be it.*"

Others had accepted the outcome in line with their religious faith. Mike Kollmansberger, a thirty-six-year-old salesman and evangelical Christian from Lexington, South Carolina, was certain he would die. "I'm okay with that," he said. "I'm going to hit this water and go see the Lord Jesus in fifteen seconds."

Some, like Carl Bazarian, tried to mentally remove themselves;

others, like Jim Whitaker, found the experience, "so tactile"—such an on-your-plate feeling—that it was impossible to escape into some non-world. For him, this was as real as life can get.

Still others, with a flash of a blush when they talked about it later, found themselves profoundly interested in finally answering life's ultimate question.

Dan Vinton, a Charlotte auditor, didn't think he would make it. He felt grief-stricken for his family but not particularly afraid of death. "I just hoped we wouldn't take out a whole city block of New York with us." He looked with some fascination at "the chance to watch myself die. Are the lights just going to shut off? Now I'm going to find out: Do we go to Heaven or do we just turn to dust?" (Vinton was reluctant to tell that tale later until he found that others shared a similar curiosity. Bazarian came up to him once, after a television show, and told him he hadn't been able to tell that story about himself till he heard Vinton tell it.)

Others were doing what the Pentagon calls "contingency planning." No matter how remote the possibility, they were charting best-odds plans for their personal response to what was coming.

Jay McDonald was typical in that regard. Having had his survival odds tested once before with his brain tumor, McDonald thought, *"Maybe, just maybe, I can survive this."* He was sure everyone had had their nightmares about being trapped underwater or caught in a fire. *"Okay, the plane is going to break apart,"* he said to himself. *"An onrush of water. Swim toward the light and pray to God there is a crack in the fuselage overhead. Now, don't get tangled up in the wiring up there. How do I make it through such an obstacle course?*

"You have to try to move the macabre thoughts aside. So I did have some logical thinking that went from 'This is the end,' to 'wait, I've seen this movie before. I'm going to be one of those guys who gets out,'" McDonald said.

Jim Hanks, the Baltimore lawyer, also ran a whole course of

thoughts through his head as they got closer and closer. At sixty-five, he was one of the few on the plane old enough to have a childhood memory of *Life* magazine's 1956 rescue photographs of Pan American Flight 006's ditching in the Pacific with all lives saved. He was twelve years old when he last looked at it, but, while most passengers were flashing on the terrifying Ethiopian Airlines cartwheel, Hanks thought of the old black-and-white photos in *Life*.

The brace position, ordered ninety seconds before the crash, became so uncomfortable for him that he sat up at least twice and looked around. The cabin, despite the chant, despite Josh Peltz's countdown, was "just tensely, almost explosively quiet." He remembers thinking it was the kind of situation he had occasionally faced in legal negotiations: "If one person snaps, that's going to legitimize everybody snapping. But if no one snaps, it will hold together." The key, he thought, came down to this: If someone *does* snap, there must be cool heads nearby to quickly quiet them down.

At the same time, twelve rows ahead, March Dolphin had a similar thought: *"Calm can be just as contagious as panic."* If they survived the landing, they were going to need some people who could nip panic in the bud.

Peering up out of his stiffening brace position, Hanks looked around out the windows and saw cars and condos on both sides of the river, so close now he thought he could see the people in them. It was a beautiful day. New Yorkers and Jerseyites were going about their business, living their lives, dealing with their problems, loving their loves.

"How could a huge, big tragedy happen in this sea of normality?" Hanks asked himself. "It's a totally irrational thought. Of course something could happen on a perfectly normal day. But I just didn't think it would." Still, when he finally saw that they had descended to the level of the West Side Highway, Hanks, a six-footer, "bunched up in as small a little ball as I can be."

Outside, people were looking in. Vince Carter, the All-Star guard for the New Jersey Nets, stood transfixed at his Jersey-side condo window as the huge jet passed by just above the water. "I couldn't believe it," he told the New York *Daily News*. "It was like watching television."

Meanwhile, text messages and cell phone calls began pulling thousands of New Yorkers to the windows of their offices, and Jerseyites like Carter to the windows of their apartments, all witnessing the strange sight out there—a long white Airbus in flawless landing mode now skimming the length of Central Park, then just feet above the Hudson at a sink rate, to the distant and untrained eye, scarcely faster than a normal airport landing. In reality, the plane had indeed slowed down to a nearly conventional landing speed of about 150 miles an hour, but was descending three times as fast as it should—13.5 feet a second.

INSIDE THE AIRBUS, the passengers had gone deadly silent but for the murmur of a few whispered prayers.

Sitting near the front in seat 7A, Casey Jones, in charge of marrying the technology of the two merged financial giants, BoA and Merrill, had just finished the Act of Contrition—the Roman Catholic prayer of preparation for death—followed by a Hail Mary, then he began hearing the off-putting sounds of the cockpit warning system, a robotic computer voice punctuated by chimes and bongs that rose in volume as the danger grew nearer.

Caution! Terrain!

Too low! Terrain!

Caution! Terrain!

Terrain! Terrain! Pull up! Pull up!

Pull up! Pull up! Pull up! Pull up!! Pull up!! Pull up!!

The loud sound of chimes continued.

Caution!! Terrain!!

Terrain!! Terrain!! Pull up!!! Pull up!!! Pull up!!!

Jones had found the flight attendants' *brace-brace* chant creepy, but the rising, robotic audibles of the computerized cockpit warning system emerging from behind the door didn't faze him at all now. "There was no way to escape what was about to happen," Jones said. "All hope for avoiding a crash was lost, and I had to focus on survival."

If Jones had been able to hear any other sounds from the cockpit, he might have been more concerned. He would have heard the last exchange between Sullenberger and Skiles.

Sullenberger: "Got any ideas?"

Skiles: "Actually, not."

A few urgent but commanding voices caromed back and forth in the center of the cabin. "Ready on the doors! Ready on the doors!"

The last number anyone remembers coming from Josh Peltz was four.

Then the tail struck the Hudson. Hard. At the front of the plane, still barely above the water and before all the other noise rushed over him, Barry Leonard heard the plane's tortured airframe groan.

"Honestly," he said, "it groaned."

7

A Crash in Weehawken,
a Bow to New York

THE TAIL OF FLIGHT 1549 TOUCHED DOWN HARD IN NEW JERSEY WATERS straight out from Manhattan's West Fiftieth Street. The fuselage and nose settled quickly into the water and the aircraft hydroplaned five or six blocks farther downriver. Then, as its left engine was shorn off by the water's drag, the plane made a dramatic left turn to point its nose at West Forty-fourth, the ferry docks, and the *New York Times* Building.

The moment of impact came at 3:30 and forty-two seconds in the afternoon, five minutes and nine seconds after the plane took off from LaGuardia.

It came down about five miles from the airport. But, considering the large loop it had taken, Jeff Kolodjay joked later that he should get fourteen miles on his next frequent-flier report.

So ended the 16,300th flight of the ten-year-old Airbus A320, tail number N106US. On takeoff, US Airways would have expected to fly the plane at least ten more years, and then sell it to another airline for perhaps ten further years of use.

The demise of N106US would go down in the record books as an "unplanned water landing" in Weehawken, New Jersey. But, as if the plane had a public-relations mind of its own, the now totaled sixty-million-dollar aircraft could sense where its afterlife lay and positioned itself in that direction—toward the myth-making, story-hungry media capital of the world, which already had begun flashing the drama around the globe.

Not that any of those thoughts—and what they might mean over the next months for the individuals inside—had penetrated the thin aluminum skin of the floating, but leaking, hull of the Airbus.

Inside the plane the drama was far from over, and the next few seconds broke down into another of those time warps in which the blink of an eye mentally passed as slowly as the opening and closing of a drawbridge. For the first five or six seconds—at least until the plane stopped and began its methodical drift downstream on the Hudson's four-mile-an-hour current—the passengers were frozen, hit amidships by a range of sounds and sensations described later in wildly different manners. During this brief period, many still thought they would cartwheel, and when the plane took its unexpected left turn, they braced against what they thought was the inevitable breakup.

Many may have been briefly unconscious or stunned when their heads struck the seats in front of them. Others had gone so deeply into altered-mind states, preparing for death or simply shutting out reality, that they have no memories of the landing. Some thought they were dead already and the landing itself was the act of death. Many watched the entire event as if from outside of it.

At least one, Mary Berkwits, thought she had landed at Newark International Airport.

Nothing resembling even a partly consistent description has emerged from among the passengers' memories of the landing, although most found it far less violent than they expected. Most clutched their way through the few seconds of bumps and rumbles as the rest of the fuselage, and finally the plane's nose, flopped into the water, slowed, and made its unexpected turn. In those split seconds fears of cartwheeling and breaking up spiked. Aircraft often come apart at what are called production breaks—the joints where large, separately built sections such as the cockpit, tail, and fuselage units are married together. N106US groaned and moaned as tremendous forces pulled at its weak points. But it would not, did not, break.

The survivors' minds played spectacular tricks on the memories of some, especially those in the rear of the plane. Some were certain that windows broke and water poured through the openings, but stunned minds going there was not difficult to understand. Some of the windows were briefly submerged, the inner casings popping off and striking passengers' faces or landing in their laps. At the same time, icy water spurted up through the floorboards beneath them and in the aisle.

So, a relative piece of cake for one passenger quite easily became the most terrifying moment of all for another.

Once the plane was in the water, circumstances divided the passengers into three distinct universes: 1) the group in first class and the first few rows of the economy section who could use the two front exit doors, 2) those in the middle economy seats clustered around the four wing exit hatches, and 3) the economy class from about row nineteen or twenty back who normally would use the two rear exit doors. Unfortunately, the Hudson already had begun flooding through various breaks in the back of the plane and had made the rear exit doors useless.

No one recollects any human sounds—no screaming or crying out or even audible prayers—during this briefest of periods, the first five seconds. This is a slice of what they do remember, or don't:

"We made three hits," said Clay Presley, a Charlotte businessman said. *"Bam, bam, bam,* sharp turn to the left. That's when I thought, *Oh shit, here's where we are going to flip."*

"It didn't feel like a bad boom," Alecia Shuford of Matthews, North Carolina, said, "just a bad landing."

"I don't remember anything," said Amber Wells, the NASCAR executive who had counted down the takeoff. "Not what it felt like. Not how hard it was. Not what my body felt like."

"It was like landing in Velcro," said Keith Anthony, a Davidson, North Carolina, banking consultant. "You stuck."

"It made a tremendous sound," said Jim Whitaker. He was still protecting young Damian Sosa in his arms while he watched and felt it all. "Such a huge object smacking the water. It's not a pleasant feeling or sound. We had continuing repercussions as the fuselage came down and then the water came in a huge wave up past the plane."

"If you want to get the same feeling, get on the highway by yourself," Chris Rini, the drag racer, told *Racin' Today.* "Get your car up to about eighty-five miles an hour, set the cruise control, and jump into the backseat."

"It felt like Splash Mountain at Disney World," Hiroki Takigawa said.

"Like we were coming down in the space shuttle," said Joe Hart.

"I thought we might be below the surface because the water was not coming down off the outside of the window," said Molly Schugel, who was sitting in one of the over-wing exit rows.

"A very unusual sound," said Irina Levshina, who was sitting in the last row. "Not quite screeching. I thought this is it. This is the last sound I will hear. Not a very pleasant one."

"Just above a minor car crash," said Brian Moss, who sat in the same position as Levshina in row twenty-six on the other side of the plane.

"We just hit—*BAM!*—and came to a stop," Jim Hanks said. "I had this big piece of metal in my lap."

"The vibration was deafening," John Howell said. "The tail was dragging in the water. My thought was, *It's going to come apart.* This all happened so fast and when the plane spun, I thought the left wing bit into the water. The plane definitely was going to fracture, and the water would come in with such velocity that I couldn't contemplate it."

"People looked at video later and said it was so smooth," Luther Lockhart said. "Bullshit. It was a huge car wreck."

Jeff Kolodjay watched from window seat 22A. "It went very black as we went under the water. Then it got very bright when we bobbed up. It was like being in a fish tank."

Raymond Mandrell, the rap producer from Miami in window seat 24F, had video visions, complete with his own special effects. "*Woo-hoo,* man! Oh, man, that was like, you ever been through any hurricanes? I know we were going hundreds of miles per hour. All the windows shattered, all you felt was air coming through the windows. You saw a bunch of ice coming through the windows. I don't want to say it was like crashing into a wall. It was like a hurricane. Like the whole plane was going to break apart into pieces."

Alyson Bell, a Christmas and Easter churchgoer four rows ahead of Mandrell, had a different sense: "An overwhelming feeling of warmth just spread over me. It was calm. A sense of peace, that if it's my time, then it's my time."

Then her head hit the seat in front of her and she felt very cold water at her ankles.

SO MUCH FOR the first five or six seconds. After the plane came to a halt, its screeching and groans settled into an occasional metallic moan and the bobbing, sloshing sounds of a boat adrift at sea. Inside, as if hit by a stun gun or given an emotional anesthetic, the passengers remained totally silent for a moment longer. "We had this little pause," Clay Presley said. "Is this what death is like?"

With so many prepared for their end, minds reeled and unreeled, some coming quickly to clarity, others lingering longer elsewhere. Then the first click ricocheted through the cabin, then a rapid fire of others, like old rifles kicking out shells, as passengers snapped free of what had been their safety belts and now were just the opposite. A din of noise, personal, instructional, urgent, fearful, squeaks, and military-like orders, erupted inside the plane: *On the doors! Open the doors! Turn around! Close that overhead! Are you crazy?! Doors!*

Early in the din, Chesley Sullenberger emerged from the cockpit and called out loudly with now well-recognized terse certainty: "Evacuate the plane!" Not everyone heard him, but most had already begun moving.

Suddenly, the aisles bordered on bedlam.

Brad Wentzell, struggling through, saw that several people were going into the overhead bins for their luggage and valuables. A treasured mink was there. Computers with years of work. Heirlooms . . . and nothings. "Get out of the overhead!" Wentzell yelled. "Somebody's going to drown for what you are reaching for." Most stopped, as if the thought had just broken through.

Some passengers remained glued to their seats. Others either pushed past them, or helped the ones who seemed unable to respond, lifting them to their feet. The aisle became solid with people; it took a sharp elbow to break through. And in many cases, that wasn't enough; sharp elbows flew back. Some started over the top of seats "like a cat on furniture," said Diane Higgins, who had panicky feelings about how she would get her eighty-five-year-old mother, Lucille Palmer—the woman who could barely walk—out of the plane. "Just leave me," her mother said. "Ma!" Higgins shouted, horrified at the mere thought.

Up front, in first class, the passengers had taken a good thump when the nose landed. But no one was in a better position: They needed only to go out the first-class exit doors to the rafts. Still, they had their reality checks to get through.

Denise Lockie remained hunched over in the brace position as passengers began to pass by her in the aisle. Mark Hood tapped her on the shoulder and as she came up, she looked him in the eyes and asked, "Are we in Heaven?"

Hood responded, "No, and I'm no angel. Come on, we've got to go."

Just ahead of them Barry Leonard rose, and started away, then paused and looked back at his seat. "I wanted to make sure my body wasn't still there," he said.

Mid-plane, passengers jammed around the wing exits. There were two on each side. Any doubts that the passengers at the over-wing exits had about their ability to think clearly were quickly laid to rest. They opened the hatches so fast the times would go into *Guinness* if *Guinness* kept such records.

Onshore videos showed that on the left side of the plane Michelle DePonte—who took the seat for the view and the leg room—had her door out in fifteen seconds with the help of Michael Whitesides. Adelaide Horton's door followed almost simultaneously, and videos show passengers exiting through them almost instantly. On the right

side the wing hatches came out just seconds later, after a brief moment of confusion when the passenger next to Josh Peltz tried to pull
the door in as Peltz pushed out. Don Norton had the other door out
before his seatmate could express a crucial fear. Molly Schugel was
worried that they were underwater. "I started to say to Don, 'Don't
open it,' but he had it open in a nanosecond."

Schugel was more right than she thought. Safety instructions tell
passengers not to open wing exits in water landings—to avoid flooding the plane. Instead, they're advised to go to the front and back
where life rafts are stowed. But this was another miracle on the Hudson. The water was not up to the exit level, and there were no waves
that afternoon, as there had been just a few days earlier. The passengers made the right move. In fact, it was more right than they could
have imagined.

Rear-cabin passengers pushed toward the back of the plane
where the signs directed them. But they would find only terror there.

Unlike the rest of the cabin, which remained in relatively good
shape, the back looked more like a train wreck the closer you came to
the galley. Oxygen masks dangled in the air; overhead-compartment
doors were off their hinges and askew; bags had fallen out; and parts
of the ceiling had broken and fallen to the floor.

But it was worse than just a mess. At impact, water had entered
the plane below the cabin floor, then began to seep in on the passengers.

Then, it surged.

On the aisle in seat 20C, Beth McHugh was still in her head-
down brace position when the turning plane threw her to the right
and she looked down to see "water shooting through the floorboards."

In the next to last row, in Seat 25F, Laurel Hubbard, a forty-six-
year-old Matthews, North Carolina, accountant, was still seated

when she heard someone scream, "We're going to drown!" Something had wedged her into her seat, a piece of debris broken loose from the plane. She lifted it and put it behind her. As she did so, she felt icy water rising up her legs almost to seat level. She began to panic. Hubbard can't swim. She believed she would need to climb to the top of her seat to breathe, and frantically tried to calculate how much room there was to the ceiling. "I'm wondering how long it will take to drown. Two minutes," she thought. And then, "I don't want to fight it for two minutes. I just want to let go."

In this kind of panic, memories and time frames become very confused, but one thing remained clear: No one would use the rear exits. They were underwater and jammed.

Other than Doreen Welsh, the flight attendant, Vallie Collins was the first to get into the now flooding galley. When she finally turned to leave, she knew she was at the dead end of a tunnel, an army of frightened passengers coming toward her and blocking the only way out, which was in the other direction.

Despite the terror and confusion, she remembers the moment clearly: "The water is above my chest now. Right there where the cup of your bra hits your bra strap. It was like needles." Her greatest life-long fear has been driving off a bridge and being unable to get out of the car.

She turned and tried to go forward. One man came at her with his arms flailing. She stood her ground. "Go the other way!" For what seemed like eons, the gridlock in the aisle did not seem to move in either direction.

Chesley Sullenberger had done his part and gotten them down. Now the passengers would have to do theirs. Without lessons. Without guides. With flight attendants stranded at opposite ends of the airplane.

It was a strange moment. Some passengers were already leaving the plane, liberated by escape, while others were penned in and even more terrified than they had been during the descent.

The reality was that all the passengers still had deadly water problems—both inside and outside the plane.

MICHELLE DEPONTE SCRAMBLED out onto the left wing and stepped into brilliant sunshine, the first to escape what she assumed would become an underwater tomb. The Manhattan panorama, framed against a clear, cold, blue sky, never looked more welcoming. Surging with adrenaline, overcome with relief, and overjoyed to be alive, DePonte did not even feel the frosty bite of the 22-degree air. On the descent, she had stared out the window, disbelieving what she was seeing until the final seconds before impact when she had squeezed her eyes shut tight.

"I opened my eyes and thought, *Am I alive?* It was very strange. You close your eyes and think you're going to be dead and then, opening them again, it's this amazing feeling. I felt pretty good. Now I wanted to get off this airplane. If I lived through a frigging plane crash, I am not dying after it, no matter what."

DePonte and her seatmate, Michael Whitesides, had opened the door over the wing in a flash. "I don't even remember taking my seat belt off. The door flew out," she said.

Memories conflict about who first jumped off the wing. DePonte remembers stepping out onto the wing and hesitating, uncertain what to do next. Whitesides said DePonte ran down the wing and leaped in and that he followed her into the water. "I realized that she didn't take anything and I took her a seat cushion and one for myself, and jumped in after her," he said.

At any rate, the next passengers onto the wing behind Whitesides followed him into the river—a man, followed by a woman, then another woman, and then another man. Steve O'Brien worked his way forward from row fifteen, stepped onto the wing, and launched himself with both feet: "Like I was jumping into a swimming pool."

"It was like watching lemmings," said Clay Presley, who had sat across the aisle from O'Brien and arrived at the exit just after he went in. "Everyone was a lemming."

The swimmers said later they saw no other option. "You had to explode out of that plane," O'Brien said. "The passengers were screaming '*Go! Go! Go!*' You had to get out. It didn't occur to me to go onto the wing. At that point, nobody was on the wing."

In DePonte's memory, she crouched nervously on the wing for a few seconds, then jumped, uncertain what the next steps should be. There had been no advice from the crew. She had expected to see a life raft, but none was in sight. The rafts at the rear of the plane, submerged, would never deploy. The raft on the left side at the first-class cabin had not yet appeared.

DePonte was confused. *Why do we not have a raft?* she wondered. *What's going on?* When some of the passengers in the water yelled up at her to jump in, and then one of them waved a hand, "I thought, well, that's not a bad idea," and leaped from her perch. "Jumping in the water was not a hard or monumental decision. That was the easy part," she said.

Meanwhile, in the first-class cabin, where the life raft out the left door had not yet deployed, Barry Leonard had moved to the door. He saw none of his coach-class companions paddling his way; like them, he was laser-focused on his escape. The river looked to be about three feet below where he stood. A voice commanded: "Jump!" Stooping, he untied and removed his shoes, and then made the leap.

Forty-four seconds had elapsed since the Airbus touched down.

• • •

THERE WERE NOW eight passengers in the river off the plane's left side, swimming in water so cold, icicles hung like long, jagged fangs from the snouts of the ferries when they arrived. No one wore a life preserver to keep his head above the water should they become hypothermic and lose consciousness, although four had grabbed seat cushions as they dashed out the exit. Having survived the impact relatively unscathed, they now faced the prospect of drowning. From the exit, others watched as several of the jumpers swam quickly away from the plane.

"I thought they were crazy," said Michael Leonard, one of the Belk Six, who watched the group as he waited to climb out onto the wing. "It was freezing out. Hypothermia kills. Why would you possibly go in the water?"

Later, accident investigators pondered the same question, especially since the passengers on the right side of the plane quickly moved out onto the wing. But Clay Presley had it right. Passengers escaping aircraft follow the leader.

"Once somebody does it, all do it," said Nora Marshall, who analyzes aircraft evacuations for the National Transportation Safety Board.

Perhaps more significant, fear of explosion trumped fear of cold water for those who exited on the left side. With the engine sheared away from under the left wing, severed fuel lines were now leaking jet fuel, causing slicks to appear on the surface. The whole scene smelled of jet fuel, but the odor was especially pungent on the left, and it stoked the fear among the first ones out the exit that they were about to be vaporized in a fireball.

Even though most airline accidents do *not* involve fire, people tend to remember television images of accidents that do. A month earlier, just five days before Christmas, news footage showed video of spectacular flames towering over a Continental Airlines 737 that slid off the runway—*slid,* not crashed—on takeoff. The fire consumed half the fuselage and injured 41 of the 115 people on board before firefighters could extinguish it.

"We had already smelled burning," said Shae Childers. "All I could think of was: We just took off, this plane is full of fuel, fuel burns on top of water."

Wendell Fox, wearing a business suit, made a point of looking at the engine when he stepped out. "I didn't see it. It dawned on me that's where the fuel is coming from. I thought: *Fire.*"

Remington Chin, a financial analyst in New York, who had been headed to Denver for a ski weekend, refused to even *think* about the cold. "Yes, the water was cold," he said. But that fact seemed irrelevant at the time. He felt there was "no sense giving it any share of my mind. *You've got to get away from the plane. You've got to get to safety.*"

DePonte went in wearing pink Ugg sheepskin boots that weighed like anchors as the water filled them. Although she, too, immediately felt numb, she ignored the cold. "It didn't register in my head," she said. "I was literally so happy to be alive, the last thing I thought about was frostbite or hypothermia. I was determined to swim to New Jersey or Manhattan if I had to."

Pam Seagle knew she would end up in the water, cold be damned, even before the plane touched down. "I thought three things," she said. "One, it was gonna burn. Two, it was gonna sink. Three, there were a lot of people behind me and we have not yet figured out how to go out on the wing. I had to make room."

Swimming out toward the nose, Steve O'Brien felt "strangely good" in the water, if slightly detached from reality. "I knew something bad had happened and I thought I needed to tell my wife about it, because I was in the water," he said. "Then I turned and saw the fuselage floating next to me. It was a calm kind of float. The plane was not rocking, but making *bloop-bloop* bobbing noises like a boat would make when docked.

"I really expected the plane was going to blow up or sink. I thought everyone was going to end up in the water. My senses were buzzing. The plane was so vibrant in the sun, it was such a majestic-looking white and red and blue, and it was so absurd that it was next to me while I floated on a seat cushion in the Hudson, with Hell's Kitchen spread out before me."

Steve O'Brien grew up twelve miles north of Manhattan in Tappan, a hamlet that dates to the seventeenth century. He spent summers swimming in the Hudson River at Bear Mountain State Park, and crabbed at Piermont a few miles south of that. "I was in a place I knew," he said. "I wanted to be in the water from the second I saw the doors open. It was so inviting, and I was all for going into it—it meant I was still alive and would see my kids again."

O'Brien's father had been a New York City policeman for twenty-eight years. "I knew the cops and the firefighters would come for us," he said. But during those first few moments outside in the river, the passengers of Flight 1549 were utterly alone. "If you look at the pictures, we are really smack in the middle of nowhere—probably the most remote you can get in the biggest city in the world. We were alone and it was overwhelming."

At that point, the plane was being swept down the river at about four miles an hour, carried by the outgoing tide and the current of the mid-afternoon. (Had Sullenberger landed on an incoming tide, the plane would have actually drifted upstream. This phenomenon is why the Mohican Indians called the Hudson "the river that runs both ways.") It was headed toward the river mouth at Battery Park, where the Hudson empties into Upper New York Harbor and, eventually, into the Atlantic. If the aircraft had ended up there, a rescue in the churning turbulent waters, where the Hudson and East River meet would have been much more difficult.

With the fuselage perpendicular to the shore, and the left wing stretched upriver, the jumpers on the left side had to swim upriver, against the current, to escape the plane. Shae Childers made little headway, then gave up and paddled back to the wing.

Pam Seagle swiftly swam out toward the nose near O'Brien. In that section of the river, a series of docks on the Manhattan side protruded nearly one thousand feet from shore, enhancing the allure of swimming for it. At Pier 86, at Forty-sixth Street, one of the best known tourist sites, the Intrepid Sea, Air & Space Museum, housed aboard the World War II aircraft carrier, beckoned invitingly. "I looked left. I looked right," she said. "Manhattan seemed the better option. *I'm going to the* Intrepid. *I know the* Intrepid." She remembers clearly that sequence of thoughts. After that, Seagle's mind pretty much went blank.

Meanwhile, a bottleneck quickly built up inside at mid-plane. The wings have two exits on each side at rows ten and eleven. In a ground evacuation, passengers climb out both openings, step onto an inflatable slide off the rear of the wing, and slide to the ground below. The chute's bottom end inflates into a large cushion to soften the landing. But on the river, the chute had deployed like a giant air mattress against the fuselage, with its cushioned bottom end sticking up. Adelaide Horton, who had opened the exit door directly behind De-Ponte, immediately became entangled in the chute after she stepped out, stumbling and sinking to her knees. Survivors continued to pour out onto the wing, however. Some climbed over Horton to get onto the slide, using her shoulder as a handhold. A crowd built up at the fuselage just outside, slowing the human traffic backed up inside.

Clay Presley, a Charlotte entrepreneur, arrived at the exit from seat 15D at what turned out to be a crucial moment. "Everybody in front of me had jumped in," he said. "I assumed the rest of the people were going to jump in." He bent his knees and prepared to leap in himself, another lemming off the ledge. But he couldn't make himself take the plunge. He had no seat cushion, and saw none within reach on the plane. The crowd pressed in tight behind him, closing off the possibility of going back to rummage for a life vest under the seats.

"I stared at the wing and the people in the water. They were making noises like they were freezing to death. I was ready to jump, but I couldn't pull the trigger. It seemed too damn cold to go in."

Jorge Morgado, one of the golfers, arrived in time to see the last two of the original group jump in. He instantly began yelling: "Don't jump!"

Michael Leonard popped through the exit, determined to stay dry. "Go to the end, go to the end," he pleaded. A native Californian, he hates cold weather. Failed boyhood swimming lessons, in which he finished "dead last" among the five-year-olds, left him with a life-long fear of water. Leonard planned to cling to the wing until the plane sank beneath him. "Water was my last option," he said.

Clay Presley, for his part, realized the danger he faced. De-icing fluid and fuel mixed with the Hudson swirled over the wing. It would be a treacherous hike across the wing, even in rubber-soled shoes. He glanced over at the inflated slide. No matter how badly twisted, it appeared to be the only available object that floated, and he was reluctant to move too far from it. On the other hand, the tip of the wing offered a completely dry perch, for now. So Presley stepped tentatively toward it. And that started what airline accident investigators call "the sheep effect." Everyone who escaped behind Presley followed him out onto the wing. No one else jumped in.

Meanwhile, the plane continued to sink, tail first.

8

Water, Water Everywhere

FROM THE NEXT-TO-LAST ROW, BILLY CAMPBELL REACHED THE TURMOIL in the galley with the first passengers looking for a way out through the rear doors. Campbell, the television executive who had overseen the making of *The Flight That Fought Back,* a docudrama about the Shanksville crash and the passengers' battle with the hijackers of the fourth plane on 9/11, was adept in the ways of bringing vivid air-crash scenes to the screen. Now he was looking at the drama up close, personally, and seemingly as hopelessly as the passengers in his film. In the time it had taken him to move the few feet from his seat to the galley entrance, the water had risen from his shoe tops to the middle of his chest. In front of him the flight attendant, Doreen Welsh, stood, up to her armpits in water, and forcefully moved her arms in a shoving motion to go the other way.

"Turn around!" Welsh shouted at him and others pushing at his back. "Go to the front! You can't get out here! You have two minutes!"

Campbell, an athletic forty-nine-year-old, turned and faced a wedge of others still groping and pushing toward the rear exit. As far as he could see, people clogged the aisle in a stalled mass of humanity, with terrified people often pushing in opposite directions, and others still in their seats unable to elbow into the aisle or not yet fully collected of their thoughts. For a man who had spent his life visualizing drama, danger, and death for others on the screen, this all suddenly became very real. The water seeped in so slowly at first and then rose so quickly that he and everyone near him thought the plane was sinking fast.

Being part of that moment, Campbell testified later to the National Transportation Safety Board, became his "second or third bit of horror" in mere seconds. "As I looked, there was almost no way out."

It was a terrifying scene and it touched everyone in at least the last half-dozen rows, adding a grim dimension to the experience that separated them in a major way from the other survivors. Would they miraculously survive the crash only to suffer a ghastly death by drowning? There were frightening problems still ahead on the water outside, but standing in the back of a sinking airplane was a hideous prospect.

The outcome seemed so certain that Brian Moss, the easygoing thirty-five-year-old business analyst who had calmed Vallie Collins all the way down, simply froze. He held back uncertain in his bad corner, 26F, looking at the clogged aisle two seats away.

It was hopeless.

Moss reached down into the water to get his wallet out of his laptop bag and tuck it into his pocket so his body could be identified. The rising water finally forced him to climb up on the seat back in front of him, where he sat hunched against the overhead bins. Below him he could see nothing but water. Far ahead he could see light through the wing exit, but he couldn't see a way to get there.

"There was a lot of calling out," Moss said. "There was a lot of energy spent—and no movement. I just remember hoping to see this thing beside me move one way or the other. That thing, that group of people, just didn't go anywhere."

Then he had what he later called a "totally irrational" thought.

"Hunched over, I was close enough to the water to realize that was how I was going to die," he said, a bit embarrassed. "I remember thinking I should test it out and put my head under the water and see what it feels like before it happens."

He didn't do it.

"That's where someone pushed Pause on the movie and it just hovered there for a long, long time." Then the line in the aisle started to creep up and he started toward it. To his surprise, one man still emerged out of the depths of the galley.

As Moss's mind fixed on leaving, he watched the man and thought, *"Just go. Go with the crowd.* He finally went past and I stepped into the aisle."

Bizarrely, his cell phone rang. It was clipped to his belt, now underwater. He ignored it.

It was a long, slow walk—and occasionally a painful one. Moss always takes his shoes off when flying. Debris, even suitcases, floated in the water. Worse, for Moss, many of the broken pieces of the aircraft and other odds and ends had sunk to the floor, hard on his feet as he moved.

Across the way, in the other thanks-a-lot seat, 26A, Irina Levshina stopped her prayer in Russian and more or less stopped thinking, too. "I remember I was shocked to realize I wasn't dead," she said. "And the others were not dead, either. But then things get very patchy. Just flashes here and there. I don't have a very linear memory of it."[1]

Levshina still had no idea where they were. The window shade that Tracey Wolsko had wanted drawn down at takeoff was still shut. "But the liquid came in and was quickly up to my waist. I thought it was jet fuel. I can swim in water but not in jet fuel. It was really scary." She opened the shade and saw water halfway up her window. "The attendant was in the aisle saying something like, 'We have two minutes.'"

Levshina remembers almost nothing more until she reached the wing.

Bill Zuhowski, the twenty-three-year-old Long Islander who had made that long trip in the snow, saw everyone charging to the back past his seat, 23E. "So you follow the herd," he said. His glasses had been knocked off in the landing and he couldn't see, as he put it, "a foot in front of his head." "You hear all these stories now about self-lessness and caring for others," he said, "but in this half minute there wasn't much of that. Everybody was shouting and pushing."

Suddenly, Zuhowski found himself pushed into the galley, the water now up to his chest. "The water was still rising," he said, "I'm facing back and there's nowhere to go, and I thought, *I am going to drown right here in the back of this plane.*'"

Zuhowski, yelling at the top of his lungs for people to calm down, wiggled his way back to row twenty-six. He was now across from Brian Moss, who still hadn't moved.

"I took one step to climb on top of the last row of seats. Feeling

---

[1]Levshina's comments bring up the point that the stress and anxiety levels at this moment rivaled military combat and other mind-warping situations. People literally looked death in the eye and many concluded their demise was inevitable. Their memories are erratic and rarely mesh into a nicely reconstructed package. The reader might consider these memories for what they are and forgive contradictions in time and other details. The contradictions often are impossible to unravel perfectly.

how heavy it was to take that step with soaking wet jeans and shoes on, I said to myself, at some point I will have to swim and I don't want to be weighed down by all these clothes. The entire experience became so overwhelming that you don't think about how cold it is.

"In what seemed like two seconds—it was Superman in a telephone booth—I had my pants off, my shirt off, my shoes off, and I grabbed a seat cushion and climbed across the seats all the way from the last row to the front row. I went right past the wing exit doors—don't know how, maybe I couldn't see them without my glasses—and went out the first-class left exit."

Suddenly, he was in a raft, thinking, "These people are all dry." The fellow rafters took an odd look at him, too—the young man in the red boxers. He felt very cold.

SULLENBERGER'S LANDING HAD been almost picture-perfect—the attitude close to ideal, wings level, nose up about ten degrees. After the tail hit, the fuselage dropped to the water in a manner that distributed all the potentially destructive energy almost evenly against the craft's frailties. Differences of a few degrees could have snapped off either the cockpit or the tail. Still, anyone who has ever done a belly flop off a high dive knows that water is not a soft surface. It can beat up an airplane almost as surely as the ground.

So, no matter how fine the landing, the A320 took a terrific punch. Examined later, parts of its underbelly looked like a crushed tin can. Aluminum panels—the aircraft's skin—had been ripped clear from the airframe. Some of them were missing literally beneath the passengers' feet in the rear of the cabin. The tail cone had been destroyed. Most important, as the skin tore away, it ripped supporting ribs and frames with it, creating a gaping hole in the lower part of the aft pressure bulkhead. The NTSB is in possession of one photograph taken from inside the rear cabin after the plane was removed from the river. It dramatically shows blue sky coming through the broken tail cone and the hole in the bulkhead.

The pressure bulkhead is a concave construction wall just behind the galley, specifically designed to keep the plane pressurized at altitude. Puncture it, and oxygen will leak out, depressurizing the cabin. Break it when you are in the water, and it becomes a culvert bringing water in.

What seemed puzzling and terrifying inside the cabin had a simple, if unhappy, explanation. Water is heavy. As more water entered, the tail sank faster, allowing still more water to enter through the bulkhead rupture. Eventually, and fairly rapidly, it surged and the tail sank deeper.

One persistent controversy about the water issue would never be completely resolved. A few passengers said they saw cracks in the seal of the rear exit door.

The rear flight attendant, fifty-eight-year-old Doreen Welsh, had thirty-nine years of experience on the job. But when she landed, she had less knowledge of the circumstances than many passengers. She occupied a jump seat near the lavatories, facing the front of the plane but without window views. With the plane's internal phone system not working, none of the flight attendants had spoken to each other since the bird strike. Nor had they had any communications from the flight deck. That added to Welsh's isolation. She had no idea that they were in water; briefly, she still entertained the thought that they might have crash-landed at LaGuardia.

In addition to the normal jolt as they hit the water, Welsh felt a sharp pain. A steel beam had pierced the floor and ripped upward, narrowly missing an artery but severely cutting her left leg. In the emergency, she ignored it. It wasn't until she finally made it into a raft that someone asked, "Who's bleeding?"

The controversy erupted when it was discovered that the seal had been broken on the left rear exit door although the door itself never opened. Welsh said a passenger tried to open it and she had to prevent her because it was partly underwater.

Only a handful of passengers were physically positioned to see the right door in the galley and all memories conflict.

This is what Welsh said in testimony to the NTSB: "I went to the 2L door to assess the situation and to my surprise I saw water. I realized the water was too high to deploy the raft so I turned around to direct the people forward. Just then a panicked passenger ran by me to the 2L door and started frantically grabbing at the door while yelling, 'Open it, open it.'"

The passenger managed to crack the door slightly but was unable to completely open it, Welsh testified.

Vallie Collins, a frequent flyer and thirty-seven-year-old salesperson from Maryville, Tennessee, made it into the galley before other passengers. She disagrees.

"I guess no eyewitness account is perfect," Collins said, "and I know the flight attendant has a different recollection. But when I got to the galley, the flight attendant was at the exit door and the exit door was cracked. We were both pushing it to get it open. It would not open. In that situation, it says exit and you want out. That door wouldn't go anywhere."

By that time Tracey Wolsko had scooted from seat 26B around her aisle seatmate, Vicki Barnhardt, and entered the galley. She saw Welsh near the door in knee-high water. "Fuck, we're in the Hudson," Wolsko recalls saying. Welsh immediately retorted "Go to the front." To Wolsko it didn't look like the door was open, but the water was rising fast. "I don't think anybody opened the door," she said.

Barnhardt says she never made it all the way into the galley and doesn't remember seeing the door, but she heard the word to turn around into the oncoming crush of people.

Eventually, the issue faded away when the NTSB released its preliminary investigative reports showing that virtually all the water had come through holes in the aircraft, not a leak in the door.

Leaving the galley, Wolsko, a wisp of a person at five feet tall and 117 pounds, decided to play cat. She went over the right-hand seats, stopping every couple of rows where passengers in the aisle were still forcing their way back toward the galley and urging them to turn around. By the time she got to the right-wing exits, a man said with a gesture, "After you."

Barnhardt and Collins, who thought she left last, eventually made it to the wing doors through the aisle.

To Collins, the water was far more frightening than the landing. She switched to what she called her "get-it-together-Vallie" mode and, being a former high-school cheerleader, waved her arms as though she was holding pompons. In a powerful, rallying voice she tried to turn the crowd around: "Go to the wings! Go to the wings!"

Laurel Hubbard's fleeting temptation to just give in to the water was overtaken by her survival instinct. She wedged in near the end of the line. Debris, including what she thought was her suitcase, floated all around her. So did many seat-flotation devices, one of which she grabbed. "I thought I was in the ocean," she said. Many of the survivors in the far rear found the wings were clogged by the time they got to them, and pushed on through the almost empty aisle ahead to the first-class cabin, where they could slide into a raft. That's what Hubbard did.

Barnhardt, certain that she would die, phoned her husband from the rising water, shouting over the din of her fellow passengers: "I think this is it. We've crashed. I love you. I love the kids. I love you. I love you. I love you." Her husband was in a meeting and didn't hear the message until fifteen minutes later. Then he had no way to call her back. His description of hearing the call late still brings her to tears.

Eileen Shleffar, Flight 1549's preeminent phone caller, was

among the most fortunate, being seated just two rows behind the wing exits in aisle seat 13D. She had not made it to the exits before her phone rang. Her husband was home from the car wash. "Hello?" she said. "Are you still flying?" he asked. "No, we're down but there is an old lady on the plane and a toddler. Oh my God." The voice responding from Charlotte became level and insistent: "Someone will help them. Honey, get to the door. Get off the plane."

Shleffar looked up and down the plane. The front was almost normal, as if the people had just walked away. The back, she thought, looked like a madhouse, a mob. Near her, a woman desperately groped in the overhead for her handbag until a dozen angry voices stopped her. She moved on without it. Eileen Shleffar walked the short distance to the left-wing exit.

Behind her there was not a comfortable soul.

FOR A MOMENT, in row nineteen, Tess Sosa wore a half smile on her face. "I clearly was in shock and didn't make sense. Part of me forgot who I was, that I even had children. The other part of me is saying, *Run, they have your baby.*

"How do I explain? It's just the way my mind was working at that instant. We made it. Through this mission. I have this man next to me who brilliantly puts me at ease and then braces my baby. This isn't a plane crash. No one died. We didn't fall to pieces. This is some kind of grand mission. Damian was crying and I was so happy he was crying. I saw these two hands and I went, 'Oh, okay, there's my baby,' and I reached for him."

In her reverie, she lost track of Jim Whitaker, the man who had braced her son, and the man on her right, Hiroki Takigawa, the Japanese trader, and never saw them again for the rest of the day. Later, Takigawa felt great guilt about leaving the woman and child behind. "How could I ignore the mother and baby?" he asked. "Right next to me. I don't remember about my right hand and my left hand. I was so scared myself. It is human nature, but it's so selfish. What if they were my wife and my kid?"

Sosa finally elbowed through the crowd to the other side of the aisle, where she could turn to look back at her husband and daughter, four rows directly behind her. The water was coming in around them. She relived the moment, telling the story. "Martin is looking right at me but he doesn't acknowledge that I'm there. He is in total shock. Sofia is looking down and crying and wiggling. I'm shouting, 'Martin! Martin!' but he can't hear me."

Tess began to worry about Damian and the water, which was coming up the aisle. *Martin will figure it out,* she thought. She tried to make eye contact with men as they passed her. But no one looked at her and no one let her in the aisle. She put Damian under one arm "like a football" and started over the seats, scrambling. "I looked for a flight attendant. I watched men just push by me." She crawled over a couple of seats at a time, then looked for help again.

Finally, one man looked at her. "Why aren't you going to the exit?" he asked.

"I can't. Can't you see I am blocked?"

Brad Wentzell, the thirty-one-year-old salesman whose last sensation in the crash was the wonderful fragrance of his three-year-old daughter, swept them up, one under each arm, carried them to the right-wing exit, and deposited them with Josh Peltz. By then, Tess Sosa had passed out and doesn't remember anything. She woke up at the exit with Damian. A moment later her husband and daughter joined her.

Diane Higgins and her eighty-five-year-old mother, Lucille Palmer, also needed help when not much was around. Higgins could see no way to get her mother out into the crush of people.

In row seventeen, water was not a serious problem until it

The New York Waterway ferry *Thomas Jefferson* approaches the right wing three minutes and fifty-seven seconds after Flight 1549 hit the Hudson River.
Photo courtesy of AP Photo/Steven Day

The final group of passengers to be rescued floats on an escape slide attached to the left side of the sinking Airbus as daylight fades. *Photo courtesy of Eric Stevenson*

A wave to departing friends and survivors and a glance toward the Jersey shore; the rescue is almost over, a remarkable twenty-four minutes after the Airbus landed in the Hudson. *Photo courtesy of Eric Stevenson*

The ferry *Thomas Jefferson*, with icicles hanging from the bow, moves in to pick up passengers on the right wing. *Photo courtesy of Tripp Harris*

Chris Cobb hands life preservers thrown from the ferry *Thomas Jefferson* to Warren Holland and Victor Warnement (in the white shirt) on the right wing. *Photo courtesy of Tripp Harris*

Left: Eric Stevenson's boarding pass. When his original flight was canceled, he was rebooked onto Flight 1549. *Photo courtesy of Eric Stevenson*

Center: Eric Stevenson, wearing a New York Waterways crew shirt, waits at a senior center in Weehawken, New Jersey, for a bus to his hotel at LaGuardia Airport an hour after the accident. The passengers' clothes smelled of jet fuel, so volunteers washed and dried them in their nearby homes. *Photo courtesy of Jim L. Whitaker*

Bottom: Eric Stevenson, who did not expect to survive the crash landing, wrote "I love you" to his mother and sister on the back of his business card and tucked it into his pocket for rescuers to find on his body. *Photo courtesy of Eric Stevenson*

The smooth nose of the Airbus A320 is cracked and dented after its collision with the geese. *Photo courtesy of NTSB*

Pam Seagle (on the right), who jumped into the Hudson River after escaping the plane, with her sister, Jennifer Evans, and son, Cameron, before his high school graduation in Weddington, North Carolina. Two weeks later, Evans died of an aneurism. *Photo courtesy of Pam Seagle*

Eileen Shleffar, a self-described phonaholic, talked to her husband, David, on the phone during the entire descent to stay calm. One of the Belk Six, she is a merchandise manager for the department store chain. *Photo courtesy of Samantha Shleffar*

Dave Carlos, Jorge Morgado, Jeff Kolodjay, Rob Kolodjay, Jim Stefanik, and Rick Delisle take their delayed golf vacation in April, 2009. *Photo courtesy of Jorge Morgado*

Laura Zych, Michael Leonard, Lisa English, and Lori Lightner, four of the Belk Six, celebrate their survival in Manhattan a few hours after their rescue. *Photo courtesy of Michael Leonard*

Tess and Martin Sosa at home in New York with their children, Sofia and Damian. *Photo courtesy of the Sosa family*

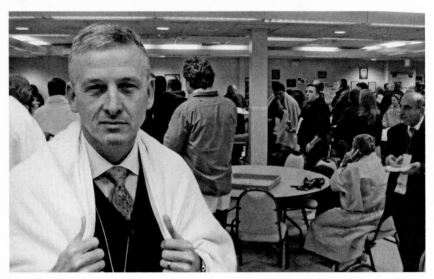

Jim Whitaker, who protectively braced nine-month-old Damian Sosa for the crash landing, wears a Red Cross blanket at a senior center in Weehawken, New Jersey, an hour after the rescue. *Photo courtesy of Eric Stevenson*

reached their knees. Then, Diane panicked. *"Oh my God,"* she thought, *"now we're going to drown. There's no way I can get her out of this plane. It's going down. It's going to sink fast. Will there be an air pocket? Will I be able to hold her?"*

Dick Richardson, a fifty-seven-year-old business executive from Charlotte, saw Diane struggling to get Lucille toward the aisle. He held off the people behind him and grabbed Lucille by the shirt, pulling her to the aisle. "The crowd will move you along," he said, in one of the day's classic understatements. By that time, as one put it, the crowd was like a rock-concert audience leaving the arena: It was crunched tightly but had its own slow, forward motion. The momentum carried anything along—as long as you didn't fall down. With Lucille in front of her and facing toward the rear galley, clutching her, Diane started down the aisle. At the wing exit they were met by one of the flight attendants from up front, Donna Dent. "I was worried about you," Dent said to Diane and led the two women to the first-class life raft.

So much has been written about the "miracle" later—not only of the landing but of the passengers' behavior as well—that anything that besmudged the image at all became distinctly unfashionable. But to expect doubly and triply traumatized human beings to be uniformly unselfish and act flawlessly was unrealistic. These were terrified people and there were bad moments in those first minutes on the river.

With a quick "I don't want to ruin a good story" qualifier, Alex Magness tells about working his way through the clogged aisle when the man in front of him suddenly turned and ripped the flotation cushion out of his hands. "That's my cushion!" the man snarled and turned back clutching it to his chest. Magness, who is six foot five, shrugged and found another.

March Dolphin, fifty-seven, had just edged herself into the aisle when a young woman did the same to her. "She will have to live with herself," Dolphin wrote in her diary. She, too, found another cushion and continued on her way.

Vic Warnement, part of the traveling BoA group, was bowled over by someone pushing for the door as he entered the aisle only two rows from the wing exits. "That's not helping much!" Warnement barked at the man as he regained his footing. Another passenger interrupted and told Warnement, "I've got him," then coolly calmed the man.

"Whenever someone panicked," Warnement said, "there were two or three people near enough to calm them down." Sullenberger had done his job. "Part two was up to us," Jeff Kolodjay said.

The last man in the rear galley of the plane, for reasons he's not sure he can fathom himself, was the Baltimore lawyer, Jim Hanks. The sixty-five-year-old attorney once represented Ralph Nader back in Nader's youthful days as an auto safety critic. Now Hanks did something that was considerably less safe than Detroit's sixties-era cars.

Pinned briefly by debris in his aisle seat three rows from the back, Hanks says the water was waist-high by the time he stepped into the aisle. Brian Moss still sat perched in the dark corner pondering his fate. But the only person Hanks remembers seeing is Doreen Welsh heading forward. "It's hopeless," he remembers her saying, which he interpreted as a reference to the exit door, not the peril. Going in the opposite direction of the flight attendant was like running a red light, but Hanks did it anyway. He wanted to see for himself.

When Hanks entered the galley, the water was well above the bottom of the exit door, which he described as twisted in its casing. According to Hanks, he could see that the door probably wouldn't open but, he said, "I tried it anyhow." It wouldn't budge, a blessing at this point. The water then quickly surged up to his neck, as if a dike had broken. The source, almost surely, was water moving higher through the unseen hole in the bulkhead as the tail sank.

By the time he had moved the few feet to the wall of the rear lavatory, the water had risen above his tie knot and almost to his mouth.

Six feet tall, Hanks looked up and figured he had less than a foot to the ceiling. With the aisle still clogged, he could see no way out.

"This is it," he thought. *"I'm going to drown. My wife, Sabine, is going to be a young widow. My daughter, Maria Dorothy, is going to grow up without a father, and she's only four years old. She's not even going to remember me."*

Hanks's voice broke as he told his story.

"Those were very sad thoughts, the saddest thoughts I have ever had in my life. It was just a certainty and it wasn't going to take very long."

The outcome seemed so sure that he briefly wondered, *What's the point?* But there is always a point. He stepped back into the aisle, which still had scores of people ahead of him. Brian Moss stepped into the aisle behind him.

As Hanks trudged slowly forward, the water level dropped evenly—down to his shoulders, down to his chest, down to his waist. Like most of the passengers in the rear of the plane, Hanks had assumed that it was sinking evenly instead of tail first. The truth came as a huge surprise and relief. "It was like walking out of the deep water at a beach," he said. "One step at a time." Eventually he walked past the wing exit doors, onto dry carpet, and into first class. Then he slid down a chute into the raft.

Moss didn't leave the plane when he reached the wing exits. He had brought a couple of life vests and flotation cushions with him and was handing them out to people who needed them. That turned out to be almost everybody. People on the wings were asking for them.

It seemed to him, as it had to Hanks, that the plane had stopped sinking. So he went back into the water to retrieve others. Another passenger, his colleague from the bank, Jerry Shanko, searched down the other side of the aisle.

"Every time I got back to the wing doors," Moss said, "hands were grabbing the vests."

So he went back again. He already was so wet he didn't think it made any difference. But it did. After several trips, and reaching repeatedly down into the water, his hands became so numb, he couldn't feel them or the life vests.[2]

"That's when I saw the captain. I took him by the arm and said something like, 'Nice job,' or 'Good landing.' I want to remember it as very eloquent. But I don't think it was. He looked at me, stone-faced, and said: 'It is time for you to leave now.'"

---

[2]Passengers complained later that even with warm and nimble hands, the life vests were difficult to extricate from under the seats. According to the NTSB assessment of the plane afterward, even with the bold efforts of Moss and Shanko, only nine life vests were removed from seats behind the wing-exit rows. In all, 49 of the 150 vests made it out of the plane, but, paradoxically, most of them came from the drier, more forward areas of the plane.

9

"Honey, I'm in the Hudson"

THE CHAOS OF THE REAR HAD NOT PENETRATED THE RELATIVE CALM UP front. When the Airbus A320 skidded to a stop, Tripp Harris, on an aisle at the bulkhead row just behind first class, picked up his phone off the floor, walked forward to the right-hand door, and put on his suit jacket. "It was very orderly," he said. Almost as if they had arrived at an airport terminal.

And then Harris called his wife.

"Hey, baby. We just crashed. We're going to be all right. I love you. I've got to get off the plane."

And then he hung up.

When he called her back from the life raft a moment later, she was crying uncontrollably. Nothing he said reassured her. After hanging up a second time, he decided to take a few photos of the scene and send them to her so she could see for herself that he was all right. But shots of people standing on the wing in the Hudson and sitting on the life raft, with the dying fuselage looming in the background, only made things worse back in Charlotte.

Later, Harris could only laugh at how ridiculous he had been. "It is really funny how your mind works in a situation like that. Thinking that a picture showing that I'm off the plane will calm her down when in fact I was sending her photos of complete chaos."

What Harris failed to convey with words or pictures was his absolute joy at being alive, outside the airplane, and safe inside a raft. He didn't have a scratch on him; his hair wasn't mussed; his suit looked newly pressed; his feet were dry. Fifteen minutes later, when he and others from the raft walked into the ferry terminal in Manhattan, their appearance astounded the first responders and became fodder for a series of Internet jokes that quickly circulated. One of the best showed a photo of the rafters floating comfortably alongside the horde lined up on the right wing. The raft bore the label, First Class, and the wing, Coach.

Others bounding into the raft felt the same exuberance. A few started cracking jokes about how many frequent-flier miles they'd earn. Ben Bostic, a former medic now working as a software developer at LendingTree, arrived with his boss, Darren Beck, and joined in. "I remember thinking, *How brilliant,*" Bostic said. "The humor let me know that the others felt the same as me, and that was reassuring. I remember thinking, *We actually survived a plane crash!* "It was something to celebrate."

Looking around, Bostic noticed others did not feel quite as confident. Amber Wells plopped down next to Charles Spiggle and announced nervously, "I need a hug." Alecia Shuford, on the BoA team, looked to Ricardo Valeriano as if she "had lost it."

"I was crying hysterically. It was horrible. God, it was so bad,"

Shuford said. "We were the first people off the plane. I noticed that the wing is sinking, and I'm thinking that all the people I work with are sinking and are dying in front of me."

The newcomers sobered the mood, a reminder to the rest that the survival of all 155 people on the flight was no sure thing. As if to reinforce the point, three of the most at-risk people on board moved into the raft next: Lucille Palmer, the eighty-five-year-old; a six-year-old Hispanic girl whose forty-five-year-old mother spoke little, if any, English; and, toward the end of the evacuation, Flight Attendant Doreen Welsh, who arrived bleeding with a five-inch, V-shaped gash in her left shin that would require surgery later that night. It was clear to everyone on the raft that none of the three could afford to end up in the water.

The temperature on the surface of the river was thirty-five degrees[1]; the temperature of the air was twenty-two degrees, seventeen with the wind-chill factor. Passengers later found it hard to convey exactly how cold it was. To Jennifer Doyle, her numb hands felt as if they were "on fire, they were burning so badly." Barry Leonard, who jumped into the Hudson from first class, had nightmares about the cold afterward, dreaming that he walked on a frozen river fifty yards from shore and fell through the ice. Larry Snodgrass said if he'd been offered a choice between a million dollars and a dry pair of socks, he'd have taken the socks. Of the many descriptions of the conditions outside the aircraft, Tripp Harris may have come up with the best: "It was Titanic-cold," he said, and no one missed the meaning.

The most immediate danger was that the plane was sinking and

---

[1] Several miles upriver, large chunks of ice held up barge traffic. Ice floated down to the landing site a day later. Three days after that, on January 18, the ice chunks were numerous enough to delay a NOAA search boat's efforts to locate the left engine on the river bottom. Michael Buckheit, a battalion chief with the fire department's Marine Battalion, later speculated in a firefighters' trade journal, *Fire Engineering,* that "the results would have been catastrophic had ice floes been off Manhattan when Sullenberger landed."

had only two usable life rafts. Neither, however, was full. About sixty passengers stood on the plane's wings, while another thirty or so sat on inflatable slides off the back side of wings—these, however, could not be detached from the plane and would sink with it. Another nine passengers were already in the water, swimming away from the fuselage on the left side. They would need to be convinced to turn around.

"One of the things I discovered was we had to be lucky more than once," said Jim Hanks, wet up to his neck after escaping from the back of the plane. "You've got to survive the crash, and then the aftermath. First the water, then the freezing temperatures. If you don't survive the first step, you don't get to find out if you survive the second step."

ONE OF THE many quirks of fate—aside from the good weather, the flat river, and so many other "miraculous" factors—was that the Airbus A320 had any life rafts on board in the first place. They are not required equipment on New York–Charlotte flights. FAA regulations require airlines to equip their planes with life rafts, life vests, and other emergency equipment *only* on flights traveling extended distances over water, at least fifty nautical miles from shore. Of the seventy-five A320s in the US Airways fleet, twenty are equipped for extended over-water emergencies, or, in the acronym-laden language of aviation, as EOW planes. Emergency equipment includes life vests for every passenger, four survival kits, and four large life rafts that each seat forty-four people, but up to fifty-five if other rafts are unusable.

The airline's remaining fifty-five A320s are equipped with four inflatable evacuation slides at the forward and rear doors, but carry no life vests or survival kits.

Water-related accidents are rare events. Still, the National Transportation Safety Board has been after the aviation agency to improve emergency flotation equipment, evacuation slides, and rescue plans since the mid-1980s. In 1985, the Safety Board reviewed forty-five years' worth of survivable water-related accidents—eighteen crash landings between 1959 and 1984—and concluded that the regulations were badly out of date and were based on "unrealistic" assumptions.

The basis for the government's safety rules is a "near-perfect" ditching in Sitka Sound, Alaska, in 1962. A Northwest Airlines DC-7, flying ninety-five passengers and seven crew, between Tacoma, Washington, and Anchorage, Alaska, lost an engine at twenty thousand feet. The pilot chose to ditch. For the next forty-five minutes, the cabin crew had such a luxury of time they moved twenty-eight passengers out of the front rows and rearranged the children throughout the cabin, seating them next to the strongest adults. They moved life rafts next to the exits and instructed those seated nearby how to open the doors and launch them. Everyone put on a life vest, and there was time enough left after all that to practice the brace, in multiple positions.

The plane landed smoothly on the Sound about 9:00 p.m. on a brisk October night. The water temperature was 56 degrees; the air was 53 degrees. Five minutes after touchdown, all on board were in the rafts; twenty minutes after that, all were aboard a coast guard cutter. In perhaps the only similarity with Flight 1549, the plane sank in twenty-four minutes. (Flight 1549 would have gone down just as quickly if firefighters had not tied lines around the tail to keep the plane from sinking.)

Water-related accidents tend to occur suddenly, with little, if any, time to prepare. They do not often take place on extended over-water flights; rather, they happen, as with Flight 1549, near an airport on takeoff or landing. The Safety Board cited 179 airports in the United States within five miles of a significant body of water and urged the FAA to update the regulations.

"Virtually none of these accidents are 'planned' ditchings," the Safety Board noted in the 1985 report. Unlike the "remarkably favorable conditions" of the Sitka incident, passengers more likely will face "injuries, panic, rising water, unfamiliar and often inaccessible water survival equipment and possibly jammed exits. . . . Those who succeed in getting out of the aircraft face dangers of drowning and often of hypothermia."

The board recommended a series of improvements and urged the FAA to require life vests as mandatory equipment on every commercial airplane. In the intervening twenty-four years, not much changed, however. The issues lived on in obscurity in both agencies—that is, until Sullenberger hit the Hudson and created an opportunity for the NTSB to revisit the old arguments once again.

At the Safety Board, investigators became fascinated with the survivors' tales. Collectively they provided the board with a rare opportunity "to reexamine many of the issues we have long been concerned about," said NTSB Chairman Deborah A. P. Hersman.

"If the ferries had not come as quickly as they had, I don't think this would have had that nice ending," said Beverly Mills.

"Ten, fifteen minutes more, there could have been many more serious problems," said Brian Moss, the BoA analyst who helped Scott Sharkey pitch life vests and seat cushions to passengers on the left wing. "I felt the water freezing on my hands when I was waiting on the wing. Scott had ice in his hair."

As it turned out, the wait for rescue would be clocked as one of the shortest in the annals of aviation lore. The city's first responders began to roll out as soon as Sullenberger radioed to controllers that he'd hit the birds. Sullenberger's alarm had passed from controllers at the New York Terminal Radar Approach Control on Long Island to controllers in the tower at LaGuardia, who passed it on to the Port Authority of New York and New Jersey in a radio call that broadcast the emergency simultaneously to operations centers at the New York Police Department in lower Manhattan, a fire department dispatch center in Queens, the mayor's Office of Emergency Management in Brooklyn, and the coast guard base on Staten Island.

By the time the Airbus glided over the George Washington Bridge, squadrons of police officers, firefighters, and medics were already converging on the river. Within thirty minutes, more than 1,200 people were working the accident—the kind of massive and swift response that few cities in the world can muster.

Scott Sharkey was still tossing life vests out the exit when police cars began lining up on the shore across the water. Stepping out, he was surprised and relieved to see the shore ablaze with blue flashing lights. "I looked on the Jersey side and could see the same thing," he said.

The mere sight of the skyline told Andrew Gray that he and his fiancée would survive. "When we were standing on the wing, I could see Manhattan towering before us," he said. "I kept saying, 'Don't worry, boats are coming.' Even though I couldn't see them, it was New York City. After nine-eleven. Their emergency response was going to be dead-on."

Al Baker, a correspondent for the *New York Times,* painstakingly reconstructed the deployment two weeks later, tracking it from the controllers on Long Island to FAA officials in Washington, to the military, to an assortment of New York first responders. A fire marshal who happened to be at LaGuardia, about to go on vacation, faxed the passenger list to department headquarters so it could be distributed to hospitals and emergency medics at the scene. John Peruggia, chief of the fire department's emergency medical service, got the call while in a car in Queens, and promptly ordered thirty-five ambulances to a staging area—twenty-five for basic life support and ten with advanced medical services.

"Any episode like this is an opportunity to check the wiring and see how things are working," Philip D. Zelikow, executive director of the federal 9/11 commission, told the *Times*. "What they had there, for a few minutes, was a series of emergency calls and a loud alarm ringing."

The NYPD Special Operations Division, which led the response, began by dispatching multiple specialized units, including its Hercules anti-terrorism team, while a police helicopter beamed video images of the plane floating on the Hudson to emergency dispatch centers around the city.

On the Jersey side, Battalion Chief Michael Cranwell, stationed in West New York, had been handling a malfunctioning alarm at a local grade school when his radio squawked: aircraft down in the Hudson. "Within sixty seconds I was headed toward one of the most extraordinary runs in my thirty-five years on the job," he wrote in *Fire Engineering*. Like many others, Cranwell equated "plane down" with a light aircraft. "The first engine company's radio report, indicating a large passenger jet was involved, was utterly discouraging. I anticipated a catastrophic outcome."

And, fortunately for the sake of history, Chris Simeone is a diligent Con Edison employee. He was making a routine equipment check at the Con Edison plant on West Fifty-ninth Street when he got the word that Sullenberger was on his final approach to the river. He dashed up to the plant's rooftop security camera, hit the record button, and captured the next forty-seven minutes on video.

Meanwhile, down on the river, something akin to a small navy assembled. Rescue vessels of every size and shape—a tug, a private mariner's vessel, a tourist cruise boat—would soon converge on the downed plane. The flotilla included fourteen New York Waterway ferries.

New York Waterway is owned by eighty-four-year-old Arthur E.

Imperatore, the son of Italian immigrant grocers. He made a fortune in trucking and real estate before buying into the ferry business—with a single ferry—in 1986. Since then, the company has expanded to a fleet of thirty-four ferries, operating on twenty routes around metropolitan New York. Ferry crews often rescue exhausted swimmers and people from overturned boats, and they train regularly, learning hypothermia treatment and CPR. The ferry company had already played a key role in earlier New York disasters. After the September 11 attacks, New York Waterway ferries spent hours evacuating 150,000 survivors from Lower Manhattan. In the August 2003 blackout, when the Holland and Lincoln tunnels out of Manhattan were closed, Imperatore's boats carried 160,000 people across to New Jersey.

Sullenberger landed the Airbus in what could be called a Hollywood parking space—almost in front of the ferry terminals, where an array of flabbergasted ferry captains, deckhands, and company executives watched the touchdown out the windows. Sullenberger couldn't have picked a more perfect arrival time if he'd scheduled it. The boats and crews were assembling to start the afternoon rush hour at 4:00 p.m. Robert Matticola, the company's safety director, saw the plane hit from his office window.

Natale Binetti, a deckhand on the ferry *Moira Smith*, told the New York *Daily News*, "I was completely shocked to see this plane going down—lower and lower and lower—and then it hit, hard, into the water. It, like, sunk down, and then kind of bobbed back up."

Vince Lombardi had just pulled the ferry *Thomas Jefferson* away from the Manhattan terminal at West Thirty-ninth Street when he saw the plane drift to a stop. "We hit the throttles," he told *Seafarers International Union* newspaper.

Meanwhile, Brittany Catanzaro, captain of the *Gov. Thomas Kean*, was midway across the river heading for Manhattan and turned back. The twenty-year-old is the company's only female captain, and its youngest. Afterward, she said the Airbus bobbing on the river looked like a child's toy in the bathtub, "like a little kid [had] just set the plane down in the water."

But few people expect to watch as a commercial airliner lands in the Hudson.

Michael Starr, a ferry captain, stood with Vincent LuCante, the captain of the ferry *Yogi Berra,* on a maintenance barge in Weehawken when their cell phones rang. "We could see it from the shore," Starr said. "The plane was clearly out of the water, all in one piece. It didn't seem like a disaster at first. It wasn't a violent plane crash. The plane just landed in the river, like it glided in."

The *Yogi Berra* was the fourth ferry to arrive at the scene.

At the Brooklyn Navy Yard, where the New York City Fire Department moors its fleet of fireboats, the crew of the twenty-seven-foot *Marine 1A* had come to work early, anticipating snow that evening. Within minutes of the emergency call, Capt. Richard Johnson and his crew launched. After the first two or three ferries, Johnson was next to arrive at the scene, rescuing twenty passengers from the left wing.

At Pier 83, a group of firefighters commandeered a Circle Line tour boat to take them to the plane. The boat had just completed a tour with *Times* writer Corey Kilgannon aboard reporting a feature about the seventy-five-year-old tour guide, John Mason, known as the "Prince of Guides." Kilgannon had gone off to write his story a few minutes before four fire engines roared up to the company's dock. "We need that boat," the firefighters barked. They ordered the tourists off and headed out, with Mason still aboard.

Downriver, Capt. Conrad H. Roy, Jr., and a three-man crew of the tugboat the *CO,* were near Governor's Island in New York Harbor when the radio crackled the news: plane down in the Hudson.

Roy was returning to his home berth in New Haven, Connecticut, after dropping a barge of construction supplies in Peekskill, New York. He immediately turned around. His tug would help keep the plane from sinking, and would then haul it south to its overnight stay at Battery Park.

In New Jersey, at the Lincoln Harbor Yacht Club, Scott Koen had just checked the engine on his boat, a converted coast guard buoy tender, ahead of the blast of cold weather forecast for later in the week. Channel 13, the ship-to-ship radio channel, sputtered with chatter in the background. Koen is a former director of operations at the Intrepid Museum, and bought the boat on eBay. He christened it *M/V Lt. Michael P. Murphy,* after a Navy SEAL who died in a firefight in Afghanistan. Suddenly, a sharp voice came over the air: "Plane down in the north river." Koen wheeled out onto the river to have a look. "I see what looks like a tail," he said. "I think it's a sail, or a smokestack on the back of a ship. I pulled out and saw it's an aircraft, a big aircraft, and I went full throttle."

On Staten Island, at the coast guard station, Jessica Wolchak, the twenty-three-year-old officer on duty, took the call, thinking it routine: a small plane down, with six people standing on the wing. She diverted two rescue boats, returning from a terrorism drill, to the scene. A second alarm call clarified the first—"commercial airliner"—and sent the station into overdrive. Crews raced to launch, as skippers shouted: "Are you on my crew? No? You are now."

At Floyd Bennett Field on the southern tip of Brooklyn, where the NYPD's Aviation Unit bases its fleet of helicopters as well as its air and sea rescue unit, an alarm chime sounded, alerting detective Michael Delaney and his partner, Robert Rodriguez, a two-man scuba diving team. The morning snowstorm had grounded the unit's helicopter, and both were winding up a slow day at the hangar. "This was one of those really cold days when you said, 'I'm done with winter,'" Delaney said.

The divers handle a multitude of emergencies. Warm months bring heavy pleasure-boat traffic and a nonstop assortment of near-drownings, capsizings, and kids on homemade rafts heading out to sea. Light aircraft and helicopters crash infrequently, but often enough so that the call "plane down" is not a surprise. Jumpers off New York's many bridges plunge in year-round. When Delaney and Rodriguez are not saving lives, they are checking boats for bombs or searching the river bottom. During Fleet Week in New York, which happens every May, the scuba team inspects every tug, barge, and non-military vessel entering New York Harbor. They also dive for guns or knives used in crimes and other evidence useful to prosecutors. "If prosecutors are sure it's there, we try to stay until we find it," Delaney said. "Most of the time we do."

When the chime sounded at the hangar, someone yelled out, "This is a real job"—no phantom jumper off the Brooklyn Bridge. "You always wonder, is this going to be real?" Delaney said. "When you get twenty calls in one go, all saying there's a plane in the Hudson, that's the real thing."

At that moment, however, Delaney was thinking Cessna, a couple of passengers, routine. Two years earlier he had helped rescue a student pilot and instructor who crashed in the middle of the river, north near Yonkers. By the time he got there, the plane already had disappeared beneath the surface. He thought of that day, as he and Rodriguez now rushed to their chopper. On a cold January afternoon, speed would be critical if they hoped to find anyone still alive. As they took off, Delaney noticed other police helicopters pulling out of the hangar, but didn't think much about it; he was still expecting a small plane.

Because the first 9-1-1 calls came in from the Bronx, the helicopter carrying Delaney and Rodriguez headed in that direction. When they reached the Empire State Building, however, they were diverted—the downed plane was near the *Intrepid*. The two divers changed into scuba gear in the chopper. "I lean over and tap the crew chief for more information, so I can make a plan," Delaney said. He is saying into his radio: "Confirm job, plane in the river." Delaney demanded: How many people? "The crew chief says, 'I have no idea.'" Delaney zipped up his dry suit just as the river scene came into view. He peered out the front window at a throng of ferries, fireboats, police boats, and other vessels.

"I look out and see all these boats in the area, and I was, like, 'What's going on? We're not even going to have to get in the water,'" he said. "That's when I saw the tail fin. A million things go on in my mind. I'm immediately thinking mass casualties. There are going to be dead people inside."

10

The Hudson Swim Team

WHEN BARRY LEONARD JUMPED OUT OF THE FIRST-CLASS EXIT DOOR AND dropped into the Hudson, the cold water hit him like a jolt of electricity. He gasped involuntarily and began to hyperventilate, gulping air in small, quick, uncontrollable breaths. The rapid breathing made it all the more difficult to swim as he could hold his breath for only a few seconds at a time.

The physical reactions Leonard experienced in the Hudson are known as cold-shock response, one of the most common causes of death after sudden immersion in very cold water. Drowning is the most immediate danger, of course—one or two involuntary breaths taken while facedown is all that is needed to flood the lungs with water.

The greater threat to the fifty-five-year-old business executive at that moment, though, was sudden cardiac arrest. Extreme temperature change can cause a rapid increase in heart rate and blood pressure, as cooled blood from the skin returns to the heart. That increase can, in turn, set off irregularities in heartbeat that can cause the heart to stop. When Leonard's blood pressure was measured at the Weehawken ferry terminal in New Jersey, some forty-five minutes after his plunge, it measured 190/110, well into stroke territory. Medics rushed him to a local hospital.

"I have never experienced anything like that in my life, as far as how cold the water was," Leonard said. "That could have killed me, just being in there. I remember thinking vividly that I have five minutes in this water."

The cold-shock reflex is often mistaken for the first phase of hypothermia, but they are different conditions. Cold shock is set off by the sudden drop in skin temperature, and it subsides after several minutes, as the body adjusts. Normal breathing returns.

Early news accounts reported Leonard jumping in to swim for it, but he jumped because he heard a flight attendant say "jump." Trouble was, the life raft on the left side of the plane had not deployed. "All I knew is we were supposed to get off that plane," Leonard said. "There were one hundred fifty-five people in there, and when somebody tells me to do something, I do it."

Leonard swam out past the plane's nose. From out front, if he had been looking up, he could have seen how the eggshell-white skin of the Airbus's nose had been smudged with black and marred with cracks and indentations after the encounter with the geese. Leonard was not looking up, however—he was looking at the shoreline. Jersey looked closer than Manhattan, which it was; the plane had landed on the Jersey side of the river. Weehawken lay at least one thousand feet, perhaps fifteen hundred feet away. If it had been one hundred feet, two hundred feet, Leonard could have swum for it—he considered himself in "pretty good shape" for a man his age. But it would have been a fool's mission, so he immediately headed back to the plane.

(In any case, swimming to shore would have been impossible. Michael Phelps himself, the fastest swimmer in the world, likely wouldn't have made it while fighting the cold and the current.)

While Leonard was getting his visuals, Donna Dent, one of the flight attendants, bent low and found the handle that manually deployed the life raft at the first-class door. Leonard's seatmate, Paul Jorgensen, hopped aboard and rode the chute down as it inflated in front of him. He expected to be deposited into the water when he reached the bottom, and was surprised and relieved when it unfolded into a rubber boat large enough to hold forty-four with an overload capacity of fifty-five people.

Two other first-class passengers, Mark Hood and Denise Lockie, bounced in behind him. All the others in the first-class cabin and many from the front of coach headed for the raft on the right side of the plane, which had properly deployed. Alone at first on the left, the trio surveyed the scene—their first look outside of the plane. "The smell and taste of the air—how good it was!" Hood said. But joyous celebration quickly turned to stunned disbelief as they watched a line of passengers file out onto the wing and another group swimming in front of the wing. Several of the people in the river swam away from the raft, not toward it, and one of the women flailed in a way that alarmed Lockie. The woman didn't seem to be headed in any particular direction. She had been in the water for less than two minutes. Was she in trouble *already*?

At once, Lockie's old high-school lifeguard instincts kicked in. She and Hood began shouting, "Come here! Come here!"

Two men from the front of the coach cabin tumbled into the raft and clamored across the inflated rubber floor. Derek Alter, the Colgan pilot, and Michael Nunn, an attorney from Florence, South Carolina, took up positions along the edge to help get the swimmers aboard—if they'd swim over. Nunn noted Hood's Citadel ring on his finger, and felt encouraged; at least their small group had a leader taking charge. Even if they got everyone out of the water, though, the swimmers would still be vulnerable to hypothermia, sitting in wet clothes in subfreezing temperatures. It was so cold, Hood had already lost feeling in his fingers.

Hood's immediate concern, however, was that none of the swimmers—or anyone in the raft for that matter—was wearing a life vest. Every successful Marine officer knows how to fashion a life vest out of a pair of pants—you tie the legs together, fill them with air and sling them around your neck. Hood had used the technique to pass a "drown proofing" exercise; one that required treading water for an hour after jumping off a high dive complete with a full pack, helmet, flak jacket, and weapon. Looking at his fellow passengers, Hood doubted anyone would consider such a step. "How could I ask Pam or Denise to take their britches off and tie them around their neck?" he wondered.

Hood's mind flitted back to the 1982 crash of an Air Florida jet in Washington, DC, on a snowy January day. That day, a Citadel graduate had performed heroically to save others after the plane plowed into a bridge and plunged into the ice-bound Potomac River. Only six survived the crash—one of them, Arland Williams, Class of 1957, repeatedly passed up the life ring so the others could be rescued first, but succumbed to the cold and drowned before the ring could get to him a final time.

"He gave his life for others," Hood said. "God, please don't let me do anything dishonorable. Help me to put myself second. I prayed for courage, judgment, and guidance."

HYPOTHERMIA OCCURS WHEN the body's core temperature drops below 95 degrees. Amnesia can begin to set in at 94 degrees, unconsciousness at 86, and death at 79 degrees. Fortunately, the human body is a marvelous machine; a normal 98.6-degree body cools more slowly than most people think. The passengers in the Hudson could have stayed in the water thirty to sixty minutes before hypothermia set in. "The body recognizes it's in an extreme situation and losing body heat to the environment," said Dr. Alan Steinman, a retired U.S. Coast Guard physician and leading national expert on hypothermia, cold water immersion, and sea survival. "It shuts down blood vessels in the surface of the body, hands, feet, arms, and legs, to maintain heat in the center for the vital organs—heart, lungs, kidneys, brain. So you've created a cold outer shell that's not critical to survival, and a warm inner core [that *is* critical]."

In the Hudson River in January, with a surface temperature of 35 degrees, the physiological wonders of the body's self-protective mechanisms were almost beside the point. The cold outer shell—the arms and legs—quickly began to malfunction. Hands became useless flippers. Any one of the survivors could have drowned without his or her body temperature dropping a single degree.

Doctor Steinman lays out the progression of steps affecting the body as hypothermia sets in: "In the first five to ten minutes, hands, fingers, feet are going to get numb, which is a real problem. You lose grip strength, your sense of touch, and manual dexterity. All of these things impair your hopes of survival.

"After ten minutes, you lose muscle strength, which affects your ability to climb. Muscles need to be at 98.6 to work efficiently, otherwise they cramp. Then shivering begins as the body tries to create heat. It's pretty uncomfortable, and totally ineffective if you're still in the water. It may slow down your rate of cooling, but you'll still get cool. Eventually the muscles get too cold to shiver. That's when you get cold really fast.

"Finally, your brain also needs to be at 98.6 to work effectively.

A cold brain loses the ability to think clearly, which can be fatal even in a survivable situation because you make bad decisions. People surviving by sitting on top of an overturned boat will jump in and try to swim for shore. Or they hallucinate."

Leonard was not in the water long enough for his brain to cool, but his thinking became muddled nonetheless. Whether this was caused by hyperventilation from the cold-shock response, when blood flow and oxygen supply to the brain temporarily decreased, or by panic or adrenaline, no one will ever know. He himself figures he would have lasted "only a couple more minutes" in the river. In the end he managed to swim back to the raft, but he has no memory of Jorgensen pulling him aboard.

Meanwhile, the effects of the cold began to wear down the others out in the water. Unfortunately, several of them still appeared to be positioning themselves to make an effort to reach the shore unaided.

Remington Chin watched the first-class raft deploy out of the corner of his eye as he swam diagonally away from the plane. To him, it looked like a slide leading to the water, not especially helpful since he was already in; he also expected the plane to explode. He put his head down and kept going.

At twenty-five, Chin is lean, athletic, and highly competitive in sports and at work. He pitched baseball through high school and college, hoping he'd make it to the major leagues. Near the end of his college career—he majored in finance at Penn's Wharton Business School—he realized that his fastball did not have enough zip to make it professionally; now, he works as a financial analyst in New York. But despite his athletic prowess, he is not strong in the water. "I'm a bad swimmer," he said. "I almost drowned once."

Still, when you're in the zone, you're in the zone, be it baseball or business, and in Chin's words, "This was that type of moment to the umpteenth degree." So Chin ignored his limited aquatic skills, and the cold, and made up his mind to swim for it. He figured he could make Manhattan; after all, he had a seat cushion. "I wasn't swimming vigorously," he said. "But I had made the decision. I was just about to turn up my effort when I looked back one more time."

There, Chin saw Paul Jorgensen waving vigorously from the raft. To this day, Chin is not so sure he would have swum over to the raft if Jorgensen had been wearing anything other than a white shirt and green tie. Something about Jorgensen's clothing said authority and knowledge.

"It was the white shirt," Chin said. "I see a white shirt and it said to me, *This guy works for the airline.* So I followed his instructions. I figure this guy knows more than I do. I don't know that I would have gone over there if he had been wearing casual clothes."

Pam Seagle and Steve O'Brien, swimming separately at first, managed to get even farther away from the fuselage than Chin. Looking back at the plane, Seagle was struck by how ironic it was to find herself in the river. She had grown up in the Hudson Valley, a place with bucolic serenity so magical that she had instructed her family to scatter her ashes at Trophy Point when she died, just where the river bends at West Point. "I knew I would end up in the Hudson," she said. "But not like this."

Meanwhile, Steve O'Brien was having another out-of-body experience. "I felt like I could see myself from above," he said. "Here I was in this huge river next to a huge plane and in front of this huge city, and I suppose my humanity just came to the forefront and I realized how insignificant I was in this situation."

O'Brien became aware of voices across the water, yelling, "Move out onto the wings!" and a nasty smell in the water. No surprise there—the Hudson is not exactly a pristine waterway. He resumed the prayers he had begun on the descent. "I tried to put my brain somewhere else by falling back on reciting a Hail Mary."

Suddenly, Pam Seagle appeared next to him, tugging at his sleeve. "That snapped me out of it. Maybe she grabbed me because I kind of wasn't there," he said.

Seagle asked: "What do we do now?"

"My brain is telling me to get away from the plane, I am expecting it to go on fire or to sink, and when it sinks, the suction will pull us down with it. Pam again asks, 'What are we going to do?' I look toward Manhattan and see a dock. I tell her we need to swim to get away from the plane and we begin to kick toward the nose of the plane and toward Manhattan. I am not sure if we make that much distance. I am not thinking, just doing."

In the forty-seven-minute Con Edison video of the accident and rescue, Seagle's and O'Brien's heads bob in the water as they kick away from the fuselage.

"The frightening thing at first was there was no one else out there," O'Brien said. "We were going to have to save ourselves. There is no doubt in my mind I was going to *try* to live, and although everyone says I wouldn't have made Manhattan, I like to think I would have."

Kicking away from the plane, O'Brien heard someone shout: "Over here! Over here!" He became aware of others in the water around him. An Asian man seemed to be hydroplaning across the surface toward the raft. O'Brien turned to Seagle; it was clear that they needed to get to that raft.

As they swam up to the side of the raft, they met Wendell Fox, the retired Charlotte-cop-turned-BoA-fraud-investigator.

Fox is taciturn, focused, unflappable; a cop's cop. He may have been the calmest person in the water. In twenty-four years on the job for the city of Charlotte, he had seen scenes far more disturbing than the one that surrounded him now. Then, as now, he knew what to do. "You do your job. Keep a clear thought. Process it."

"It never crossed my mind to swim to shore," Fox said. "I knew they would come and get us."

He tried to reassure Seagle and O'Brien. Keep moving, keep moving. Everything is going to be all right.

Seagle remembers "pieces" of her swim, but cannot recall the encounters with O'Brien or Fox. "Jumping in took my breath away. It was really cold. I wondered about taking my pants off because they were weighing me down. I don't remember anything else until I was at the side of the raft and asking Mark Hood if there was room for me."

As Hood recalls it, Seagle spoke not a word when she swam to the side of the raft, she was so far gone. "I see Pam, and I'll tell you, I've seen a lot of dead people in my life, people who've been dead ten seconds, people who've been dead much longer than that," he said. "And Pam looked to me like she was almost dead because her lips were so blue and her skin was so pale. She didn't look like she had any strength left. I bent down and grabbed her in a hook under her left leg and pulled her in, and moved her to the middle between everybody to keep her from freezing to death."

While Nunn and Jorgensen hauled the other swimmers into the raft, Hood reached over to lift Michelle DePonte to safety. A minute earlier, her surging adrenaline had launched her on a swim to shore. Now she clung to the far side of the raft, ashen-faced and in tears. She crumbled into a heap in the center, on the floor. "Once I got on that raft, my whole body shut down," DePonte said. "I could not breathe. I could not talk. My legs were blue. I was done."

As the swimmers were pulled aboard, the raft continued to fill with passengers from the back of the plane, many of them just as wet. Several inches of water sloshed on the floor of the raft, adding to the misery. The air was so cold that wet clothes froze. Billy Campbell, who'd been in seat 25A, slid in wet up to his neck. Bill Zuhowski, in only his red boxer shorts and a T-shirt, huddled over, shivering. Beth McHugh, who lost her shoes when her feet became entangled in her shawl on the floor, entered the raft soaked and frantic. "I slid into this cold water with my feet now bare," she said. "I was lying on my back in this frigid water. And I couldn't get up. It was just crazy."

Barry Leonard shivered so violently, he couldn't dial his cell phone. Derek Alter, the Colgan pilot, ordered Leonard to remove his wet top before all the warmth drained from his body, and handed over his own dry uniform shirt for Leonard to put on. Then he bear-hugged Leonard and dialed Leonard's wife. The message to her was telling: "I've been in a plane crash. I'm in the middle of the Hudson on a raft. I *think* I'm okay," Leonard said. "*Think* was a very important word," he said later. "I still was not sure if I was okay. I was so cold." (Leonard had cracked his sternum on the impact, when his knees were driven into his chest. He felt chest pain, not heart attack pain, but enough to prompt a battery of tests and scans at the hospital.)

In the Con Edison video, Seagle and O'Brien spent about three minutes in the water. At six foot three and 220 pounds, O'Brien managed to swing a leg and an arm over the side of the raft, but it took both Hood and Lockie to pull him in. He looked upriver, and then at the sky. "I was expecting boats and helicopters and I saw none," he said. "Where are they?" His disoriented, out-of-body sensation returned.

"I could see the look of panic and terror on his face. He wanted to call his wife," Lockie said. She took him in her arms, and he asked her: "Is this a dream? Is this really happening?"

"No, it's not a dream," Lockie said. "It's really happening."

Then Wendell Fox, calm and unflappable, reached out a hand and introduced himself. "Hey, I'm Wendell. Let's have lunch some time."

11

Wing Walkers

WHAT DO YOU SAY TO THE MAN STANDING NEXT TO YOU ON THE WING of a commercial airliner floating down the Hudson River? You've never met before. But instantly, you become intimate friends because he's holding you to keep you from falling in. He also offered to share his seat cushion, which is sort of like a stranger offering to lend you his car. Water is creeping up your legs because the plane is sinking as it drifts downriver and there's still a chance everyone will drown or freeze to death before help arrives. You've already gone through the "Wow, what just happened? We can't believe it" and "Ohmygosh, we're getting soaked here." Is humor appropriate?

Jennifer Doyle had no idea, but she didn't puzzle long as she looked down at her wet legs and then toward her benefactor, Craig Black, still holding her by the shoulder.

"Do you know how hard it is to find pants that fit this well?" she asked.

If riding through three minutes of terror inside the aircraft had a certain unreality to it, standing on the wing took it well into the surreal. "It was like stepping into a different world," said Doyle, a thirty-three-year-old bond trader at Wachovia. "You crouch through this little door and then you're literally walking the plank in the middle of a river."

For the first ones outside, it was so silent that seagulls above the river seemed to call full-throated. Water swirled over the wing and froze to the metal. Time sped up. "While we were waiting for impact, we were going through slow motion," Doyle said. "Then real motion started again." Optical illusions tricked frightened eyes—some who peered out at the people standing knee-deep in the Hudson assumed the plane had come down in shallow water and they soon would be wading to shore. For those already standing knee-deep, the monstrous wing suddenly seemed to be a fragile thing. Some were uncertain it would support the weight of several dozen slightly overweight Americans.

"I didn't know if it would sink or break off," said Clay Presley. And, to him, the tip of the left wing seemed to be a long way from the fuselage. Presley had the distance right. It was just over forty-six feet, more than half the distance from home plate to first base. Unknown to Presley and many others, the extra weight was an inconsequential addition to a wing designed to support, along with its partner on the right, the entire aircraft, which weighed 151,510 pounds on takeoff.

"It was an odd sensation," said Jerry Shanko, the BoA technology manager. "Here we are, apparently safe, standing on the wing, and yet there is all this freezing cold water, which was unlike anything I've ever felt. Looking at everyone's faces, I remember a look of disbelief."

"People shuffled out carefully and slowly," said Jay McDonald, the software company salesman. "It was a courteous moment. It was, 'No, go ahead, after you.'"

Stepping through the exits, many felt immense relief just to be outside the plane. "Okay, nothing can kill me now, I'm on the fuse-lage," McDonald said. Warren Holland, a BoA bond trader, became "elated" out there. "I felt like I had some control over my fate. I could use my wits and my brain to save myself," he said. "When you're strapped into the middle seat of an airplane, there's nothing you can do to affect the outcome."

Holland's exuberance about control begged the question: What exactly does one *do* on the wing of an aircraft in the middle of a river? Josh Peltz, for one, had no idea.

"Inside the plane, I became very task-oriented," he said. "Now our next step is to get onto the wing and make room for everybody. We need a flotation device. Now what's the next step? I didn't have a next step."

Peltz had efficiently opened the hatch next to his seat at 10F, but he couldn't loosen his seat cushion on his way onto the right wing. Jenny Moulton, two seats over, snagged it for him as she followed him out. "In one swift motion, she ripped the cushion out," he said. "She was like the mother you hear about who lifts the car off of her infant child. I was thinking, she's like a superhero. She's a slight girl, very slender. I'm a big guy, six-foot-four and 235 pounds."

The two walked out, holding each other up for balance, as river water washed over their feet. "We walked out as far as we could go," he said. "It was so cold, freezing cold. I honestly thought we were going to have to swim to New York."

Mary Berkwits remained unfazed by the whole experience like the New Yorker that she was, despite the move to the South. On the de-scent, she had never once glanced toward the window, concentrating instead on calming Amy Jolly seated next to her on the aisle. Stepping out onto the wing with her husband, Michael, however, she expected to see an airline terminal. "I thought we were landing at Newark," she said. "I went, 'Michael, we're in the water? I didn't know we were in the water.' And he said, 'Yeah, Mary, it's the Hudson. There's the *Intrepid* right over there.' And I went, 'Oh, we'll be okay.'"

Despite Mary Berkwits's steely confidence, the wing presented a serious new risk to everyone's survival. Irina Levshina, for one, didn't feel at all safe out there. Nor did Stewart Wallace, an investment banker at Wachovia. "None of us had life jackets on," said Wallace. "I was trying to ease myself down the wing. I knew the water was very dangerous. I thought you could last more than a minute in the water, but I knew it wasn't ten minutes."

At one point, Peltz tried to console a woman crying uncontrollably. "I was telling everyone, we crashed. Past Tense! It's okay, we're alive. Even as I thought in my mind, *We are going to drown or freeze to death.*"

THE LINE-UP OF passengers on the wings became the enduring image of the accident. From a distance, the wing walkers looked composed, patient, calm—everything they were not. Fulmer Duckworth, forty-one, a computer graphics designer for Bank of America, watched the plane hit the Hudson from the twenty-ninth floor of his office building at West Forty-second Street and Sixth Avenue. Peering through binoculars, he counted eighty people standing on the wings. "It looked like everybody was really calm," he told the *New York Times*. "Like on the subway platform when it's really, really crowded . . ."

Up close, there was a certain sense of subway-station togetherness. . . .

"I remember everyone being kind of tight, close together," said

Jorge Morgado, one of the golfers who ended up with three of his companions on the left wing. "There was someone touching my right shoulder, my left shoulder, and someone right behind me. There was no room to go anywhere. I had to shift myself forward and out, which put me at the front of the wing. If anyone had bumped me, I was going right in the water."

A sense of calm was another matter. In Fulmer Duckworth's binoculars, Susan Wittmann and Dick Richardson probably appeared as ordinary subway commuters. But their accounts of the same moment hardly bear out such a description. While Richardson did, indeed, remain outwardly calm, Wittmann was less sanguine. She had become separated from her bank colleagues, Scott Sharkey and Jerry Shanko, and walked onto the right wing alone and scared.

"I was probably tenth or eleventh out," she said. "I never went over knee-deep water. My foot slipped and slid down the wing. I realized I couldn't get traction. I looked at the guy next to me and said. 'I'm slipping.' He grabbed my hand and pulled me back next to him and said something like, 'Not today. It's not gonna happen.' He said, 'Hi, I'm Dick,' and I said, 'Hi, I'm Susan' and something stupid like, 'nice to meet you.' He said, 'Why don't you just hang on to me?' I think I was in shock."

Richardson had paid little attention to Wittmann until she grabbed his sleeve. He was preoccupied with his own emotions, trying to cope with two lifelong anxieties—a plane crash and drowning. But the woman next to him clearly appeared to be terrified. "Her eyes were like a couple of saucers. She said, 'We're sinking.' I had been watching the water level on the windows. We were indeed sinking, but slowly. I said, 'Hang on to me and we'll get through this.' She goes from holding my jacket to now grabbing my arm. I can't swim. I'm thinking, *Oh shit, I said the wrong thing. Now I have a 130-pound weight on my arm.*"

The surface area of each wing measures around 650 square feet. To some it seemed as narrow as a balance beam, especially when they lost sight of it as the wing sank beneath the surface of the river. Although the effervescent Mike Berkwits rallied his companions on the left wing to dance in an effort to keep warm, most considered the wing a precarious perch and more than a few lost their footing. Kristy Spears, one of the BoA merger team, fell, banana-peel style, as soon as she stepped through the exit. She scooted the rest of the way toward the tip on her backside.

"You couldn't see under the surface of the water. You were blindly feeling with your feet, trying to stay on the wing," said Chris Cobb. "You didn't know where the tip was, you didn't know where it started to slant down. I didn't feel secure at all."

"I had Uggs on, thank God," said Amy Jolly. "I was not having a hard time, even though it was very slippery. Every time the water would wash over, it would immediately ice up."

"I had on leather-soled shoes, which made for it being very slippery," said Stephen Lis, a partner with KPMG. "My footing got better as the water came up."

At least eight people tumbled off the wings into the river. Heyam Kawas had followed her seatmate Wendell Fox to the left wing. "The next thing I know I'm in the river. I can't swim," she said, though she has no memory of how she got there. Debbie Ramsey also fell off the left wing. "I was just grabbing, trying to grab onto anything. I had my cushion. I could swim. And yet I was scared to death," she said. "A guy got hold of my hand and said, 'Calm down. I'll help you up.' He got me up on my feet. He said: 'Hold on to me, I won't let you go and you won't let me go.' And with that we took baby steps out on the wing."

To her everlasting regret, Molly Schugel, the sensible Iowan, was wearing new red shoes with three-inch heels. In the airline terminal, they had received *ooh's* and *ahh's;* now they had become a curse. Halfway down the right wing, she took off the shoes and chucked them into the river. She fell in anyway.

The man who hauled Schugel up did not look especially strong, but he pulled her up onto the wing as if she was a feather, leaving Schugel to marvel at the power of adrenaline.

A few moments later, in another surreal moment, one of the red shoes floated by Jenny Moulton as she moved out toward the tip, clutching Josh Peltz. She recognized the shoe as it glided by as one she had admired at the security checkpoint. She wondered what had become of its owner, having no idea that Schugel stood a mere ten feet away.

On the other side of the plane, Beverly Waters, traveling with her workmate, Jim Clark, watched a woman's boot float by. "It freaked me out. We didn't know if anyone had died. I pointed it out to Jim. 'Somebody didn't make it,' I said."

Jim Clark: "I just said, '*Shhhh,* don't say a thing. No reason to draw attention to it.' In my mind, someone took their shoes off. We had a lot of people on that wing and we didn't want anyone to panic. If someone starts freaking out . . . while we weren't dry, we were at least safe at that point."

ON THE LEFT wing, separate mini-dramas played out every few feet as groups of passengers bunched together. Some cried, while others soothed the criers. It was a comedy act, an emergency room, *M*A*S*H.* The group that had jumped in swam in front of the wing, adding to the desperately anxious mood.

"As I first stepped out there, it was so bright and so sunny and I remember thinking, *I'm on a plane in water,* like a dream sequence almost," said Amy Jolly. "Then I saw another passenger named Joe Hart. He had a bloody nose, and that snapped me back into reality. That's when I started screaming Shae's name, and I think she said my name back, and that's when I saw her pretty far out in the water.

"Another passenger came out behind me. I remember her saying, 'Help me, I'm going to die.' We were all very scared. We all were at that point when we didn't know what in the heck was going on. I remember seeing a man crying. I had a father who never cried. It was very upsetting.

"The crying man sobbed: 'My son, my son.' I thought: *Ohmygosh, people have died.* That's when I saw Shae and thought: *Is she alive?* I remember thinking, *Has she died?*"

The crying man was Rob Kolodjay, the elder statesmen on the golfing trip. He had helped pull Debbie Ramsey back onto the wing and calmed others standing near him. But he was also overwrought about the fate of his 31-year-old son, Jeff, and his fears eventually gave way to tears.

Joe Hart, meanwhile, became fixated on the rising waterline, trying to gauge how long he could hold out on the wing before he would end up in the water. It seemed to him as if there would be enough time for rescuers to arrive before the plane sank.

"Most of the panic didn't occur until you got outside the plane," Hart said. "It was odd to me, once you got outside the plane, it was simply logical that you were okay. Amy is next to me on the wing and she is absolutely terrified. She's talking to me. 'Are we going to die?' That kind of panic was in her voice, and I looked at her and said, 'If I were you, I'd ask for an upgrade next time you fly.' She looked at me in disbelief, almost like, *What an asshole.*"

Amy Jolly found Hart strangely comforting. "Joe Hart told me panicking isn't going to help. I just started crying. I was really getting upset. He says, 'Are we going to cry?' He was, like, 'Calm down. Panicking isn't going to help anything here. The worst thing that can happen is we will get wet.'"

Jolly had briefly considered jumping into the river to join her friend Shae Childers.

She scooted down, then heard another calmly reassuring voice, an unknown man, caution: "Stay on the wing as long as you can. This plane will float for at least an hour." Twenty to thirty minutes was more like it.

"It was enough to stop me from getting in," Jolly said. "These voices, thank God for them. It's great how some people can stay so level-headed in a situation like that. Had I jumped in the water when I thought I was going to swim with Shae, I don't know how long I would have made it, because I didn't have anything to float on."

Jolly saw someone talking on a cell phone, and she in turn pulled out hers from her purse on her shoulder. "I wondered if I should call my mom. This was before any of the ferries got there. I didn't think that would be very smart, so I called the guy I was dating at the time. I felt like I needed to contact somebody."

Hart, who travels with two cell phones, pulled both out of his pockets. He called his boss, his mother, his ex-wife, his son, his twin daughters (simultaneously, one on each cell), and his brother. His daughters and mother began crying hysterically. His boss and his ex-wife thought he was joking. His brother said, "Are you on that flight? How fucking cool. Tell me what it's like."

A few steps away, on another section of the wing, Michael Leonard tried to hand Lori Lightner, his boss at Belk, a seat cushion. She had beat him out onto the wing from her exit row seat, but had left her cushion behind. The two have been friends since their under-graduate days at the University of California, Los Angeles. Neither of them likes cold weather, but Lightner is so sensitive to it that when she travels, she often wears her coat inside the plane. Standing outside now in her full-length down coat with its fur hood, and wearing leather boots, a scarf, and cashmere gloves, Lightner seemed better equipped for the cold than anyone on the flight. Just looking at her made Leonard, in his shirtsleeves, shiver more. But Lightner was a doer, not one to wait. As Leonard watched in astonishment, she jumped off the back of the wing.

Lightner saw it like this: Stand on the wing and sink with the plane. But off the back of the wing, an inflated escape slide floated like a raft.

"I go for a boat. I'm a very strong swimmer," she explained later. "It didn't occur to me that the water was very cold, that I had no life jacket and was fully dressed in a full down coat, jeans, and boots."

As she swam to the slide, which was upside down and twisted, one of the exit hatches floated by. "I thought I'll sit on the door, which was stupid—it immediately sank. So I swam to the back of the raft. By that time I had been in the water three or four minutes. You can really start to feel your bodily functions slow. My hands wouldn't grip. I was completely bogged down with the full down coat, the jeans, the boots, sweater, scarf. My coat was zipped up. I was adrift, going with the current toward the back, toward the tail of the plane. I thought: I need to get out of the water. If I don't get out of this water, I'm going to drown. I can't stay afloat much longer, and I am a strong swimmer."

Lightner scanned the wing, looking for someone to help her out. "That's when I saw Michael Leonard and swam over. There was no niceness about it. I shouted at Mike: *'Pull me out!'*"

Meanwhile, Eileen Shleffar strode along the wing, still on the phone with her husband. At fifty-six, Shleffar had worked at Belk for ten years. She is respected by colleagues, and is generally so good at her job that the company president dubbed her the "Queen of Retail." Her descriptions of the accident and her efforts to calm herself are among the most compelling, if occasionally comedic, of anyone on the flight. When she first escaped onto the wing, the scene unnerved her, even as she continued to talk on her cellphone.

"People were gingerly walking down the wing, and I saw people in the water. The slide seemed to be stuck behind the wing. I'm thinking, *Crap. How am I gonna get away from the plane? It's going to explode.*

"I had bad shoes on for a wing walk. Three-inch heels. Pumps. My only comfortable pair," she said. "I could feel myself slipping. I could feel pressure on my waist, like somebody was behind me, and I dropped onto the wing and slid into the water."

So ended perhaps the most remarkable phone call in the history of the flight. As she hit the water, Shleffar's cell died immediately, still in her hand. "The next time my husband knew I was okay he saw me on TV on his Jet Blue flight to New York. I was wrapped in a Red Cross blanket."

In the water, Shleffar, like Lightner, tried to climb onto the exit hatch bobbing nearby. "I hurled myself onto the floating door and it immediately sank and I'm, like, *Crap, this is not a good option,* and let the door go and started working on the slide to get it out. The front part of the slide had been pulled away and two people were in it, a lady in the front and the Australian singer lady. I was trying desperately to get into the slide. The lady in the front must have been in total shock. She had her legs hanging over the front of the slide and was staring ahead. The singer girl was not so stoic.

"I was looking for someone to help me get onto the slide between them, and I was determined to get out of that dirty, stinky water. I heaved myself up and landed in between them. The singer is shouting, 'I have to get on the plane. I have to get on the plane.' I was trying to calm her down.

"Someone is standing in the door of the plane throwing little plastic bags out, and I didn't have any idea what they were. Lisa [English, another Belk buyer] tossed me one and said, 'Here, you'll need this.' Seeing my puzzled face she said, 'It's a life jacket.' My hands were so frozen, I couldn't get my fingers to pull the thing apart, and she leaned over and ripped it open. And then I put it on and someone helped me pull the cords because my hands were so stiff, they wouldn't move."

Both Lisa English and Shleffar tried to calm the Australian, twenty-six-year-old Emma Cowan. "You cannot get back on the plane. She says, 'I must get my passport. I am not from here. Let me back on the plane. I don't live in this country.' We were saying, 'Calm down, people will help you.' She was very agitated, and as it was, I didn't have my balance anyway, so I just slid right into the water again, but at least I had a life jacket on.

"I thought, *Great, I guess I'll swim to the wing.* The wing is farther away from the body of the plane than the raft is. I swam to the wing and someone pulled me up on the wing, and we stood there waiting, and someone yelled, 'Boats! The boats are coming!' and I heard a helicopter. All right, we're going to get rescued. If we don't explode, we'll get rescued."

THE AIRBUS A320 lay tilted in the river, with the right wing weighed down by a 5,250-pound engine, low in the water. The left wing, shorn of its engine, floated just above the surface. When Casey Jones, who stood on the wing for seventeen minutes, reached the tip, his feet were completely out of water. But on the right wing, the water rose from the ankles to the thighs to the waist in minutes. Larry Snodgrass charted the progression. "The wing was above the water when we got out. By the time we started loading the ferry, the wing's about four feet under water. By the time I got to the bow of the ferry, the door that we came out had three inches of air space left. That's how far that wing was below the water. The fireboats had already clamped onto the plane. If they had not clamped on to hold it up, that plane would have gone down in a hurry."

Don Norton, who opened the exit at 11F and was the first one out, found it discomforting that the wing moved beneath his feet as he ventured toward the end. "It pushed farther and farther down," he said. "I'm surprised I didn't go up to my neck. I didn't know where the wing ended. The water was about halfway between my ankles and knees when I came out and quickly got much deeper."

Like others, Freida Muscatell, the software saleswoman for IBM, also wondered if the wing would break. "I couldn't believe how many people were on the wing," she said. "It seemed like there were a hundred of us out there."

For at least two women, wading along the wing became an especially grueling ordeal. Both well-traveled professionals, Beverly Mills, approaching her sixtieth birthday, and Laurie Crane, at fifty-eight, lacked the stamina of their younger colleagues.

Mills didn't even want to leave the warm cabin. She had occupied a seat in one of the over-wing exit rows. Mills and her husband had spent twenty years in Florida, and dived in the Keys and the Caribbean. Mills had been certified as a rescue diver, and knew well the dangers lurking just outside. "As I looked sideways, as the man was opening the door, I was horrified. I couldn't imagine how we would survive it," Mills said. "If you were in the water, which was where I assumed we were going, you would have a minute, possibly. Maybe two. I remember thinking, *I'll just stay in the nice warm plane and let everyone step over me.*" But she had to make way.

So Mills became the third person out the exit. "I was really concerned about my ability to hold out as long as I had to hold out. I had to maintain all of my focus on keeping my balance. At some point, my mind drifted off. The effects of the cold were already hitting me. I was in water up to my knees. I said, 'I'm cold, I'm cold.' The man next to me looked alarmed. I thought, *Okay, I can do this thing.* But then, not long after, about thirty seconds later, I said again: 'I'm cold,' and I doubled over a little bit. It was so painful."

The man alerted the group and began maneuvering Mills back toward the fuselage, where several other men were trying to untangle the inflated slide off the back of the plane. As with its twin on the left, the slide had to be righted before anyone could get onto it. "The raft is flipped over and out of reach," said Jay McDonald. "You can't get to it or get in it. It's wedged into and under the plane. There's a tether there, and we couldn't get it loose."

Dan Vinton tried to grab for it, but fell in. Alex Magness, Brad Wentzell, Carl Bazarian, and several others formed a chain to wrestle it down flat on the water.

"I grabbed Carl's belt and another guy grabs me," said Keith Anthony. "We do this human chain to walk out over the edge of the wing, and the water is going deeper and deeper, and we lean him out over the water to span between the wing and where the raft is."

Bazarian's arms were too short. They pulled him in and Anthony, who is six foot six, with longer arms, got a hold.

McDonald also reached out. "I asked the guy to hold my left arm, and I grabbed the raft and was tugging on it, freeing it and flipping it. There was an onrush and people just dove in." Then the raft began filling fast and McDonald said "Let's get the women in the raft first. As I'm saying something like that, a woman taps me on the shoulder, and I scoot out of the way and let her through."

Tracey Wolsko heard somebody say, "Hey, you're tiny." The next thing she knew, she was "chucked into this raft. I was grateful for not having to stand on the wing, but sitting in the raft in fifteen inches of water didn't help either."

One of the men shouted to Beverly Mills to jump aboard. She wasn't sure she could leap over the gap between the wing and the slide. "My brain was trying to think, *How am I going to perform this physically impossible feat?* When I hesitated, they threw me into the slide," she said. She remains grateful to the man who helped move her down the wing toward the slide. "If that man hadn't helped me, I was going to go into the water. I didn't have anything left to stand up anymore. I was out of gas."

Mills sat facing Carl Bazarian. He describes himself as hyperactive, and manages to appear energetic during even the most somnolent business meeting. On the slide, he was on an adrenaline high, helping people.

"Carl is sitting there in a perfectly pressed suit," Mills said. "He looks like he belongs in a boardroom. He didn't even have a hair out of place. He smiled and nodded like we were being introduced. I said, 'I'm so cold.' He took my hands and said, 'You're going to need your hands.' He was just as cold as I was, so it didn't help, but it was a nice gesture."

And so it went, calm and panic. When Robin Schoepf stepped onto the slide, she felt like giggling. "It was complete elation," she said. "A guy to my right pulled out a phone and started taking pictures. He got on the phone and called somebody. It wasn't a frantic call, it was a 'Holy crap, you're never going to believe this' call. I made eye contact with him. He was having the same kind of feeling I was. Very happy to be alive."

And yet the jet fuel still worried them. Alex Magness tried to calm nerves. "Our raft was very close to the right engine. I remember saying, with no credibility or authority whatsoever, 'We're fine, the fire went out in the air, we're in water now, it's totally extinguished.' I've since learned that fuel can burn on water, but it sounded good at the time and nobody wanted to disagree. It seemed that they were perfectly happy to treat me as the authority on the subject."

Meanwhile, Laurie Crane, one of the Belk buyers, and the only one of the six who had not escaped onto the left wing, emerged with her arms full. She carried her mink coat, a briefcase, and her purse.[1]

"I'm holding all the stuff in my left arm," she said. "I couldn't even fathom putting on the coat, because I was shaking so violently. A woman at the door behind me noticed and said, 'She's up to her waist. She's freezing.' She told me, 'Don't worry, we're going to be okay.' I looked around and I saw the first New York Waterway ferry coming toward us."

At that moment, Josh Peltz had been trying to call his wife on a borrowed cell phone. At home, she was watching a video of *Horton Hears a Who* with their toddler and newborn, and she didn't recognize the 917 area code of the caller and didn't pick up. He left a message. As he hung up, the ferry boat chugged toward the plane. It looked like a giant blue and white box, not a sleek marine vessel. "No offense to my wedding and the birth of my children," Peltz said. "I thought it was the most beautiful sight I had ever seen."

[1] Aircraft evacuees commonly retrieve belongings, according to Professor Ed Galea at the University of Greenwich. It helps calm them down. The handful of passengers who attempted to remove their belongings from the overhead bins had been shouted down by others, and most left the plane empty-handed. In Crane's case, her coat was on her lap and her bags were at her feet.

12

All Aboard

IF IMAGES OF THE CARTWHEELING ETHIOPIAN AIRLINER STUCK IN THE mind's eye of the passengers inside the cabin, the mental image of the sinking *Titanic* loomed large and roiled fears once they stepped outside.

Craig Black, watching several men wrestle with the twisted slide off the right wing, thought immediately of the *Titanic*'s shortage of life rafts. "All these people near the door trying to get this thing fixed," he said. "There were three people for every seat on that device."

Mike Kollmansberger, the sales manager, recalled James Cameron's 1997 version of the legendary sinking, and Leonardo DiCaprio's hypothermic swim before he disappeared beneath the surface. "I'm thinking I need to keep moving," Kollmansberger said. "My legs were not responding. It was like walking through Jell-O, and I'm thinking this is hypothermia."

As the tail continued to sink, others focused on the more obvious parallel and what that might mean for the group.

Dave Sanderson had stationed himself in the door frame of the right-wing exit to assist. "What crossed my mind was when, in the movie, the boat went straight down and sucked everyone down with it," he said. "That's when I said, I have to get off this plane."

"If you've ever seen the movie, the weight of the boat sucked everyone under, and I was thinking if this starts to go under, we'll have to swim away," said Stephanie King. "I was hoping everyone could swim."

Fears of being sucked down by a seventy-five-ton aircraft were natural, but the concept of the swallowing vortex is largely a myth— the product of Hollywood producers, dime novelists, and hyperbolic sea stories dating back to Homer. The last man off the *Titanic,* a radio operator, did not go down with the ship, but survived and tes- tified to Congress.

What was more likely to happen to the Airbus in the Hudson was what happened to that Northwest Airlines Stratocruiser that ditched in Puget Sound in 1956. After the pilot performed a "beautiful" ditching, according to witnesses, the plane simply sank. Mrs. Helen Wilkings, thirty-three, of Ladd Air Force Base in Fairbanks, escaped from the plane onto a wing with her four-year-old son, Lester. "The wing began to sink so we crawled up onto the cabin," she said in a United Press account of the accident. "We were there about two min- utes and then it went down. That's when I thought we had had it. I watched the tail come up, and the plane nosed over and sank. I was worried about being pulled down with it, but there didn't seem to be any suction. Lester and I were on the floating cushions. As soon as

Lester got into the water, he said, 'Mommy, I gotta go potty.' I told him he could do anything he wanted."

Mother and son were rescued a few minutes later. Still, five of the thirty-eight people on board drowned. Only the speedy arrival of rescue boats—the fastest rescue on record at the time—kept the death toll from going higher.

The passengers on Flight 1549 needed nothing as melodramatic as a vortex to turn their remarkable survival into a full-blown disaster. They just needed a little more time in the water.

Fortunately, a new speed record for rescue was about to be clocked.

ON THE CON EDISON video, the New York Waterway ferry *Thomas Jefferson* arrived at the right side of the plane three minutes and fifty-seven seconds after Sullenberger hit the river. The ferry picked up fifty-six people from the wing and the life raft, a feat of such alacrity that it caught even the airline, which already knew that Sullenberger had lost both engines, unprepared.

As the ferry pulled up to the life raft on the right side of the plane, the rafters waved it over to the sinking wing. "We said we're fine," Amber Wells said. The ferry stopped eight to ten feet from the wing, putting the metal ladder that had been lowered from the deck out of reach. "The ferry guys are going 'Come on!' and nobody is moving," said Molly Schugel. "I was already wet. I'm thinking, somebody's got to go first. I jumped in, swam to the boat. My hands froze to the ladder, and the deckhand is going, 'Let's go,' and I'm saying, 'I'm stuck.'"

And then she was up on the deck, the first passenger from Flight 1549 to be rescued, the first to make the transition from passenger to survivor.

Inside, ferry passengers swarmed around her. A hat was pulled over Schugel's head; someone gave her a pair of gloves. Two passengers handed over their coats. A woman offered her a tiny cell phone, the smallest Schugel had ever seen.

"I remember trying to dial and I could barely do it, my fingers were shaking so much. I called my husband and left a message. That was at 3:37. Eleven minutes after takeoff. I was safe and calling someone. It was amazing."

Schugel's husband picked up the message and quickly dialed US Airways customer service line and asked: "What's the plan?"

"They told him, the plane's fine, it took off, nothing's happened," Schugel said. "He's saying: 'Ma'am, I respect that you might not know this yet, but I'm telling you my wife just called me. She is on a ferry boat in the middle of the Hudson River and she told me her plane crashed.' And as he's talking to the operator, the phones in the background started ringing off the hook. Everything goes crazy."

One of the passengers on that ferry, Janis Krums, of Sarasota, Florida, shot the first close-up photograph of the scene and posted it to Twitter, helping to spread the news of the accident around the globe almost instantaneously.

The boxy ferries were not built for the kind of large-scale rescue operation they were about to undertake. They had difficulty negotiating the curves and angles of the jet, especially with the current factored in. Craig Black watched with trepidation as the *Thomas Jefferson* sped toward the wing. "I hoped he would slow down. He was coming at a good pace and I thought he would hit the wing a little hard," Black said. "He stopped the thing on a dime."

The water was so deep around Jennifer Doyle, next in line on the wing, that she had only to "lean" into it to swim. As she started up the ladder, the ferry began backing away to reposition itself. "Where is that boat going? I don't remember if I said anything. I don't know if

I *could* have said anything. When you hit the water, it took your breath away. You could feel the air get sucked out of you."

After a moment, the ferry stopped. Doyle said, "I pulled myself onto the bottom of the ladder. My clothing made a crunching noise as soon as I came out of the water, a sound I'll never forget. The deckhands said, 'Don't climb. Just lift your arms.' I reached up, and the next thing I know, I'm in the boat."

Climbing up, Warren Holland could hardly contain himself as he stepped onto the ferry deck. "I was giddy with relief. I could not believe that I was all in one piece. I'd won the lottery. It was a one in a million chance."

The ferry backed up again as Stephanie King climbed the ladder. She screamed as her fiancé Andrew Gray yelled, "Go! Go! Climb the thing."

"Once Stephanie got up, I was four or five after her," Gray said. "I clambered up, looking. Where's Stephanie? I ran up to her. I was holding her, trying to use my body heat. I pulled my phone out and called my parents, made it real quick. I said, 'Hey, first of all, we're okay. We've been in a plane crash. Turn on the news. Gotta go.'"

Meanwhile, in the life rafts jutting out from the first-class doors, the passengers anxiously watched the rising waterline on the side of the fuselage. Windows at the last few rows of seats were no longer visible. Water is heavy, a gallon weighing 8.3 pounds. As the aircraft filled, the sinking accelerated. (At one point during the rescue, as the fire department boats tried to tie mooring lines around the tail, a fireboat tied itself to the starboard side, but stationed a firefighter with an axe nearby to cut the lines free if the plane became unstable.)

"I heard the plane making groaning-type noises and then that gurgling sound as it was settling down in the water," said Beth McHugh, who huddled in the life raft on the left. "Once I was on the raft, I thought, *This plane is going to sink and we'll still be attached.*"

No one in the rafts, including the crew, could disconnect either raft from the plane, and, of course, in the post–September 11 world of air travel, none of the passengers had even the smallest pocket-knife, which would have done the trick.

"That was my final big fear that day," said Bill Nix, who sat in the raft on the left side of the plane. "I kept watching the plane sinking, and in my mind's eye, I saw it taking us with it."

Sullenberger appeared at the right door and pulled a Velcro strip, but the raft remained tethered to the plane. At one point, Jeff Kolod-jay became so desperate to unleash the raft from the sinking ship that he tried chewing through a nylon cord that connected it to the door frame. "I rubbed the cord against the door to get some friction. Then I tried biting it to tear through it that way. But I could taste the gas on the rope, so obviously I stopped that."

The deckhands on the *Thomas Jefferson* had knives. "There was an older gentleman with a black mustache who looked like someone you'd see from the old country," said Douglas Schrift. "We started shouting at him for a knife. He pulls out his knife; it's six to eight inches long. I remember thinking, *Don't drop this into the Hudson.* He tosses the knife, and I know there's one other guy behind me. I let it go over my head and the guy caught it. He opened it up and cut the cord."

On the left, Alyson Bell caught another knife with a one-handed catch that wowed the macho road warriors in the raft. She handed it over to Sullenberger who cut them free from the plane. Until then, the passengers had known their captain only by his clipped voice as he uttered those seven chilling words on the descent. Few even recognized him.

Sullenberger had been the last to leave the aircraft and the last into the left raft. He had inspected the cabin before stepping out, and tried several times, unsuccessfully, to get a head count. The first count on the left didn't go very well, said Steve O'Brien. "One, two, eleven. It passed me by. Somebody said twenty-four, someone said two again." But now, seated with copilot Jeffrey Skiles and flight attendant Donna Dent, the passengers got their first opportunity to look over the man who had pulled off such a feat.

"It almost seemed like it was no big deal to him, like he had parked a car in a parking space," said Ian Wells, the University of Miami senior. "He was calm, extremely collected. I was, like, This guy is incredible."

Wells thanked him. "I said, 'I owe you my life,' and he said, 'It was just my job. We were very fortunate.' I said, 'No, I owe you my life,' and he goes, 'Thank you. That means a lot.'"

Sullenberger made an identical impression on Bill Elkin, a Charlotte executive returning home from an overseas trip. "He was cool as a cucumber. He had his hat on, his clipboard in his hand, his jacket buttoned up. He slid down the raft and sat next to me. He was just sitting there. He didn't say anything, but was very calm."

"I gave him a one-armed hug. I said, 'Thank you, you saved my life. You're my hero.' He said, 'You're welcome.' I sat next to him for twenty minutes, and that's all he said."

"I was terribly impressed," said Jim Whitaker. "He was completely unflappable."

To Steve O'Brien, the man with the clipboard under his arm seemed so serene that O'Brien initially mistook him for one of the rescuers. "I thought this guy came off a ferry or was a fireman or a cop and he was here to rescue us. There was no way you could have told me that he was on the plane. This person had to have come from outside the plane to be that much in control. I didn't realize he was Sullenberger. Remarkable."

Back on the right, the *Thomas Jefferson* moved into position next to the life raft and prepared to take on eighty-five-year-old Lucille Palmer and Doreen Welsh, who was bleeding all over the raft.

The aircraft's door had refused to lock into an open position, and Douglas Schrift had spent much of the evacuation as a doorman, holding the door open and helping people into the right life raft. He had eased both Palmer and Welsh in.

"Lucille's lips were quaking and there were tears in her eyes," he said. "With Doreen, there was blood all over me. I asked her where she was injured and she had no idea. Then I saw her pull up her pant leg. It looked like someone had taken two dull tomahawks to it. It was a bad bash, real bad and went right into her flesh big-time."

The frail octogenarian reminded Jeff Kolodjay of his grand-mother. She shivered so violently, he wrapped her in his sweatshirt and hugged her tight.

"My whole mind was blank, blank, blank," Palmer said. "All I re-member is lying down in that raft and this man put his arms around me to keep me warm."

Someone asked the proverbial question—Is there a doctor on board?—and Alberto Panero, about to graduate from medical school in May, moved over and elevated Welsh's bleeding leg on a pile of seat cushions. Welsh went up the ladder to the ferry first, pushed from below and pulled from above.

"Her mascara was running down her face. She was totally wet. She was crying," said Nick Gamache. "We kept yelling, 'Get her up. Get her up.'"

The deckhands threw down a couple of lines, and several men in the raft jury-rigged a rope chair to hoist Lucille Palmer up next. After Palmer, the six-year-old clamored up, then her mother, and then it was the rest of the women onto the boat.

Jim Hanks, sixty-five, lingered until the end. "We got all the women off, and then I'm still holding onto the ladder, so I'm looking around to see if there are any other women, and I heard this voice. 'Get the old guy up, get the old guy up.' I looked around to see if there's some elderly gentleman we've missed and the guy is pointing at me."

No one is sure how the passengers decided that women should leave first. Perhaps it was because it was a plane full of Southerners; perhaps it was because everyone was so well behaved. But moving women onto the ferries first when they had to crawl over the men in the rafts, or step precariously around the men on the wings, perplexed several recipients of the courtesy.

"It was not practical," said Pam Seagle. "Steve was closer to the net."

Theresa Leahy, one of the BoA merger team, was surprised to hear the phrase "women and children first," something she considers an arcane notion.

"Certainly children first and those who needed assistance, the elderly and injured," she said. "I appreciate the humanity that's happening there, that people are putting someone else ahead of themselves. But in an evacuation situation where time could be lost or other things could happen? What if the plane had sunk right then and there, when seconds count? You have to do the thing that's most efficient. I am not trying to be critical. I know they were trying to do it out of genuine love for other people."

The Japanese traders, Hiroki Takigawa in the left life raft, and Kanau Deguchi on the left wing, waited through the rescue as cultural outsiders. In Japan, Takigawa said, the courtesy would not be used in a similar airline disaster.

"Small children first, yes. But they would never ask, 'Ladies, you go first,'" said Takigawa. "There would probably be someone giving orders." Then, in a joking reference to the cultural difference, "You know, seat number one through ten."

Both men thought the evacuation went very smoothly, by American standards, although it was not as efficient as it would have been in Japan. "In Japan, it could be even more orderly. Japanese people are more obedient."

After five years in New York, both men wryly acknowledge they have taken on certain American ways. "We are practicing 'Ladies first,'" said Takigawa, with a smile. And during the rescue, Takigawa found himself caught up in the American habit of hugging strangers.

"I got so excited on the ferry, I hugged the other passengers and shook hands with many of them. I usually never do that kind of thing. Actually, I got kind of high. After I reached the pier, there was Mayor Bloomberg and Governor Paterson, and I had a chance to talk to them, so that made me even more excited."

Indeed, the *Thomas Jefferson* pulled in to what would become a New York moment, if ever there was one. The passengers were besieged by a throng of waiting police officers, firefighters, medics, FBI agents, and other first responders at the terminal. But if one group was more shocked than the other about what they saw, it was the group on shore.

John Peruggia, chief of Emergency Medical Service, was so amazed to see the first survivors walk into the terminal in business suits, he asked several of them if they had really been on the plane.

"Because you would not know they were just in a plane crash in the Hudson River," he told the *New York Times*. "They said, 'Yeah, we were on it.' One guy said, 'I stepped out of the plane, onto the wing, and then onto a boat that brought me to this building and then two of your paramedics took great care of me.'"

The scene replayed in St. Luke's Roosevelt Hospital emergency room when Diane Higgins and Lucille Palmer arrived to get checked out. "They were so prepared for mass trauma, when we walked in, they were dumbfounded," Higgins said. Palmer, who bruises easily as a result of the blood-thinner she takes daily, had nary a mark on her, save one bruise from the rope. Higgins's reading glasses were still on top of her head, right where she'd put them before takeoff. "One of the nurses came in and said, 'Were you the ones in the plane crash? Your hair is perfect, your nails are done. Who knew?'"

13

Saving Shae

SHAE CHILDERS HAD SURVIVED ONE OTHER NEAR-DEATH EXPERIENCE before Flight 1549. Fourteen years earlier, while she was working as a management trainee at a small finance company in Gaffney, South Carolina, a man in a black cap and sunglasses, holding a pistol in his hand, burst into the office and threw down a hand-scrawled note: *"There's a bomb in the building. You have ten seconds to give me all your money."*

The robber shoved a pillowcase at Childers, waved his gun, and commanded her to empty the cash register. Until January 15, 2009, that had been the scariest moment of her life. What could be worse than staring down the barrel of a robber's gun? She now knew that the prospect of being in a plane crash, surviving, then almost drowning in the Hudson River was worse.

A cheerful mother of two, Shae Childers had managed to skate through the security checkpoint, no questions asked, with two dozen cupcakes in her carry-on for her sons at home. They were fancily frosted minis from Crumbs Bake Shop—a celebrity bakery known as the cupcake baker to the stars—and she had carefully tucked them under the seat. Fifteen minutes earlier, her only concern had been to keep them out of squish-range in the jam-packed overhead bin. Now, here she was in the Hudson, clinging to the wing of the plane that had been carrying them all home for dinner. She had no idea what to do next.

"Keep moving, keep moving," a man's voice instructed from nearby.

Childers looked left, startled to see a man next to her in the water. The voice belonged to a spry sixty-seven-year-old business-man named Donald Jones, of Jacksonville, Florida. He was wearing a shirt and tie and was methodically pumping his legs beneath the surface. "Keep moving, keep moving," he instructed.

Shae Childers describes herself as someone who "won't jump into a cold swimming pool." Her leap off the wing was therefore just a rote response to years of pre-flight safety briefings: Exit the aircraft; move away from the plane. She exited, she moved away, expecting the plane to quickly erupt into flames. "I didn't think of hypother-mia," she said later. "I didn't think of that as life threatening."

Childers hadn't seen Jones until he appeared out of nowhere next to her at the wing. Then again, she hadn't seen any of the others who jumped lemming-like into the river with her. She hadn't seen the slide off the back of the wing, nor had she seen the life raft when it popped out from first class. She didn't even look back at the plane until Amy Jolly, her work companion, called out to her. "I couldn't believe people were standing on the wings. They were full of fuel," Childers said. "By that point, I figured that if it hasn't blown up, then it's not going to. That's when I turned around and swam back." Through chattering teeth, she called up to Jolly: "I'm so cold, I'm so cold."

Donald Jones had swum over from first class. The CEO of a medical society of endocrinologists, he had traveled to a thyroid conference in New York, and was on his way home, comfortably ensconced in an aisle seat in row three when the birds struck. He slid into the left-hand life raft a little too vigorously, bounced into the water, and swam back to the wing to await rescue. He found the wing too cold and slippery to grip, so he tried to swim back to the raft. "I didn't get ten feet in that current. I was deadweight," he said. So he paddled back to the wing and pulled up next to Childers just as the cold began to nibble away at her stamina and confidence that she'd done the right thing by jumping in.

SHAE CHILDERS WAS born in Blacksburg, South Carolina, a one-stoplight town named for a Confederate soldier, ten miles from where she lives now. She married her high school sweetheart and earned a degree in elementary education, though she never taught. Instead, she started at her local department store, Hamrick's, as a Saturdays-only cashier and worked her way up. Now, as a buyer of women's plus sizes, she traveled to New York six times a year. As a Baptist, Childers's life is anchored by her faith. Prayer had helped her hold it together on the descent, and she began to pray now as she held onto the wing. *Lord, in the name of Jesus, save me.*

"Keep moving, keep moving," Jones said.

Jolly leaned down with an update. "The ferries are coming. Hold on. It won't be much longer." But to Jolly, Childers looked to be losing strength.

By the time Michael Leonard, one of the Belk Six, arrived at mid-wing, Jolly had begun to cry, and Childers's prayers had become a wail. *Lord, in the name of Jesus, save me!* When Leonard heard her cry out that she was going to die, it startled him and he moved quickly to help. With a great tug he managed to pull her onto the wing, but he wasn't certain how to calm her.

Leonard, who lives in Charlotte, is a transplanted Californian, more comfortable in New York than the Bible Belt. "I honestly didn't know what to say to Shae. I know she needs to calm down. If she doesn't calm down, she will die. You can't panic in a situation like this. You have to think rationally."

Leonard helped Childers to stand on her wobbling legs, already stiffened by the intense cold. Her hands were a throbbing shade of scarlet and utterly numb. He blew on them, in a useless effort to warm them. There wasn't much else he could do, although this, at least, seemed to calm her.

Meanwhile, the ferry *Moira Smith* approached. Named for a policewoman killed in the September 11 attacks, the ferry was the second New York Waterway boat to arrive at the scene, and the first to the left side of the plane. Everyone on the left had eagerly watched over the top of the fuselage as the first ferry picked up fifty-six passengers from the right wing and the first-class raft, then steamed off to the safety of the Manhattan shore.

Things did not go so smoothly on the left, however. Over the next eleven minutes, the *Moira Smith* fought against the current and managed to pull only fourteen people off the wing to safety. The ebbing tide constantly dragged the vessel toward the plane, and it throttled backward and forward as it struggled to hold position long enough for the passengers to climb up the netlike Jason's Cradle. At one point the ferry pulled in behind the wing, but was able to hold only long enough for one or two passengers to scamper up. It then maneuvered around to the front side, nosing in so close that the bow rode over the edge of the wing. "I was afraid he was going to knock us all in the water," said Jorge Morgado, one of the golfers who stood at mid-wing.

The passengers were so grateful to see the ferries arrive that months later they broke into tears as they described the rescue. Ultimately, a remarkable bit of maneuvering was on display that day—by boats not built for such tasks. Still, the view from the water's surface to the deck towering above seemed an insurmountable climb to some. To Jim Clark, it looked to be thirty feet. And the engine noise and the closeness of the props terrified many.

"The ferry was coming toward us, and the ferry can't really stop, and so we're watching this giant blue wall come closer and closer," said Eileen Shleffar. "We're yelling, 'Stop! Turn it! Turn it!' We thought we'd be crushed as this great, giant thing approached. It was making the wing bob more, and again, I slipped facedown on the wing. I'm sliding back into the water; my feet and knees were in, almost to my waist in fact. Someone—I don't know who—pulled me back up."

Out at the end of the plank, Clay Presley felt the ferry clip the wing tip. "It was amazing watching those guys maneuver the boats and try not to run over anybody. They'd hit the wing and it would go down a little bit. It was very scary. I said, 'Oh man, they're going to break this thing off. Someone is going to get killed by one of these boats around here.'"

The *Moira Smith* changed positions so often that many of the passengers thought several ferries had come and gone. At one point, its stern drifted sideways and collided with the first-class raft, causing temporary panic on it. Michael Nunn was convinced they would be crushed between the ferry and the fuselage, which was a widely held view among the group huddled there.

Steve O'Brien pushed against the ferry to hold it back.

"There was a big blue wall right on top of us," he said. "The out-flow valves caught the gray rubber on the raft, and I thought it was melting it. The spinning propellers were out of the water. I couldn't believe it. You survived the crash and get killed in the rescue?"

The scene grew more chaotic as other rescue vessels arrived on both sides of the plane. "It was like a mall parking lot the day after Thanksgiving," said Michael Starr, a ferry captain who arrived in the *Yogi Berra*.

Two ferries joined the *Moira Smith* on the left side of the plane. Then the twenty-seven-foot fireboat *Marine One* motored up. The fireboat was more agile than the ferries and eventually slipped in and parked next to the fuselage in front of the wing, rescuing the wing walkers who had been unable to get onto the ferry.

At one point, as Donald Jones and Childers tried to climb the ladder, the ferry pinned Jones's leg to the wing. "We started up the ladder at the same time," he said. "It was pretty difficult. The ferry kept bouncing up against the wing. My foot got caught between the ladder and the wing, and they had to back away so I could get my foot out. I was having great difficulty. I had no feeling in my hands. It was like having a nightmare and you're running from something and you can't move."

As the ferry backed up, Childers lost her grip and fell back into the river. She is not a small woman. At five foot seven and 195 pounds, pulling her out in wet clothes proved difficult.

Joe Hart wanted to keep her from slipping back in again. "Finally after two or three times of pulling her out of the water, she is on her butt on the wing. She is soaked. She is very cold, very scared. I tell her she has to take her frigging shoes off," he said. "She looked up at me with puppy dog eyes. She said, 'I can't. I can't. I don't have any energy.' She has ankle boots on. I unzip the boots, and—I am openly angry, because she keeps falling in the water—I release that anger by taking her boots and heaving them as hard as I could into the river, like it was their fault that we had this problem."

The ferry, meanwhile, moved around again to the rear of the wing. Michael Leonard positioned himself to help Childers up the ladder.

"Because of the currents, the ferry ends up lunging at us," Leonard said. "I have two choices. I can either get knocked into the water, or I can grab on for my life. I was not going to get off that wing until Shae got rescued. But I wasn't going to go in that water. I jumped and grabbed the ladder."

Leonard tried to leap back onto the wing once he caught his balance. But the deckhands grabbed him and slung him onto the deck. Childers stayed on the wing.

About that time, the NYPD helicopter carrying the divers appeared overhead. Michael Delaney, the lead diver, looked down, perplexed, at boats going every which way. "The scene is huge. And it's moving, moving at four knots, which is pretty swift. I'm thinking, *Where do we start?*"

The *whump-whump-whump* of the chopper's blades drowned out all conversation. Delaney and his partner, Rob Rodriguez, used hand signals to formulate a plan. The chopper looped around again, and Delaney opened the side door.

"I'm thinking, *There is so much boat traffic in the area,* there was no way we can get in the water without getting run over. The size of the boats—*they'll never be able to see us. We're two little specks in the water.*"

Meanwhile, the *Moira Smith* attempted another run at the front of the wing. Childers grabbed onto the ladder, but all of her strength had vanished in the cold water and she could not climb. No one could push her up from below, either. Joe Hart clamored up the ladder to the deck, determined to pull her up from above. "I reach down, and they're trying to push her up and I'm trying to pull her. With that the boat drifts away from the airplane. Now it's just me and Shae, and I'm losing her and she has no strength. We've got this eye contact just like in the movies, like, *Hold on*. And with that, she slips through my hands."

As Childers remembers it, this was the most frightening moment. "When I lost the ability to move my arms and legs, when I couldn't pull myself up in front of that ferry, that's when I became afraid for my life."

Others watched helplessly from the wing as the ferry backed away with Childers dangling from the ladder. Then, when another ferry passed between the *Moira Smith* and the wing, she disappeared from view. Amazingly, many of her wing mates did not see her again until their reunion for the *Sixty Minutes* taping in February.

"My final haunting image of her was when she was holding onto the ladder and the boat turned away out of my line of vision," said Casey Jones. "It eerily reminded me of the closing scene in Moby Dick where Captain Ahab was trapped in his own net as the boat turned away."

The helicopter now hovered almost directly overhead, its blades churning up an icy rotor wash on the passengers below. They waved it off. "The backdraft sucked all the heat out of our bodies," Gerry McNamara said.

"If you were soaking wet, that extra fifty-miles-per-hour wind just froze you to death," said Bill Nix, who was indeed soaking wet after escaping the deep water in the back of the plane.

From the open door in the chopper, Delaney caught a tiny flash of red sweater in the traffic jam of boats. "By chance," he said. "Out of the corner of my eye, I see one of the passengers holding onto the ferry."

He signaled the pilot, and pointed. He ripped off his weight belt and air tank to increase his speed and agility in the water. "That's where we need to go. Put me there. That's the person we have to get to. I remember yelling it as loud as I possibly can."

The helicopter couldn't go much lower. "We would have blown the people off the boats and off the wings," Delaney said. He stood out on the skid and jumped in from twenty feet up, high for a rescue jump.

Meanwhile, Childers had grabbed on to the ladder for her life as the ferry backed away. Unable to control her arms or legs at this point, she was frantic. "When I tried to climb up the front, I couldn't," she said. "When the ferry backed away, it pulled me back into the water. I was hanging on to the front of the ladder. The thought going through my mind was, *God, I've lived through this plane crash, but now I'm going to fall under this boat and be killed by this ferry.*

"My right arm slipped off and I'm hanging by my left," Childers said. "There was a helicopter to my right, and every time I looked that way, I would get a face full of the breeze with water off the helicopter. I almost gave up. I thought I'm just not going to make it. I can't hold on any longer."

At that moment, Delaney, himself now in the roiling waters, tapped her on the shoulder. *Lord, in the name of Jesus, thank you.*

The boats had churned up a pretty respectable chop in the water, and the engines and helicopter sounded, as someone described later, like a "wall of noise." The cop in Delaney spoke in a deliberate, easy-going manner, as if he'd approached Childers on the street. "How are you? . . . What's your name? My name is Michael. . . . We're going to get you out of the water." Shae Childers was able to tell Delaney her name at least.

A deckhand lowered a life vest. Delaney showed Childers where to put her arms so the crew could hoist her up. But in Childers's eye, the vest somehow morphed into the most confusing contraption she had ever seen. The arm holes looked too tiny for human arms. She held on to the ladder tighter.

Delaney gave up on the vest, and any thought of getting her onto the *Moira Smith*. "For me to help, you have to let go. You have to trust me," he coached. "The boat is not going to run over us. You have to let go."

Finally, Childers relaxed her hold. She lunged for Delaney and bear-hugged his torso. Off to the side, away from the cluster of boats, another ferry, *George Washington,* idled. Delaney signaled the captain, and then swam over, with Chiders wrapped around him. His dive partner, meanwhile, met them at the *George Washington*'s bow. A deckhand climbed down to the small two-foot platform at the base of the ladder. Delaney coached Childers again, this time his voice stern. "I said, 'Listen, I need your help. You have to help me get you out of the water.'"

The two divers and the deckhand moved Childers onto the platform, six feet below the deck.

Delaney: "She was standing there like she was completely useless, like she could not help herself. I said, 'Listen, you've got to stand up.'"

Childers: "I tried to lift my legs. I couldn't feel them."

Delaney smacked his hand on the platform: "I yelled, 'Shae, you have to get yourself up! Put your foot on here. You have to go one step at a time.'"

Childers remained immobile. "I could not make them move."

Delaney: "She looked down at me and I said one more time, 'Shae, you have to help. One step at a time.'"

Pushed from below, Childers slowly began inching up the ladder, and eventually made it onto the deck. As the ferry sped toward Manhattan, a deckhand pulled his black cap around her ears, stripped off her wet sweater, and wrapped his jacket around her, then cuddled her to keep her warm. Childers was the only passenger on board.

On shore, she was tucked into an ambulance and taken to New York Downtown Hospital, where doctors quickly transferred her from the ER to the ICU. NYPD officer Ray McCann, who sat with her at the terminal, rode with her in the ambulance, her own special escort. McCann helped her call her husband, her office, and find her colleague, Amy Jolly, who had been taken to the Weehawken side.

Childers's New York experience would not involve an evening of celebratory toasts to survival with new friends. She spent the next three days wired to machines. "There wasn't a lot of good sleep," she said.

Her core temperature had dropped to 92 degrees, the lowest of the seventeen passengers to be treated for hypothermia. The hospital put her inside a high-tech warming blanket, and she received breathing treatments because her asthma complicated her recovery. She had severe bruising on her right leg, and numbness in her fingertips and thumbs, which were painful to touch. The prolonged violent shivering had even caused temporary muscle damage. When muscle tissue breaks down so severely, muscle enzymes, or creatine phosphokinase, leak into the bloodstream, creating the potential for kidney damage. Childers's CPK levels shot to 2,400, from a normal range of 150. CAT scans of her lungs and legs raised concerns about possible blood clots, and would delay her release until Sunday.

Meanwhile, back on the Hudson, Delaney and Rodriguez kicked away from the ferry as soon as Childers moved up the ladder out of their reach. Near the plane, Heyam Kawas, the UN Arabic specialist, who earlier had fallen, was now back in the river, flailing limply. She could not swim. Delaney swam to her and pushed Kawas onto the fireboat, then turned his attention to the plane.

Until then, none of the rescuers had gone inside to check for trapped passengers. Delaney and Rodriguez, who wore full scuba gear, moved to the over-wing exits. Delaney signaled his partner.

"Listen, go inside, we're in and out, two minutes. No more." Water levels were rising precipitously. "We got to the aisle and started heading to the back."

And that's when I yelled, "Rob, we got to get out, this plane is going to sink!"

14

"Throw the Baby"

FLIGHT 1549'S YOUNGEST PASSENGER, NINE-MONTH-OLD DAMIAN SOSA, had survived the day, so far, with the good-natured élan of a well-traveled frequent flier. Earlier, he had cooed and burbled in the departure lounge while the ladies admired his baby Ugg boots. Later, during the crash, he had been "quiet as a church mouse," Jim Whitaker said, as he had braced the little boy for impact. Now, grasped in his mother's arms at the exit to the right wing, Damian was about to undertake the most dangerous part of his journey back to dry land.

"Throw the baby!" someone yelled.

Tess Sosa recoiled. "I wasn't going to throw him and risk him falling into the frigid waters. I ignored the shouts. I made it through all of this and you think I'm going to throw my baby now? No. I'm fine holding him."

She did not look fine to those watching. Bedraggled, her eyes wide with fear, she seemed unwilling to commit fully to the move from the door to the wing—let alone detach herself from Damian. Her blouse was torn. Still, the voices on the inflated wing-exit slide continued, insistently, "Throw the baby!" The slide was overflowing. It did not look like there was room even for Damian, let alone his mother, father, and sister.

Douglas Schrift, hanging out of the open door above the life raft at the first-class cabin, tried waving her over. "She's not quite on the wing. I can see the young baby. I'm terrified. If the baby's in the water, the baby's dead. I'm screaming to her to come back into the cabin and up, that we have room on the raft. I'm shouting to her."

Until then, Schrift maintained a forced calm about escaping the plane and waiting for the coming rescue. He defined the experience as merely a sequence of doable tasks: Hold on to your seat cushion. Don't panic. Huddle tight. Let's get it done. But the sight of the Sosas at mid-plane caused Schrift to choke up.

"Tess was looking right at us. I'm thinking, *Can't she hear me? Or is she too terrified to go walk back through?*" He turned to Sheila Dail, the flight attendant, and said, "There's a baby back down there, you've got to go help." Sheila disappeared and returned with half a dozen men, but not the Sosa family, he said. "One guy barreled through the door so fast," Schrift said, "I was afraid he was going to knock people off the raft into the Hudson."

Martin and Tess said later they were in a daze at that point, and heard only the continuing calls for them to throw their baby. "That was absurd," Martin said. "We were not going to throw our baby." Martin doesn't remember how his wife and children moved onto the slippery wing and onto the jam-packed slide. Tess is not sure either. "It's all a bit hazy," she said afterward.

Other memories also are blurred, and many did not even realize

Tess Sosa was standing with her husband. Karin Hill saw only a mother with an infant and her young daughter in distress just inside the exit.

"She was paralyzed," said Hill. "I said, 'Give me your baby. Let me hold him. You have to get out of the plane.'"

From outside: "Throw the baby!"

Alex Magness watched nervously from the slide. "Tess for sure was very upset and very frantic," he said. "We wanted to make sure that her baby was safe. I remember clearly there was this discussion, and a lot of teamwork going on about what we were going to do about this baby."

Dave Sanderson, a salesman for Oracle, remembers less organization, more chaos. "She was trying to get on the slide. I knew if she tried to do that—it was so slick with jet fuel and cold water—she would probably fall and something bad was going to happen. She's either going to lose the baby, or she'd be in the water. That's why we were yelling, 'Throw the baby.'"

About that time, Vallie Collins, after her long walk out of the water in the back of the plane, stepped out onto the wing. The call to throw the baby gave her a start. "I was, like, *Whoa, whoa, whoa, that doesn't sound like a good idea to me.* I see the husband and he had a kind of panic. He is in complete shock. The mother, Tess, was obviously very distraught, but here's her husband, who's kind of frozen. There's a man in the slide. He's in the center, and he made eye contact with me and he said, 'Get those kids.' I step onto the back corner of the slide, the corner away from the fuselage. There's not enough room in the slide anymore. I'm kind of half in, half out. I have one foot on the back and one foot on the wing. I look at Tess and say, 'Give me your baby.'"

Something in how she said it must have made Tess finally give Damian over, and immediately Vallie handed off Damian to a man on

181

the slide. Turning back to Tess, she asked for Sofia. "I took the little girl and I just sat down cross-legged with her in my lap. I looked up and one of the ferry boats was coming. They're throwing life jackets into the water. Real hard, rigid ones. Four inches thick. I'm going to grab one of those. I've got my seat cushion on my right arm. I can swim, but Sofia can't. I felt at any moment we could fall into the water. Her mother climbs on. The father is still out on the wing, still in the water. Tess is panicked. She's screaming at him. The way she's standing, I'm afraid she's going to knock us in. I said, sternly, 'Lady, you have to sit down.' She sat down. At least I didn't feel as vulnerable anymore. I said, 'This little girl has to be scared to death.' I asked her mom, 'What is her name?'

"She did not cry, did not say a word. The only reason I knew she was alive is she kept biting my arm through my sweater. She kept chewing on my arm. Just kind of in a nervous way, kind of nibbled on my arm. Not chomping down."

In Dave Sanderson's view, Vallie Collins saved the moment, and staved off a traffic jam on the wing. "It had to be a woman," he said. "That's the difference between guys and girls. Guys just want to get it done; women nurture. God had to give Tess faith to give up her baby to somebody. And, logistically, Tess had to move. Nobody could move past her on that wing until she moved."

Keith Anthony watched the hand-off from the slide. "I remember her looking at me as I watched her make that decision of giving her baby up," he said. Damian, in a diaper and T-shirt, passed through several pairs of hands. "And then to me," Anthony said. "He had had these Ugg boots on, brown, fuzzy boots, but when I sat down, he didn't have the boots on anymore. I held his feet in the palms of my hand trying to keep them warm. Carl Bazarian was sitting on my lap, and I was sitting on another guy's lap. By the way, I'm six-six, two hundred and thirty."

Damian was handed around the raft until his mother wedged herself in between others who made room. "Someone literally handed me the baby," said Beverly Mills. "He was just priceless. He screws up his face like he's gonna cry, and he looks at me. And I'm going on about 'Isn't this a great day, what a wonderful adventure this is.' And he looks over the water, and looks like he's going to cry. He comes back to look at me, and I'm telling him what a wonderful day it is and what a good time we're having. He starts playing with my earring. Now he's totally absorbed with this earring. Isn't that typical? We're stable, we're safe. The rescue hasn't started yet. There's no danger and no stress. He's totally in the moment.

"I turned to the other people on the raft and said, 'Guys, I don't know how the rest of you are doing, but the baby is playing with my earring.' A few people reacted, because frankly, it was just silent everywhere. Everyone was so absorbed in what they needed to do, no one was really talking to anyone else. I think maybe for a couple people it broke the tension a bit. We spend a lot of time worrying about the future and regretting the past. We don't spend much time in the moment, and he was in the moment. It was pretty cool."

With Tess and the children on board, the space in the raft closed up tight and Martin was left to stand on the wing. He edged farther out, stopping finally when he stood waist-deep. He stayed there, hands turning blue-black from the cold, until rescuers arrived on the eighty-six-foot *Yogi Berra.*

THE ACCIDENT SCENE became more chaotic as more vessels surrounded the plane. A privately owned converted coast guard buoy tender pulled in front of the wing, and its skipper, Scott Koen, jumped off and started helping people onto the ferries.

Michael Starr, one of the ferry captains on the *Yogi Berra,* said the toughest task of the rescue involved negotiating the traffic jam around the plane. "The boats are highly maneuverable. They're easy to drive. They're jet boats. They'll turn on a dime," he said. "The most difficult part was having all the equipment out there with you. Who's behind you, who's to the left? Who's to the right? It got a little crowded."

Meanwhile, Vallie Collins did not feel secure holding Sofia on her lap while balancing on a sliver of space on an overcrowded slide.

"I was very scared about falling in the river," Collins said. "The ferry boats were creating a lot of chop. The helicopters were coming. The slide was bouncing around. I was afraid we were going to float out into the river and she and I would fall off. It felt safer to have the slide up against the plane. Worst case, if we did fall off, somebody on the wing could grab her and pull her back up. If we had floated out and she and I fell off, then it was going to be totally up to me. I also knew I couldn't handle watching this girl drown."

For this reason, Dave Sanderson, a big lug of a man, spent the next fifteen minutes half submerged in the water, gripping the plane with one arm, and the slide with the other, a human mooring line, keeping the slide flat against the fuselage. By the time the *Yogi Berra* motored up to the wing, Sanderson was as frozen as a cod. He lunged for the boat, six, seven, eight strokes away, and gave out at the bottom of the ladder. "I can't climb. I got one foot into a little stirrup. Two people grabbed my arms. This is seven, eight feet up they pulled me."

Once on the deck, he was unable to move. "I don't want to die this way," he said. "A gentleman came up. He was dry. He said, 'You need to call home.'"

The Jason's Cradle, unfurled off the ferry decks to aid in the rescue, confounded almost all the passengers who climbed it. It consists of a plastic grid, or "scramble net" of squares, and is considered the industry leader in man-overboard equipment. A weakened or injured person can lie in it and be rolled up inside it onto the deck. Most of the passengers on Flight 1549 simply climbed it. "Like Spiderman," said Kristy Spears. Martin Sosa, who could no longer feel his legs as he climbed up, called his effort, "the most harrowing thing." Almost everyone had trouble with it, and Laurie Crane, the petite, fifty-eight-year-old Belk buyer, had more trouble than most.

By then, Crane could barely move. She stood on the wing in water up to her bra cup. She still had her mink coat, a small document bag, and her purse. Now she tried to climb with them. "The ferry people said, 'Okay, lady, it's your turn.' My legs are not feeling too good, so I'm sort of floating over to the ferry. Somebody yelled from the raft, 'Lady, let go of your things, they're dragging, holding you down.'

"Everybody was staring down to see what I was doing," she said. "The mink coat? I just flung it. I think I even chuckled at that point."

Chris Rooney, the Colorado engineer, asked for her purse. "He was perturbed that I was holding up the process," Crane said.

Rooney had pulled Crane back up onto the wing when she slipped off once. "She was not going to be able to climb up the net with stuff in her arms," he said. "Grown men were struggling to climb up this. Everyone was freezing and it was not an easy climb. I saw this woman with her purses and she was kind of sideways tangled up in the net. I grabbed them from her, but they were really heavy because there was so much water in them. I had to let them go."

Someone on the raft cheered.

Sheri Nejman watched apprehensively as Sosa, Sanderson, and now Crane struggled to climb the ladder. "You can tell that after a few minutes, they are getting somewhat delirious," she said. "They're getting panicked. They can't move. They want to, but their bodies just can't move. Martin got a little panicked. Laurie was holding on to her laptop and her purse for dear life. She couldn't climb. It wasn't that she wasn't trying. Hypothermia was setting in."

CRANE LOOKED DOWN at the murky waters and thought she would drown. She described her climb as a "comedy of errors."

"I had a bulky gray sweater and there was a huge metal hook on this rope thing and in trying to stand up, the sweater got hooked. I'm trying to get loose. The raft people said, 'You can do it.' And finally, I took the sweater off. I always wear black underwear, and I was trying to get this thing over my head without the use of my hands. The raft people were rooting for me. I turned and climbed up the rungs and realized I didn't have the strength. I looked up to the guy and said, 'I can't feel my fingers. I can't grip.' I could see his face. He said, 'Don't worry, lady, I'll hoist you up.' That is my favorite word in the world now. *Hoist*."

Once Laurie Crane was safe, the crew then moved to get Tess and Damian aboard. A deckhand called down for the baby to be passed to the ferry. Chris Cobb looked over at Tess from the wing, dubious.

"The only way we can pass the baby to him is to pass the baby down a line of passengers on a submerged wing," he said. "It didn't feel like it was a good idea. I looked at the mom. I'll do whatever she wants, but I'm hoping that she doesn't want us to pass this baby down the line. She said, "No, I'm keeping the baby with me on the raft.'"

As tension rose, Josh Peltz solved the problem by scrambling up onto the ferry's deck, and leaning over the edge over the water.

"Someone is holding my legs and my torso. I was stretched out with both arms. They get her close enough to me. She's clutching her baby so tightly. I said, 'You have to give me your baby. I'm a dad and

I know how to hold your baby. I'm not going to drop your baby.' It clicked with her. I took the baby with one hand, and held the shoulder and grabbed the pants and made sure I had a good grip and I said, 'Okay, I've got the baby.' And she let go. To see that baby in my hands and to know for a nanosecond I'm the only thing between that baby and the water, it was an unbelievable emotion."

Tess and Sofia climbed the net to safety and the embrace of Martin, who quickly gathered his family together in the warm cabin. So ended the Sosa saga. As the *Yogi Berra* pulled away and headed to Weehawken, Damian nestled in his mother's arms and suckled at her breast, among a crowd of wet and shell-shocked plane-crash survivors.

"You're so pumped with adrenaline, that's the one force that got someone through this thing," Martin Sosa said. "I've never been so pumped up. It gives you superhuman powers. I was thinking of survival. I was thinking of my family. I was thinking that I didn't die of a heart attack. So many things that could have happened didn't. When I finally made it over the side, that's the first moment I felt okay."

The ferry inadvertently left behind a handful of stranded passengers when a deckhand holding the ladder in one hand and the slide in the other lost his grip and the slide and the ferry drifted apart. "I'm the last one in the raft," said Freida Muscatell, "But I wasn't really worried, because by then, rescuers were everywhere." A pair of coast guard rescue boats hovered off to the side, in sight, and one of them quickly nosed in as the ferry pulled away. Muscatell crawled on board to safety.

The other coast guard boat raced around to the left side, where the last seven passengers of Flight 1549 waited on the slide in the waning light. The current had picked up in the ebbing tide and the whole accident scene was now moving more swiftly down the river.

"It became much more quiet once the passengers were rescued from the wing and the front rafts, and the ferries and the helicopters distanced themselves," said Laura Zych, one of the Belk Six. "I did not feel alone with the other passengers, but it felt like loneliness was lurking around us in the form of cold air and the darkening sky as we waited."

There wasn't a lot of talking. Emma Cowan, the Aussie singer, had calmed down and stopped screaming about her passport. Adelaide Horton, one of the first to escape, and now one of the last to be picked up, remembers someone saying it felt like they were in a movie. Everyone agreed.

"The *Zodiac* pulls up," Horton said. "They were so excited, and they said, 'Just a minute, we have to stow the machine gun.' He was stowing the gun on the front and we got into the *Zodiac*. One of the coast guard guys said, 'This is my first rescue.' I said, 'Well, you got a good one.'"

Zych doesn't remember the faces of her rescuers. "But in my mind, each one closely resembled Superman," Zych said. Their rescue had one hitch, when the boat's motor sputtered and died—*one of those go-figure moments,* Zych thought, considering how the whole episode began. Within seconds, the other coast guard boat returned, and the transfer was made. Then coast guardsman Ian Kennedy hit the throttle, and the little orange boat roared away to the New York shore.

Exactly twenty-four minutes had passed since Flight 1549 had hit the Hudson River.

15

Night in New York

EVEN BEFORE HE GOT TO SHORE, JORGE MORGADO HAD BECOME A VERY hot media commodity. The carpet-store manager had phoned his wife from the left wing to tell her about the crash and that he was okay. Within five minutes of his call, the phone at Morgado's house in Chicopee, Massachusetts, began ringing nonstop.

"My wife got calls from network after network, show after show. The best," Morgado said. One caller said, 'We know Jorge has been in a plane crash. We know he's asthmatic. We can go find him and help him. We'll protect him.' That was their approach."

Across town, Rob Kolodjay's wife, Jane, fielded a similar on-slaught of media calls. "They knew everything about Robbie," Jane said. "They knew all about his medical history. They knew Robbie was diabetic and needed insulin. They said they could go get it. This was crazy. All this stuff is supposed to be private. They always talk about the power of the media, but until you go through something like this, you really don't know how crazy it can be."

The networks began calling Morgado directly on his cell phone around the time he stepped ashore at Chelsea Pier with his brother-in-law, Jim Stefanik. Up until then, the two men were still absorbing what had just happened to them, had no idea of the media blitzkrieg they were about to walk into, or that the 155 people on board Flight 1549 had become a New York—not to mention world—sensation.

A triage center had been set up on a nearby dinner boat, and on their way inside, the two men picked up the first hint of their new status when an FBI agent collared them three steps off the fireboat that delivered them to the pier. "He was right there pushing us along. 'How did the plane go down? Was it taken over? Was it this, was it that?' I said, 'No, it wasn't any of that. We heard it was birds.'"

Inside the dinner boat, enough firefighters gathered to man a three-alarm blaze, and they wrapped survivors in linen table cloths. Morgado, Stefanik, and the other survivors were then ushered to a police van, which delivered them to a shuttle bus to the Crowne Plaza Hotel at LaGuardia, where US Airways had reserved a block of rooms. The cops wanted a smooth, quick transfer from van to bus. "They literally said, 'We don't want these people's feet to touch the ground,'" Morgado said. "They didn't want us to be exposed to the media. They knew what was about to happen."

On the drive to the Crowne Plaza, Morgado gazed out at still more media and helicopters flying by overhead. "There were police cruisers all around our bus, blocking the roads so we wouldn't even have to stop at a red light. We were king of the hill."

Meanwhile, NBC had retrieved the inconsolable Rob Kolodjay

from the Weehawken ferry terminal and ensconced him at the Westin, where they reunited him with his son, Jeff. The Kolodjays were working out the details of their *Today Show* appearance when Morgado tracked them down via cell phone. Soon NBC dispatched a car to the Crowne Plaza to fetch Morgado and Stefanik, expanding the NBC exclusive on the golfers. The producers offered to send limos to Chicopee to pick up their wives. "They paid for everything," Morgado said. " 'Guys, whatever you need. It's on us.' "

The golfers were to meet their producer in the hotel lobby at 4:30 a.m. He gave an unusual instruction. Don't leave the lobby. "There will be vans and other vehicles waiting outside," he told Morgado.

" 'They will say they're with us, but they will actually be from a competing network.' I said, 'So you're telling me they're going to kidnap me?' He said, 'No, they are not going to kidnap you, but they'll kidnap your story.' It made me think, *Are these guys serious? We're just average Joes.*"

So began the instant celebrityhood of Flight 1549. The bizarreness of the golfers' New York experience played out a dozen different ways that night and for weeks afterward. The new celebrity status—fifteen minutes of fame for everyone, Andy Warhol had said in a cynical moment forty-one years earlier. But even *he* couldn't see the 24-7 television and celebrity society of today that hit the passengers faster than Red Sox fans hit the streets after the end of the eighty-six-year-old Yankee curse in 2004. Nor could he have foreseen the circumstances—a feel-good, round-the-clock story arriving at the height of the world's big downer that kept delivering a daily pounding of bad news about everything from people's jobs to their homes and their futures. New York had taken the brunt of the beating for months. Political embarrassments, spectacular bankruptcies, and financial scandals such as the one involving the breathtaking audacity of scam artist Bernie Madoff had soured almost everyone. A planeload of made-to-order heroes could not have arrived at a better moment.

It was one of the few times that reality made better TV than Reality TV. The images from the river were mesmerizing, hypnotic, and more riveting than anything that *Survivor* or *Fear Factor* could dish up. These were real people—your next-door neighbor. The hoopla that followed could only happen in New York—a city with a history of floods of ticker tape and a reputation as the classic creator of heroes. A city that bows to nobody and has seen it all, swooned. Captain Sullenberger walked into the ferry terminal a made-for-TV hero and was lionized to mythological heights by sundown. (A couple of hours later, a Captain Sully cocktail had been introduced in every bar in town: two shots of Grey Goose vodka and a splash of water.)

The main action played out at the ferry terminal in Manhattan, which Charles Spiggle said was lit up "like it was having a rock concert." Mayor Michael Bloomberg arrived with an entourage of twenty, who passed around their cell phones so the phoneless could call home. Gov. David Paterson did his bit to enhance the story line, too—standing before a bouquet of microphones, he uttered the phrase that gave the accident its name: "Miracle on the Hudson."

Craig Black, wrapped in a Red Cross blanket, watched from the sidelines. "The whole New York experience was underway," he said. "The media, the pols-kissing-babies kind of thing. People were asking us, 'Can you be on camera with the governor?'"

"I must have had a dozen people take my name," said Jim Hanks, the Baltimore attorney. "The mayor shows up. He asked me where I was from. Baltimore rings his bell. He graduated from Johns Hopkins. We talked."

On both sides of the river, it seemed as if every survivor had his or her own personal cop. By her count, Sheri Nejman, who ended up in Weehawken, figured she gave interviews to seven or eight police officers. "They were all very nice," she said. "I asked, 'How many are there of you guys?' They laughed. 'For this type of incident? In this city? You have no idea how many agencies are involved.'"

On the Manhattan side, the first survivors through the ferry terminal door wandered around trying to keep warm. A coffee stand opened up and served hot drinks. They hugged, they stood on a heat grate, and exchanged high fives.

"The next thing I know, there's a lot of FBI, a lot of police," Laurel Hubbard said. "They're telling us to get in one place and sit down and don't move. They had a hard time getting our attention. They wrapped crime scene tape around the group and confined us to one area. At one point, the head guy at my company called and wanted to come and get me. His driver couldn't get within two miles of the terminal."

The survivors were given color-coded tags to wear around their necks, depicting their condition. Most found the tags creepy and unnecessary, given the outcome.

"The tag had perforated sections that could be torn off," said Josh Peltz. "White was for uninjured. Green was minor injuries. Then other sections for more severe injuries. The black one was deceased. I remember looking at that and saying *'wow.'*"

In the Manhattan terminal, Mark Hood dropped to one knee and said a quick prayer. Overcome, he could barely speak. "I could not believe this had just happened. Which led to another round of thoughts? Why did it happen? Why were all of us spared?"

As he stood on a heat grate drying his feet, Billy Campbell, who had gone to high school with Hood's wife, recognized him and walked over to shake hands. Comparing notes, they learned that not only were they on the same flight, they had also shared the same life raft, although neither man knew it at the time.

"What are the odds of running into a guy who you haven't seen in twenty years on a plane crash?" Hood asked.

Warren Holland endured the wait in the terminal with uncharacteristic aplomb. "Usually I get very upset and angry about politicians and thrill seekers," he said. Not that day. "I stood at the ferry terminal in wet clothes for three or four hours without losing my temper. I had a different perspective on life. I was just happy to be there."

But Jim Hanks grew impatient to get to LaGuardia. By then, he wore a blue sweat suit and was carrying his worldly possessions wrapped up in a big ball inside a Red Cross blanket. Hanks declined the offer of a bus ride to the Crowne Plaza at the airport, and headed toward the door to hail a cab. A policewoman stopped him. "Once you go outside the yellow tape, sir, you're on your own. You might want to think about how you'll look to somebody that you might want help from." Hanks looked at himself and thought, *She's right. I look like a homeless person.*

The officer assured him it would be a fifteen-minute ride. "It's rush hour," Hanks objected, thinking it would be more like two hours. "She said, 'Trust me, it's going to happen.'" It did.

Craig Black had his own homeless-person moment at the Waldorf Astoria Hotel, where his boss had booked him a room. He showed up during dinnertime in blue sweats and white tube socks, carrying a crumpled, wet T-shirt, a jarring sight in a lobby full of well-heeled guests on their way out. The clerk at the front desk eyeballed him disdainfully when Black asked to be directed to the tower and its pricier rooms. But the entry to the tower lobby was locked, and Black returned to the desk clerk. "I could really use your help," he said. "I was in that plane in the Hudson." With that, he reported, "The guy practically jumped over the desk to assist me."

Twenty minutes later, Black was taking a hot shower in a suite stocked with wine, cheese, and chocolates, and a new phone.

The generosity of strangers amazed Denise Lockie. An anonymous donor who saw her on TV sprang for a new set of clothes for her at Ann Taylor, so she'd have something to wear home.

If New York rolled out the red carpet the way only New York can, then Clay Presley took the weirdest walk on it. Presley bulled his way through a herd of television cameramen in the driveway of the Crowne Plaza Hotel at LaGuardia. "You would have thought I was Britney Spears," said the bald, mustached father of four.

"How was it?" the reporters shouted.

"Harrowing," Presley told them.

"How do you feel?"

"Exhausted."

Inside, Presley stopped for a quick drink in the bar and talked briefly to several policemen. One of those "If you're ever in New York and need a cop, give us a call" conversations. When he got to his room, he found his phone's message light blinking. A woman who had just watched his hotel driveway interview on the news was offering to come over and sit with him to keep him company. "You're here without your family. I feel so sorry for you," she purred into the message tape.

Not everyone was caught up in the euphoria that night. Frank Scudere, a native New Yorker and litigation attorney for Skadden Arps, worked in the New York office and commuted to Charlotte. He had spent the night before Flight 1549 at his dying father's hospital bed. Three hours after the accident, Scudere caught the train back to his mother's house on Long Island. He didn't tell anyone what had happened to him, and the next morning, when he went into the office, he discovered that he was about to be laid off as part of a large downsizing by the firm. The unlucky ones got the bad news over the phone.

"They started calling people alphabetically," Scudere said. "In this particular instance, you didn't want to have a message on your voice mail." He did have one, from one of the firm's partners, whom he didn't know. "It was a stranger calling me, with a friendly voice, who was not a friend."

Scudere returned the call. "I said, 'If this is about layoffs that are happening, I want to let you know that I was on the plane that went down in the Hudson yesterday,'" Scudere said. "He stumbled with his words and said he'd get back to me. That's when I knew that was the call for me to be laid off." Scudere did not lose his job that day. The firm kept him on until March 26, when they laid off another round of attorneys.

The scene in Weehawken was every bit as surreal as the one across the river. Steve O'Brien felt like he'd been invited to a party where he didn't know anybody. Josh Peltz wanted to "kiss the ground" when he walked inside. He didn't; instead, he feigned calm and tried to nonchalantly buy a cup of coffee. "You're in a state of shock, but you're acting like it's an everyday occurrence. I went up to the coffee stand and asked how much do I owe you? The guy laughs and says, 'It's on me, buddy.' I say, 'Thank you so much.' He looked at me like I was crazy."

The wettest survivors were ordered out of their clothes and handed chef's pants—three sizes too large—from Arthur's Landing, a restaurant next to the ferry terminal. "Mom always said wear clean underwear," said Pam Seagle with a silent thank-you to her mother.

Dave Sanderson, who was one of the wettest and coldest, watched in horror as the color-coded tag was looped around his neck and a blood pressure cuff clamped around his arm. "I'm thinking *M*A*S*H*. They tagged me. I thought, *I am dead,*" Sanderson said. "I'm looking around. What's going on? A lady next to me is naked. She's just crying. The nurse comes back. She says, 'Your blood pressure is 190 over 120. You're gonna die of a heart attack or a stroke. We've got to get you out of here.'"

Walking off the dock in Weehawken, Adelaide Horton overheard a firefighter talking into his radio. "He said, 'The survivors are coming in,' and I remember thinking that was a strange word, *survivor,*" she said. "It put it in a context I didn't have until that moment."

OFFICIALLY, THE SURVIVOR list of passengers included ninety-five men, fifty-two women, three children, and five crew members. Fifty-two were treated for injuries, most of them minor cuts, scrapes, bruises, and sprains. Horton tore tendons in her shoulder, and Shleffar fractured her arm and tore the rotator cuff. Barry Leonard's cracked sternum was X-rayed to see if it had nicked his heart. It hadn't. Seventeen cases of hypothermia were treated, none as serious as Shea Childers's.

"I have never had that experience of someone looking at you like you were supposed to be dead," said Bill Wiley. "I think they must have called out every cop and fireman in the area. As we were walking up to the hotel, the firemen and the police were on either side of us and they were looking at us almost mesmerized. They couldn't believe that we were alive."

Later, standing in a hospital hallway, Nejman overheard police officers and firefighters marveling at the good condition of the survivors. "They were so fascinated that we lived. For what they do—deal with crashes—I think they were somewhat startled. I could hear them saying over and over, 'They're in really good shape and everyone seems so happy.' I thought, *Well, who wouldn't be?* I'm extremely happy."

Meanwhile, behind the scenes, for the lucky passengers attached to corporate America, human resources aides popped up all over town doing what HR types are supposed to do, but rarely get the chance. The big employer on the flight, Bank of America, booked up the Marriott Marquis in Times Square and started buying clothes and shoes and cell phones.

When Nejman got to the hotel, she ran into a therapist the bank had provided. "The minute I came up the escalator, there's this ther-apist who fits the description—wild glasses and wild hair. She intro-duces herself and takes me aside and says, 'Do you want to talk?' About ten minutes into it, I am thinking, *Who is this person? Is this some covert press operation?* I said, 'If you don't mind, I just really want to go to my room.'"

Susan Wittmann, after being hospitalized briefly, reconnected with her work pals, Scott Sharkey and Jerry Shanko, in Shanko's room at the Marriott. Sharkey by then had become one of the faces of Flight 1549 on the cable shows. "You're gonna laugh your ass off," Shanko told her. "Scott is all over CNN. He is everywhere. You can't watch five minutes. That's what happens with the cute guys."

The three ordered room service and a bottle of wine and watched themselves on TV for the rest of the night. "Scott and I drank the bottle without any problem," she said. "Jerry would lay on the bed. 'I was in a plane crash and I lived.' He would just scream. We would say, 'Yes, we know. We were there, Jerry, we were there, shut up about it.'"

Tripp Harris also ended up at the Marriott and had another one of those "Am I in Heaven?" moments. Earlier that day, at a meeting at Accenture, where he works, he'd bumped into his best friend from high school, who works in the firm's Chicago office. They hadn't seen each other in ten years.

Later, after the accident, the friend left him an urgent message on his cell. When Harris returned the call, his friend sounded relieved. "Oh good, you weren't on that flight." Harris assured him he was. "It totally shocked him that I was so calm," Harris said.

Two hours later, Harris and his friend were downing beers in the Marriott bar. Upstairs in his room, Harris had a new phone, battery charger, and three bags full of new clothes in his sizes. The room was stocked with wine and cheese and fruit.

"It was surreal. I was with my best friend that I hadn't seen in ten years. My company had taken care of everything. I was thinking, *Did I really make it or not? Maybe I crashed and now this is my dream of what's going on,*" he said. "It just seemed too weird. I thought, *Maybe this is Heaven.*"

Across town, the Belk Six celebrated the night away drinking Captain Sullys at a bar at the Casablanca Hotel. "The whole time, we were, 'Holy crap, this pilot, how did he do that? This pilot rocks,'" Shleffar said.

Jay McDonald, Nick Gamache, and Charles Spiggle got a policeman to drive them to Brooks Brothers where McDonald and Gamache bought new clothes. Spiggle ran an errand for his wife at Saks, where he bought her two favorite lipsticks, then walked to St. Patrick's Cathedral, where, he said, he lit a votive candle and said "a thank-you prayer that I was still alive."

Casey Jones went off to Jos. A. Bank for some new clothes, had dinner, and watched the coverage until 3:00 a.m. in his hotel room. Asleep eventually, he dreamed that he'd slipped on ice, a dream he's had a dozen times since.

The experience seemed surreal enough, but the speed with which it had happened only made it stranger. Many found it so mind-boggling, they couldn't think clearly for hours. Joe Hall, a BoA manager, had dinner that evening with two colleagues who'd also been on the flight. "Math has always been easy for me," he said. "I couldn't add the tip on. Twenty percent of $20 is four dollars. I just know that. I couldn't get it to come out right. I couldn't focus."

Many wanted nothing more than to sleep in their own beds. Stephen Lis's assistant sent a car service to drive him home to Philadelphia. In the backseat he found some chocolate, a bottle of Glenlivet, and ice. "I drank half of the whiskey before I got home," he said. "The driver was terrific. He said, 'If you want to talk about it . . . ' The more I talked, the better I felt."

The LendingTree group, plus Molly Schugel and Jennifer Doyle, headed for Teterboro and a flight home on a private plane. "Five of us got into a police van," said Darren Beck. "We started driving and hit traffic. We said, 'Can you turn the siren on?' The officer driving says, 'Yeah, no problem.' We were flying after that—fastest trip out to Teterboro we've ever had. Minus the one stop at a mall Dunkin Donuts. They gave us the police discount."

At the mall, Ben Bostic ran over to a liquor store and bought a bottle of Maker's Mark. "I wanted to celebrate life right there," he said. "I offered everybody a drink and took a couple of swigs, and then I realized I was drinking from this open container in the back of an NYPD van. I know nobody is going to say anything, but I don't want to be that obnoxious guy. I put the cap back on it. The cops laughed."

Joe Hart may have set a minor record in the annals of fear-of-flying literature. He booked his return—a 9:30 flight back to Charlotte that night—from the deck of the *Moira Smith*.

"My ferry is backing away from the aircraft and it is a scene to behold. A helicopter was there, we're surrounded by boats now. I called US Air, the Chairman's Preferred line. I said, 'I don't know if you know this, but my plane went down in the Hudson,' and she interrupts: 'Ohmygod, are you on it?' I said, 'I'm fine. I need to know what's the last available flight out of LaGuardia or Newark?' There was a 6:00 p.m. out of Newark. I looked out at that scene and said, 'There's no way I'm gonna make a six o'clock.'"

Hart was joined by seven others. The bus to LaGuardia whizzed through Manhattan, "like a hot knife through butter," said Paul Jorgensen. By then, some of the magic had begun to wear off. The bus driver got lost, for a start, and there was an argument with a cop who wanted them to go to the Crowne Plaza. Jim Whitaker, who had held Damian Sosa through the crash, finally reached his breaking point when he tried to negotiate some basics with US Airways.

"He started screaming to the person on the phone. 'We were just in an airline crash. Can't you make some provisions?'" said Freida Muscatell.

As Whitaker explains it: "As we say in the South, this was a moment in life where you show your ass. I went nuts."

Inside the terminal, Paul Jorgensen and some of the others stopped at a bar in the concourse for a beer. The TVs were all tuned to ESPN; Jorgensen asked the bartender to change the channel to CNN but he refused. "The bartender told us someone came around from US Air and changed all the TVs to get it off the coverage of the plane crash. They didn't want other passengers panicking," Jorgensen said.

The plane home was a smaller aircraft, with seats in pairs on either side of the aisle. The 1549 group, wearing their Red Cross blankets like shawls, retreated to the rear, almost giddy in their reverie, a sight that, several said, they were sure alarmed the other passengers on board.

"We took off on the same runway. Same flight plan. No luggage. We're wet, disheveled. It was very, very quiet until we passed the point of impact with the birds," said Joe Hart.

"At three thousand feet, it was dead quiet. You know what everyone was thinking," said Larry Snodgrass. "When we got up to ten thousand feet, and that chime went off, somebody yelled, 'It's time for a drink.' It was the most enjoyable flight that I've ever had in my life."

"I said my prayers," said Mark Hood. But he wasn't nervous about getting back on a plane. "When it's your time to die, it's your time to die. It just wasn't our time."

Fame, Faith, and Fear of Flying

The Airbus A320 spent the night secured to a pier at Battery Park wharf, near the confluence of the Hudson and East Rivers and the ghosts of the World Trade Center towers. Mostly underwater, only the plane's left wing and part of the cabin remained above the surface.

For two days the sunken shell became one of New York's favorite tourist attractions as hometowners and visitors lined up for a last look. Several passengers visited the plane, too, one woman tearfully concluding the now-dead plane was female, and "a very sad girl" at that.

On the third day after the crash, the plane, whitened with snow, was hauled by barge to the New Jersey side of the river through new ice floes in the Hudson. From there it was trucked to Jersey City for the beginning of its autopsy by federal accident investigators.

Inside the cabin, investigators found that the floor had buckled at row twenty-two. But all the seats in the cabin remained anchored to the floor. Despite the recollections of several of the passengers, none of the windows had actually broken out, although the casing had broken off several. Among a handful of laptops, coats, and purses left in the cabin, investigators found a pair of men's jeans, size 32 × 32, at row twenty, near where Bill Zuhowski had stripped to his underwear.

FOR WEEKS AFTERWARDS, even the most sure-footed among the survivors felt that life had been completely upended. Some lost the ease of their nightly routines to the curse of insomnia. For three days afterward, Paul Jorgensen burst into tears without warning at least twenty times, and for five full nights did not sleep. Then something clicked. "I said to myself, *Hey, this is a positive thing. This is a happy story. You helped people out of the water. You did everything you would have wanted to. You were tested. You did good.*"

Douglas Schrift found himself daydreaming about the accident almost daily.

Susan Wittmann could not concentrate at work. "I was totally distracted." At meetings, it seemed like her colleagues "were speaking a foreign language. I was listening, but I couldn't understand them. It was very weird."

Several others felt that their identity had been lost in the accident—that the person who stepped onto Flight 1549 was not the same person rescued from the river. Denise Lockie, for one, consulted a therapist on a search mission to relocate her old self. "The Denise that I knew previous to the accident," she said.

The night of the accident, for the first time in decades, Bill Nix dreamed that he was back in the deadly highland forests of Southeast Asia in 1968, where he had patrolled the Laotian border as a soldier in the Vietnam War. It was one of the worst places to be in the worst year of the war. "I lay there and thought more about the fears I had in Vietnam than I had on the plane," he said. "It was almost like the two were related in some strange way. It was just the fear that brought it all back to the surface."

Mike Berkwits had gone through the whole ordeal calmly, then got emotional when he made an appearance on *60 Minutes*. "Then the angst arrived," he said. And it hung on. "There's a fear that comes over me absolutely, like, God, somehow I've been spared. Why was I spared? And why didn't I recognize how dangerous it was at the time? It could have been different. I'm still trying to assimilate it."

Heyam Kawas, the Arabic language specialist at the UN, who had twice fallen into the river from the left wing, remained traumatized for months. Kawas was flying to Charlotte for the birth of her granddaughter. But panic set in among the Charlotte relatives when they heard the plane had gone into the Hudson. Kawas's daughter, who had booked the flight, knew her mother couldn't swim. "She called her husband, and told him 'my mom is dead,'" Kawas said. Meanwhile, Kawas, who is divorced and lives alone, had been hospitalized in shock and couldn't call anyone to tell them she'd survived. In Charlotte, the family gathered and began making Muslim burial arrangements. "For two hours, my daughter was going crazy," Kawas said.

Two days later, Kawas flew to Charlotte for the birth, but her daughter had been so upset, the baby was not born until January 27. "I had to pretend for my daughter that nothing was wrong, but I went through a very difficult time," she said. "I'm not like the same as before. I forget things. Any noise I hear, I get scared. I'm always tense. Sometimes I can't function really like I used to." She cannot get on an airplane without taking medication for anxiety. She returned to work in late March. "I thought, 'Maybe I'll get rid of these things when I get busy again,'" she said. "But I'm still struggling."

Others felt euphoric, energized as never before. The sun seemed to shine more brightly; food tasted better. "It's my rebirth," said Luther Lockhart. "I will forever celebrate January 15 as my second birthday. I got a second shot."

Eric Stevenson returned to Paris with a mix of strange feelings—at times he felt like a phantom, at times invincible. In the famously unyielding traffic of Paris, he felt "like I could step in front of any bus or walk across a freeway, and traffic was certain to stop for me," he said. The feeling lasted about a week.

Carl Bazarian stopped having the recurring plane-crash dream that had plagued him since his twenties. Five days after the accident, he flew to Miami, where US Airways helped him replace his passport, and then flew on that night to Chile on business.

"I am still the same person," Bazarian said. "But my tolerance for bad people is now zero. If I walk into a room and I feel the chemistry is not right, I'll walk out. I don't want to be with bad people. Life is too short. How am I going to live my life now? The same way: I'm going to go like hell. I do appreciate the sun coming up over the beach. But I'm also walking fast on that beach while the sun's rising."

"Every day of my life is a free option," said Ricardo Valeriano. "I'm not supposed to be here."

Eileen Shleffar went right back to work—too soon, she realized. When a colleague checked on her, Shleffar confessed she needed to "find my happy place," a zone of comfort she hadn't yet discovered. "I have this little ball of hysteria, this little hysterical person bouncing around inside of me," Shleffar said.

One day, Shleffar called her husband and told him they were going to Disney World. Always previously afraid to ride on roller coasters, she told her husband and daughter she planned to sit in the

"It's a Small World" ride for three days. "I'm going to be a crazy lady," she joked. Then she discovered she had to release the little hysterical person. "I needed to scream as loud as I could until I had no breath in me," she said. To her daughter's amazement, Shleffar decided to ride every roller coaster. "My daughter kept saying, 'Who are you? Where's my mom? Really, you want to go on that?' I had my arm in a sling, and I said, 'Let's just do it. I am not afraid. I can't be afraid of anything.'" It was the best therapy she ever had.

A week after the accident, Tripp Harris went to see his pastor in hopes of making sense of it all. "There were so many things that had to line up. The right pilot on the right plane. The weather going from horrible to being good. The fact that the ferry boats were right there," Harris said. "My biggest question to my pastor was, 'If God put all these things together, why not just move the birds?'"

Harris was not being flip. His pastor told him that God moves birds for a lot of other planes. "But this was a time when God needed to show that he can make miracles happen," the pastor said. "This was a time when everyone around the world needed a miracle."

ON FEBRUARY 12, exactly four weeks after the demise of Flight 1549, the remarkable run of thirty months without an airline fatality in the United States came to a spectacular and gruesome end. A Colgan Air commuter plane crashed as it approached a landing in Buffalo, New York, killing all forty-nine people on board, as well as a man on the ground.

The Buffalo crash seemed almost a reverse image of the all-souls-saved incident of Flight 1549. Losing speed, the Colgan pilot had attempted to climb, putting the plane into a stall and then a nose-first dive into the ground. The last human sound on the cockpit recorder was the scream of the copilot.

In contrast, Sullenberger, losing thrust and rapidly slowing in his takeoff climb, immediately put the Airbus into a deep, banking dive to regain speed and avoid a stall. By the time he was two-thirds of the way back to the ground, Sullenberger had enough control to attempt a crash-landing glide.

Little of this—the luck of the draw that life had given them—was lost on the still-recovering survivors of the US Airways flight. The Colgan crash traumatized them again, just as many were getting over the first stages of their ordeal.

"My single worst day? The Friday morning after the Buffalo flight," said Joe Hart. "I was comatose. I could not deal with it. I still can't. I don't understand it. Up until the Buffalo thing, I felt kind of special."

"I was feeling better until the Buffalo crash happened," said Don Norton. "I'm definitely feeling post-traumatic stress. I'm obsessed with airplane crashes, scouring the Internet, listening to cockpit stories and audio."

Beverly Water's husband, Don, heard about the crash before she did. "Don't turn on the TV today," she said he warned her.

Larry Snodgrass said he couldn't watch the TV coverage of the crash. "That was a terrible morning. The biggest thing was: Why them? Why not me?"

"I'll bet 90 percent of the people who got on that Buffalo flight thought, *Boy, I'm glad I wasn't on Flight 1549 three weeks ago*," said Bill Wiley. "Would you rather be in a large jet that loses power low over Manhattan or a plane with de-icing equipment landing in a snowstorm? I would choose the other plane. They had a better chance."

The Colgan crash brought issues of faith strongly to the surface in many ways.

Wiley, a Presbyterian who no longer attends church, considers himself deeply religious but is troubled by the view that God was watching over him but not the passengers in Buffalo. "I don't believe God micromanages things like plane crashes."

"God's hands are on the plane," Alex Magness, also spiritual, thinks aloud about the famous drawing of heavenly hands setting Flight 1549 safely into the Hudson. "It's a really wonderful drawing. But it hit me the opposite way. I felt so much pressure from it. It means we went through the trauma for a reason. Then Buffalo happened. Where were God's hands on *that* plane? I know it's not for us to explain. There is a spiritual aspect that is hard to understand."

For many believers, these are unanswerable questions you take purely on faith.

"How can I explain it?" asked Mike Kollmansberger, a member of what he calls "your typical evangelical church," near his Lexington, South Carolina, home. "I don't know. The Bible says the Lord giveth and the Lord taketh away. He gave us one more day. He didn't give them one more day. This is where you move into the element of trust. I can't explain it. Some have tried, but that's a little presumptuous."

A few months later, the Colgan accident was followed by two other horrendous crashes taking 380 lives and leaving a sole survivor. The tragedies were markedly different but left haunts that once more slowed the emotional recovery of the Flight 1549 survivors. Both planes were Airbuses, and both went into water.

On June 1, 2009, an Air France A330 caught in a freak storm while flying from Rio de Janeiro to Paris, fell 35,000 feet into the Atlantic, killing all 228 persons aboard. Only a few bodies and scraps of metal were found. A report that the plane may have fallen intact from that altitude ran chills through the 1549 group.

A month later, an old Yemenia Airlines Airbus 310 crashed into the Indian Ocean while trying to land at Comoros, not far from where the hijacked Ethiopian plane, of cartwheeling video infamy, went in. A single fourteen-year-old girl was found alive after clinging to wreckage for thirteen hours.

All told, by mid 2009, more than five hundred people had died in commercial air crashes around the world, making it the worst year for aviation fatalities in seven years. It was a year that made fear of flying, whether a long-held phobia or one enhanced by the events on the Hudson, difficult to subdue.

BILL WILEY JOINED the Xanax crowd, medicating for anxiety before flights. Casey Jones no longer has those relaxed travel days when he'd enjoy a cocktail and a nap.

"The first time I flew after the incident, I had a dream that we were headed for a midair collision," Jones said. He woke with a start and looked out the window. "I can't relax when I fly now. I won't have a drink. I want total awareness at all times, just in case."

Luther Lockhart doesn't even have to board a plane to become unnerved. "I live very close to LaGuardia Airport. I never noticed air traffic before. Now I cannot stop looking up every time a plane goes by. Is that plane going to blow up, or fall out of the sky? It's a really shitty feeling. I hate it," he said.

As with any large group, the fear of flying, and even the incident on the Hudson, gave way to larger traumas for some.

On Father's Day, Pam Seagle's younger sister and only sibling, Jennifer Evans, died suddenly of an aneurism at age forty. Evans, the top prosecutor in the South Carolina attorney general's office, had been Seagle's best friend. As Seagle raced to the hospital, she thought back to the day of the accident when Evans and her mother waited for news, fearing that Seagle may not have survived. Now, it was Seagle's turn to comfort her mother.

After Seagle returned home safely, her mother wrote "profound, touching" letters to both daughters. "My sister and I discussed the letters as well as our feelings about what might have been," Seagle said. "I told her the role I wanted her to play with my children should something happen, and she told me her wishes should something happen to her. Never before had we discussed things like that, but I'm so grateful we did. Upon her death, there was nothing left unsaid."

Her sister's death changed her perspective on Flight 1549. "Before this, January 15 was my worst day," she said. "Now, I'm done with it." By her own reckoning, Seagle is not a big believer in organized religion. But in coming to terms with her sister's death, she has become more religious. She has asked herself again the same questions she asked in January: Why was she spared?

"Every day, I struggle with how these two events are connected," she said. "Perhaps God knew she was going to leave, and my parents couldn't handle the loss of both their children. I had to survive."

Frank Scudere, who sat at his father's hospital sickbed the night before the accident, sat with his father the following week when he died. Then in March came the layoff from Scudere's law firm. That day was a repeat of January 16, the day his firm had originally planned to lay him off, but held off because of the accident. "I kept checking my voice mail," Scudere said. When the call came through summoning him to a conference room, the firing played out in the same awkward way. "Same HR woman, but a different law partner," Scudere said. "I did everything but get on my knees and say, 'Pretty please, can I keep my job? Can you make an exception for me? I'm working and making money for you.'"

Back in South Carolina with his family, Scudere has absorbed the upheaval and described this stage of his life "as a journey" leading to a destination yet unknown.

As for life-altering change, perhaps Lori Lightner has experienced the greatest transformation. One of the Belk Six, Lightner had put in eighty-hour weeks as a vice president and division merchandise manager in charge of a group of buyers. She and her husband, Eric, always planned a family but couldn't conceive, and fertility treatments failed. They talked about adoption but hadn't gotten around to it. "It was always, 'Okay, in two years we'll have enough money. . . . Okay, in three years . . . ' " Lightner said.

After the accident, Lightner no longer wanted a career, but she wanted a baby.

"Lori was never the same after the crash," said Michael Leonard, one of the Belk Six and Lightner's longtime friend. "Her killer instinct was gone."

In the spring, Lightner left Belk and joined the Red Cross as a volunteer. She and her husband are actively pursuing adoption. They downsized, cutting their living expenses to adapt to their new lifestyle.

"I was a classic Type A. Work, work, work. Now there is nothing I want to do more than help other people and raise a family," Lightner said. "I want to be a stay-at-home mom. It's not important to me whether anyone shops for T-shirts and dresses. I don't care. I got a call from a job recruiter, who told me he can pay me twice as much as I used to make. I told him, 'Where you are located is colder than the Hudson River.' Money is not important. What's important is that my husband is happy and we have a family. It's made every day so much brighter."

For Michael Nunn, the accident confirmed that his plan to walk away from his law practice and seventy-hour weeks was the right thing to do. In April 2009, he signed on as general counsel at the Florence, South Carolina, sheriff's department. "The day-to-day pressures of a private law firm are not present in this new job," Nunn said. "It was a significant pay cut, but it was time for a change."

Irina Levshina, who had long delayed starting a family, thought it was time to make plans to do so. "We were just putting it off, because so many things have been in flux for a long time," she said. "I remember hearing somebody say, 'Maybe none of the people on the plane will do anything big, but their children are going to go on and do wonderful things.' So maybe that's part of it. Even if I don't do something great, maybe my children will. So that made me think about having kids."

Eric Stevenson expects changes, just as his life changed after his near-death experience on the Delta flight over the Pacific so many years ago. That event led him to his life in Paris, and he expects that Flight 1549 will lead him in a new direction. What that will be, he can only guess.

But for the others, so far at least, life-altering changes have not yet come, and may never. Many survivors are not looking for big changes.

"I haven't booked an island destination where I'm going to go practice yoga for the rest of my life," said Craig Black. "But I don't pay attention to the stock market anymore. If it goes down, it goes down. If I lose my job, I'll find something else. It's not the end of the world. I sleep better at night."

Adelaide Horton said she did not want Flight 1549 to redefine her life. "But you find it defining your life anyway," she said. "Everybody asks you about it because everybody is afraid it's going to happen to them. They want to touch you and talk to you because they realize that you could live through something like this."

Theresa Leahy said she likes life the way it is. "I'm not going to run off and go to an ashram, or climb Kilimanjaro. I am who I am. I am comfortable in my own skin."

While some aboard Flight 1549 feel a burden now that they've been given a second chance at life—a feeling characteristic of people who go through near-death experiences—Molly Schugel disagrees.

"People should think about it another way," Schugel said. "Rather than 'I have to do something,' the people on the plane *have* done something. They lived. Theirs was a story of inspiration and hope. This story has touched millions, maybe a billion. Everyone I talk to, whether I know them or not, sheds tears that I was on that plane. Maybe they met me once; maybe it's the thought that I could be their daughter. There was this miracle so the world could continue to have hope."

Martin Sosa still sees the accident "as a metaphor for what's happening in the country. We were in free fall with no outcome in sight," he said.

The outcome jolted some others, including some of those who gave their most to help the people who came out of the Hudson.

Three weeks after the accident, Arthur's Landing, the restaurant next door to the Weehawken ferry terminal, and the place where the staff had handed out dry chef's pants to wear, free drinks, and hot coffee, and had helped soothe frayed nerves, filed for bankruptcy and closed.

For most, however, life went on, if a little differently. Michelle DePonte had her dream wedding in February in Hawaii, although the reception didn't go exactly as she'd planned. It was better. Despite the bad economy, virtually every friend she'd invited spent the money to attend the ceremony. "Half the people who came couldn't afford to be there," DePonte said. "Everyone was there to celebrate more than Dave and me getting married. It was a celebration of me being alive. Every speech talked about me living after that plane crash. Do you ever wonder how many people are going to attend your funeral? I feel like I have an idea."

The golfers took their golf vacation in April, driving rather than flying to Myrtle Beach. Their holiday coincided with the worst wildfires to hit the coastal region in thirty years. Seventy homes were destroyed and at least one hundred more were damaged, and two thousand residents were forced to evacuate.

In August, Andrew Gray and Stephanie King got married in Wisconsin—with Jeffrey Skiles, Flight 1549's copilot, as one of the invited guests.

Amy Jolly wrapped up her airport therapy and got back to flying, nervously. "It doesn't get any easier," she said. "I just know how to control my fear now."

Josh Peltz took his first flight a few months after he popped out the exit hatch from seat 10F and ran down the wing. By chance, he again ended up in an exit row, this time on Delta Airlines. Asked by the flight attendant if they were comfortable handling exit-row duties, Peltz's seatmates all nodded, half-listening the way Peltz once did, and went back to their newspapers. Looking up at the attendant, Peltz smiled and replied "Yes."

With that, the miracle on the Hudson, at least for Peltz, began to recede into the past.

Passenger List

TRACEY ALLEN-WOLSKO: Seat 26B. *Age:* 37. *Home:* Huntersville, NC. *Quote:* "When we landed, I didn't even know where we were. But you get this tunnel vision of what you need to do to survive."

DEREK ALTER: Seat 6E. *Age:* 25. *Home:* Matthews, NC. *Quote:* "It was a fantastic landing. It felt like we were water-skiing."

KEITH ANTHONY: Seat 7F. *Age:* 39. *Home:* Davidson, NC. *Quote:* "It's a miracle and everyone's safe and that's great. I still wish it had never happened. We came this close to not being here."

KEVIN ANTON: Seat 23C. *Age:* 49 *Home:* Knoxville, TN. *Quote:* "What I've learned from this experience is the importance of taking accountability for yourself and always being aware of what is going on around you . . . and have your cell phone charged," he said in an article posted on www.knoxvillechamber.com.

VICKI BARNHARDT: Seat 26C. *Age:* 38. *Home:* Huntersville, NC. *Quote:* "I spent all day near my kids or hugging them. My eight-year-old daughter reminded me that her prayers to 'keep mommy safe' had been answered."

CARL BAZARIAN: Seat 16B. *Age:* 62. *Home:* Amelia Island, FL. *Quote:* "I remember going to the end of the wing, and I remember the tranquility of that. Seeing the sun. I thought *This is beautiful. No noise, no movement, no ferries.* Thank God I saw the sun. It was so peaceful. Then my adrenaline kicked in."

DARREN BECK: Seat 3A. *Age:* 37. *Home:* Charlotte, NC. *Quote:* "When I got home, my ten-year-old had this little medal that he won in a youth iron-man competition. He put it in one of those gift bags. He wrote, 'This is your medal for being a survivor.' I travel with it. I put that medal in my standard-issue carry-on that I fly with."

ALYSON BELL: Seat 20D. *Age:* 49. *Home:* Matthews, NC. *Quote:* "I have a special-needs child, severely handicapped. She is the joy of [husband] Ron's and my life. That was my concern with Ron, how is he going to handle everything? We are such good partners. What could he do on his own?"

MARY BERKWITS: Seat 14B. *Age:* 52. *Home:* Matthews, NC. *Quote:* "We're all holding on to each other, all of us to keep each other warm. Michael starts saying 'Dance, everybody, dance.' So we're all like this on the wing, dancing, to keep ourselves warm."

MICHAEL BERKWITS: Seat 13B. *Age:* 55. *Home:* Matthews, NC. *Quote:* "We were coming in by the *Intrepid.* Couldn't be a better place. There's nothing but police rescue boats, ferries. I didn't think about the plane flipping, breaking—I didn't think that there could be ice in the river, that we could hit a boat. Everything seemed like this was supposed to happen this way."

FRED BERRETTA: Seat 16A. *Age:* 41. *Home:* Charlotte, NC. *Quote:* "You had this feeling, I'm possibly going to die here. I'm going to die next to this man and I don't even know him. I remember thinking how strange that was to be in that situation and thinking how they might be feeling about that."

CRAIG BLACK: Seat 9C. *Age:* 46. *Home:* Charlotte, NC. *Quote:* "I'm happy with my life. The biggest thing I learned was I was okay to die that day. Once you have that perspective, you're okay to go, it makes everything else seem pretty nominal."

BEN BOSTIC: Seat 20A. *Age:* 38. *Home:* Fort Mill, SC. *Quote:* "I don't typically consider myself a great public speaker. I have been gifted with a great story to tell."

MARYANN BRUCE: Seat 5D. *Age:* 48. *Home:* Cornelius, NC. *Quote:* "People say, why do you still go on planes? Obviously, there's the practical matter. I met my husband on a plane, so I remember the positive things. That was Thanksgiving. We were engaged by February. We have been married twenty-six years. That's why I love planes."

BILLY CAMPBELL: Seat 25A. *Age:* 49. *Home:* Los Angeles, CA. *Quote:* "I can't believe I'm sitting in this raft. This plane is sinking. We just landed in the Hudson and survived. It quickly hit me afterwards."

DAVID CARLOS: Seat 7C. *Age:* 35. *Home:* Chicopee, MA. *Quote:* "I flew to Vegas about a month afterward. It was tough . . . scary at some points. I love to travel and now would rather drive to my destinations."

GLENN CARLSON: Seat 6B. *Age:* 47. *Home:* Charlotte, NC. *Quote:* "This is the new mind-set. Glenn is a little more nervous, with a bit of uneasiness. That's just the way it is. This has become a new way of travel."

SHAE CHILDERS: Seat 13C. *Age:* 38. *Home:* Gaffney, SC. *Quote:* "I give Sully credit for being experienced. But I think those people were put there by a higher power in order to save us."

REMINGTON CHIN: Seat 11B. *Age:* 25. *Home:* New York, NY. *Quote:* "I feel, like, right now, I'm in extra innings. It's all bonus."

BRENT CIMINO: Seat 20B *Age:* 24. *Home:* New York, NY. *Quote:* "You don't have control over your life like you thought you did. You've got to be a little more wary and more appreciative because it might not be around forever."

JAMES CLARK Seat 21F. *Age:* 44. *Home:* Huntersville, NC. *Quote:* "I'd like to say, all of a sudden I do everything right and I'm perfect. I try to say I need to be better or more tolerant. But it didn't change my life, as it did to some people. I kind of am back to my life. I'm a big workaholic."

CHRIS COBB: Seat 15B. *Age:* 32. *Home:* Matthews, NC. *Quote:* "I slept like a baby that night. I haven't had any problem sleeping. Had a few dreams and a few plane crashes in the dreams. But nothing that consumes me."

VALLIE COLLINS: Seat 26D. *Age:* 37. *Home:* Maryville, TN. *Quote:* "I remember seeing people way out in front of me with water at their ankles. And it took a few minutes for my brain to figure out that they're standing on the wing. I could see the ferry boat was almost to us at the end of the wing, and I remember thinking, *Okay, I'm not dying today.*"

EMMA "SOPHINA" COWAN: Seat 13F. *Age:* 26. *Home:* Perth, Australia. *Quote:* "If it's my time, it's my time. I'm very blessed to be alive," she told *USA Today*

LAURIE CRANE: Seat 9D. *Age:* 58. *Home:* Charlotte, NC. *Quote:* "I don't know who I am sometimes. I don't want to go back to the life I've had. I was a shopper. I was a workaholic. When I wasn't working, we were in the mall looking for the deals. I'm trying to figure out where I'm going."

MICHELE DAVIS: Seat 24D. *Age:* 23. *Home:* Olympia, WA. *Quote:* "Probably the scariest part of it was the thirty seconds before we hit and the thirty seconds after we hit," she told the *Seattle Post-Intelligencer.*

KANAU DEGUCHI: Seat 25C. *Age:* 36. *Home:* New York, NY. *Quote:* "I was surprised that after I got out of the airplane that people did not panic anymore. People tried to help each other on the wings. I saw some pushing inside the airplane and some people climbed over the seats. But it's kind of normal, and maybe that could even happen in Japan. But after I got outside, people cooperated with each other."

RICK DELISLE: Seat 5A. *Age:* 54. *Home:* Chicopee, MA. *Quote:* "It's great to be here, but if I knew what I know now before getting on that plane, I wouldn't have done it. Nothing's worth going through what we went through," he told www.southcoasttoday.com.

MICHELLE DePONTE: Seat 10A. *Age:* 30. *Home:* Charlotte, NC. *Quote:* "I was shivering so badly I couldn't catch my breath."

MARCH DOLPHIN: Seat 12B. *Age:* 57. *Home:* Brooklyn, NY. *Quote:* "After we're on shore, some of the passengers are talking about how the exit door in the back of the plane would not open. One gentleman reports that a rescuer told him that it was a blessing in disguise, because the plane would have filled up with water much more quickly."

JENNIFER DOYLE: Seat 9E. *Age:* 33. *Home:* Charlotte, NC. *Quote:* "It's a healthy reminder that people are good and people do look after each other and care about each other, a plane full of strangers, from CEOs to moms."

STEVE DOYLE: Seat 10E. *Age:* 45. *Home:* Charlotte, NC.

RICARDO ELIAS: Seat 1D. *Age:* Withheld. *Home:* Charlotte, NC.

BILL ELKIN: Seat 18B. *Age:* 41. *Home:* Mooresville, NC. *Quote:* "I may be unique, but I'm not special. Lots of people have near-death experiences every day. Lots of people survive heart attacks, car crashes."

LISA ENGLISH: Seat 8C. *Age:* 38. *Home:* Cornelius, NC. *Quote:* "In my mind, if we crashed in the water, we would sink and would drown and I would never see my son again. I had no idea that a plane could float like that."

LEE FAZZI: Seat 7D. *Age:* 56. *Home:* Charlotte, NC.

WENDELL FOX: Seat 9A. *Age:* 56. *Home:* Cornelius, NC. *Quote:* "We had so many things in our favor that day. The most stellar crew that US Air has. It was midafternoon. It was sunny. There was no maritime traffic on the river. We were going with the current. The Hudson has ferries. It happened in a city that is the most well-prepared and equipped to handle emergencies than any city in the world and they train constantly and their skills were evident."

NICK GAMACHE: Seat 17B. *Age:* 32. *Home:* Raleigh, NC. *Quote:* "My three-year-old is coming up with new words every day and riding her scooter. I cannot believe I almost missed out on all of this."

BALAJI GANESAN: Seat 20E. *Age:* 30. *Home:* Fremont, CA. *Quote:* "You could say I do feel that I cheated death. I look at it more positively. I'm destined to make it for a long time."

DAVID GRAHAM: Seat 12D. *Age:* 54. *Home:* Columbia, SC. *Quote:* "This is an example of God, his hand over all things. That it had a positive and happy ending doesn't change the importance that God is still in control."

ANDREW GRAY: Seat 14F. *Age:* 28. *Home:* Fayetteville, NC. *Quote:* "I didn't fear what was going to happen on the other side of death. I knew my soul was saved. I didn't spend those last few moments crying out trying to get things right, or scared of what was on the other side."

LINDA HAHN: Seat 5B. *Age:* 53. *Home:* Anaheim, CA. *Quote:* "When we got on the little boat and everybody was getting panicked, and calling on cell phones and calling their family and saying all kinds of things, apologizing to them, sending them love, and I figure, their life is going to be ended soon, so that's why they are doing this. . . . And then I looked up and there was a big ferry coming to us. I thank God."

JOE HALL: Seat 22C. *Age:* 37. *Home:* Charlotte, NC. *Quote:* "The one image that is very powerful to me is the ferry and the people in the cold weather, wet, helping each other. It was twenty-one degrees outside. . . ."

JIM HANKS, JR.: Seat 24C. *Age:* 65. *Home:* Baltimore, MD. *Quote:* "I went from thinking I'm about to drown to realizing I'm going to get out of this aircraft. I did think as I was walking forward because there was so much water in the cabin, *I better get out of this aircraft as quickly as I can. The water is rising and this aircraft may sink very quickly.* I was very purposeful."

TRIPP HARRIS: Seat 4C. *Age:* 37. *Home:* Charlotte, NC. *Quote:* "It has changed my outlook on being at home. I'm a workaholic. I work a ton of hours. I'm tired on the weekends. When I get home, especially when I'm traveling, I just want to relax and take it easy and recharge. It's totally different now. I want to get home so I can spend time and play cars with my son or go the park."

JOE HART: Seat 7B. *Age:* 50. *Home:* Cornelius, NC. *Quote:* "I never knew what happened to the woman in the water, Shae Childers, after she slipped out of my hands trying to climb up the ladder onto the ferry. Fast forward to the *Sixty Minutes* taping. She walks toward me. This could be a disaster. I'm thinking this woman is going to come over and slap me and say 'You left me there to die, you bastard.' So as she's approaching me, I'm nervous. She embraces me in one of the warmest bear hugs ever, and then pushes me back against the wall, and says, 'You owe me a pair of boots.'"

DIANE HIGGINS: Seat 17E. *Age:* 58. *Home:* Goshen, NY. *Quote:* "Oh yeah, I was scared. When I get on a plane I have this thing with angels, 'Please take care of us, let us have a safe journey. Bring this plane up and protect us and bring it back down.'"

KARIN HILL: Seat 18E. *Age:* 24. *Home:* Boulder, CO. *Quote:* "This solidifies my faith, but I think it also just reminds me of just how thankful I am that I'm alive. I don't think the crash was a wake-up call for us. It was solidifying in our hearts that we have our priorities right."

WARREN HOLLAND: Seat 16E. *Age:* 40. *Home:* Charlotte, NC. *Quote:* "I am better for the experience. I have true inner peace and I think I'll always carry that sense of peace with me. I don't dwell on what could have been."

MARK HOOD: Seat 2A. *Age:* 48. *Home:* Charlotte, NC. *Quote:* "You've got to know where you're going when you die. Never leave the house without letting your family know you love them. And always think about the next step to increase your chances [of survival]."

ADELAIDE HORTON: Seat 11A. *Age:* 58. *Home:* Mooresville, NC. *Quote:* "The hostess at Arthur's Landing took off her socks and gave them to me. The waiter gave me a lucky scarf. A fireman came up to me and said I should go buy a lottery ticket. I told him I already won."

JOHN HOWELL: Seat 2D. *Age:* 40. *Home:* Charlotte, NC. *Quote:* "I was immediately back on a plane the next Monday. If I stayed home, I'd probably not be able to do this anymore. I could stay at home and change everything, but that seemed cowardly at the time. I thought I'd keep doing what I do and not live frightened by what could have happened. As time passes, by insisting I'm not letting this change anything, am I missing a chance to change everything? I am still debating it with myself."

LAUREL HUBBARD: Seat 25F. *Age:* 45. *Home:* Matthews, NC. *Quote:* "It was a very frightening experience and traumatic, I'll agree with that. But the feeling that we had when we reached that pier was not trauma, but sheer joy, happy to be there."

NICO ILIEV: Seat 22E. *Age:* 32. *Home:* New York, NY. *Quote:* "I wouldn't say I cheated death. I would say I looked at death face-to-face."

ANDREW JAMISON: Seat 25E. *Age:* 26. *Home:* Charleston, SC. *Quote:* "I really had peace that God was in control of it, and worst case scenario, I meet Christ today, and that's okay," he told www.wsoctv.com.

AMY JOLLY: Seat 14C. *Age:* 29. *Home:* Gaffney, SC. *Quote:* "It still amazes me that the wings held us and kept us relatively dry as long as they did. I like to think of it as angel's wings."

CASEY JONES: Seat 7A. *Age:* 48. *Home:* Jacksonville, FL. *Quote:* "I used to wake up and tell myself I was going to have a good day. Now, I wake up every morning knowing I'm going to have a good day."

DONALD JONES: Seat 3C. *Age:* 67. *Home:* Jacksonville, FL. *Quote:* "When I tried to climb the ladder to the ferry, it was like I was in one of those nightmares where you're trying to run from something but you can't. My body didn't want to move."

PAUL JORGENSEN: Seat 1A. *Age:* 38. *Home:* Charlotte, NC. *Quote:* "There was a time where I was really just in shock over it all. I did not sleep for five days and then something happened. Hey, this is a positive thing. This is a happy story. You helped people out of the water. You did everything you would have wanted to. You were tested. You did good."

MATT KANE: Seat 24A. *Age:* 38. *Home:* Bridgeport, CT. *Quote:* "My whole life was built up for that moment. It was almost like a test of who I was, what I've done, all the tough things I've gotten through in my life with the family and my dad being tough on me. It was for that moment, to get through it."

HEYAM KAWAS: Seat 9B. *Age:* 48. *Home:* New Jersey. *Quote:* "I was so lucky that a scuba diver jumped from the helicopter right away and pulled me up from the river. I was drowning at that time. I couldn't move. I was freezing."

STEPHANIE KING: Seat 14E. *Age:* 29. *Home:* West Bend, WI. *Quote:* "I don't think that because we survived this we are going to live a long life. I don't know when my time will be. It wasn't January 15 2009, but that doesn't mean it couldn't be tomorrow."

MIKE KOLLMANSBERGER: Seat 12E. *Age:* 36. *Home:* Lexington, SC. *Quote:* "It's given me lots of opportunities to talk to people, not only customers, friends, family, people I've lost contact with who've wanted to regain contact. I have had a chance to share not only what happened, but how—it's been neat."

JEFF KOLODJAY: Seat 22A. *Age:* 31. *Home:* Norwalk, CT. *Quote:* "I thought, okay, in a couple seconds it will be over and I'll get to see what's at the end of the tunnel. I wasn't ready to see it."

ROB KOLODJAY: Seat 6C. *Age:* 60. *Home:* Chicopee, MA. *Quote:* "It was an out-of-body experience. I really thought I was dead," he told a local newspaper, the *Republican*.

THERESA KRUSE LEAHY: Seat 5C. *Age:* 49. *Home:* Charlotte, NC. *Quote:* "This has been portrayed as uplifting. It's funny that something I was personally involved in could have been a confidence booster for the country."

BARRY LEONARD: Seat 1C. *Age:* 55. *Home:* Charlotte, NC. *Quote:* "Ten years ago, my son got hit on the head by a baseball and almost died from an epidural hematoma, which is what killed Natasha Richardson. That night he said, 'Daddy I have a headache.' I took him to the hospital. They had to move him to another hospital. They told me he could die on the way there. That was the worst thing that happened to me in my life, not this. That changed my life."

MICHAEL LEONARD: Seat 12C. *Age:* 37. *Home:* Charlotte, NC. *Quote:* "My memories are black and white, like it wasn't real, like I was watching a movie or something."

IRINA LEVSHINA: Seat 26A. *Age:* 37. *Home:* New York, NY. *Quote:* "In all kinds of relationships with people, if you want to express something, your appreciation, your love, you shouldn't delay those things; and just do them."

LORI LIGHTNER: Seat 10C. *Age:* 35. *Home:* Tega Cay, SC. *Quote:* "At Arthur's Landing, the first thing I do is strip off all my clothes down to my underwear. I remember peeling my jeans off and my legs were this weird blue-purple, and I think that's not normal. Someone zipped me up in a down coat. Someone wrapped me in a table cloth. They brought out hot tea. I was shaking so much I couldn't get it to my lips. I've never been so cold in my entire life. After the accident I went on YouTube to make sure I wasn't naked anywhere."

STEPHEN LIS: Seat 14D. *Age:* 42. *Home:* Chalfont, PA. *Quote:* "People ask me if I thought I was going to die. I don't know. I did think of how the plane would crash. I do know that I said a prayer and tried to keep my wife in my mind as we hit. Then I was on the wing. Manhattan in front of me, beautiful blue sky."

LUTHER LOCKHART: Seat 23D. *Age:* 32. *Home:* New York, NY. *Quote:* "I'm still dealing with that right now. I need to accept it. This is part of my life. This is something that will be with me forever. You naturally want to denounce bad things, to say they never happened. But this really did. I have a hard time accepting that."

DENISE LOCKIE: Seat 2C. *Age:* Withheld. *Home:* Charlotte, NC. *Quote:* "You have days that you don't understand because you have emotions that sometimes you cannot control and you have a little disorientation, and forgetfulness, and sleeplessness, a lot of things that are off kilter that take time. But every day is a good day."

ALEX MAGNESS: Seat 17A. *Age:* 38. *Home:* Rockville Centre, NY. *Quote:* "I feel much less risk-adverse now. Much freer."

RAYMOND MANDRELL: Seat 24F. *Age:* 30. *Home:* Miami, FL. *Quote:* "It took a long time for it really to sink in. When we walked into the Crowne Plaza and there was the newspaper with the plane on the front page. I couldn't believe this just happened. That's when it came to me."

CLAUDETTE MASON: Seat 22D. *Age:* 46. *Home:* Memphis, TN. "There were some real men on that plane," she told the Memphis *Commercial Appeal.* "Their [own] safety seemed secondary."

JAMES "JAY" McDONALD: Seat 14A. *Age:* 39. *Home:* Charlotte, NC. *Quote:* "Why did I survive [a brain tumor] to go down in a plane crash two years later? It didn't make any sense. Now having had the plane incident, I'll always be asking why. Was I changed? Yes."

BETH McHUGH: Seat 20C. *Age:* 64. *Home:* Lake Wylie, SC. *Quote:* "From the ferry, I had to look back at the scene. Did we really land in the river? Is that the plane sinking? Ohmygod. Was I really on that plane?"

GERRY McNAMARA: Seat 8F. *Age:* 54. *Home:* Charlotte, NC. *Quote:* "I've come since to realize that it is an incredible gift that we've been given and it's a very, very good thing and I feel called to share it."

BEVERLY MILLS: Seat 11D. *Age:* 59. *Home:* Sherrills Ford, NC. *Quote:* "Climbing up the rescue ladder, the man on the boat grabbed my arm and pulled me up till he got me to his chest, and he just— poof, and then he was bent over getting the next person up. I felt like a salmon that had just been beached."

JORGE MORGADO: Seat 5F. *Age:* 32. *Home:* Chicopee, MA. *Quote:* "I stepped onto the wing and realized it was stable. How far we were from shore. Can I swim this?"

JAMES "BRIAN" MOSS: Seat 26F. *Age:* 35. *Home:* Charlotte, NC. *Quote:* "The water was awful. I didn't feel safe even at the point at which I was safe. I was on a rescue boat alive in a fully functional boat, and I felt like if I don't get out of this water, I'm going to die."

JENNY MOULTON: Seat 10D. *Age:* 27. *Home:* Charlotte, NC. *Quote:* "We hit the water and it was an incredible force. It's the one piece of this story that I'm at a loss for words to describe. I can't explain how everything inside my body moved an inch and then went back into place."

FREIDA MUSCATELL: Seat 8B. *Age:* 49. *Home:* Lake Wylie, SC. *Quote:* "How many people can this wing hold before it snaps off? This wing wasn't designed to hold that many. I was not thinking that we were in the water."

SHERI NEJMAN: Seat 18A. *Age:* Withheld. *Home:* Charlotte, NC. *Quote:* "I had so many emotions from the time I hit the ferry, when you're finally feeling you are safe. That's when there's a flood of emotions. I was overjoyed and felt extreme happiness."

BILL NIX: Seat 25B. *Age:* 62. *Home:* Charlotte, NC. *Quote:* "I thought it was the end about three times. I thought there was going to be an explosion. I thought we were going to crash. The third time, in the back of a plane full of people, the water just got deeper and deeper. We're going down, so this is the way it's gonna be. I'm going to drown."

DON NORTON: Seat 11F. *Age:* 35. *Home:* Matthews, NC. *Quote:* "I told my wife, 'Put a message on Facebook, I'm okay and going back to Charlotte.' It was just unbelievable."

MICHAEL NUNN: Seat 6F. *Age:* 53. *Home:* Florence, SC. *Quote:* "This thing did not catch these people unprepared. They knew what to do in the event of a situation like this."

STEVE O'BRIEN: Seat 15C. *Age:* 44. *Home:* Charlotte, NC. *Quote:* "I'm still kind of scattered. Everything that was big is little and everything little is big. There are places in your life when there is a very thin veil between you and God. I was at a very thin place."

SUSAN O'DONNELL: Seat 3D. *Age:* 51. *Home:* Winnsboro, SC. *Quote:* "Although it was a stressful incident, the successful outcome and the assistance and support I received afterward have been truly humbling and inspirational," she said in an account to the Allied Pilots Association.

LUCILLE PALMER: Seat 17F. *Age:* 85. *Home:* Goshen, NY. *Quote:* "I could swim if I had to. My whole vision was blank, blank, blank. All I remember is getting into that raft and laying down in the raft and this man put his arms around me to keep me warm, and said 'I'll take care of you.'"

ALBERTO PANERO: Seat 16F. *Age:* 26. *Home:* Pembroke Pines, FL. *Quote:* "Once everyone realized we were going to be okay, they settled down," he told *The Australian*.

JOSH PELTZ: Seat 10F. *Age:* 39. *Home:* Charlotte, NC. *Quote:* "We're finally on the ferry and we're all asking: Did everyone get off the plane? Is everyone okay? And I thought to myself, please don't let anyone die, please don't let anyone die today."

CLAY PRESLEY: Seat 15D. *Age:* 54. *Home:* Charlotte, NC. *Quote:* "You see that light coming in, and you say that's pretty heavenly, I'm getting out of here. I stood there for a few seconds before I stepped out, trying to figure out, do you go back and get a cushion, or do you go? I elected to go out onto the wing."

DEBBIE RAMSEY: Seat 13A. *Age:* 48. *Home:* Seymour, TN. *Quote:* "It's changed my life as far as looking at stuff differently. Now I make sure instead of zooming by people, I smile at them and hug them. Before, I was busy. I didn't have time for nobody. It's put me where I need to be, as far as my heart."

DICK RICHARDSON: Seat 18F. *Age:* 56. *Home:* Charlotte, NC. *Quote:* "I'm in the terminal after the rescue in wet pants and a Red Cross blanket with a cup of coffee. All these EMT people and firemen are starting to settle down. This woman, also in a Red Cross blanket, comes up and says, 'I don't know if you remember me, I'm Susan Wittmann.' I start busting a gut. 'I will never forget you. We almost died. We were just standing on the wing of an airplane in the middle of the Hudson River ten minutes ago.'"

CHRIS RINI: Seat 22B. *Age:* 37. *Home:* Holmes, NY. *Quote:* "What I do for a hobby (race) is risky but it never feels like it, since everything around you is built and calculated for a crash. On that plane, I realized that a fraction of an inch could be the difference between an abrasion and death," he told www.faststreetcar.com.

CHRIS ROONEY: Seat 18D. *Age:* 23. *Home:* Colorado Springs, CO. *Quote:* "We had the perfect crew and we owe them so much and they're the reason why we're alive."

DAVE SANDERSON: Seat 15A. *Age:* 47. *Home:* Charlotte, NC. *Quote:* "The big lesson is the power of working together as a team, 155 people had to come together in less than a minute to pull it off. No one had an ego on that plane."

ROBIN SCHOEPF: Seat 9F. *Age:* 40. *Home:* New Braunfels, TX. *Quote:* "I would look at one person and we would laugh, and look at another person and cry."

DOUGLAS SCHRIFT: Seat 6D. *Age:* 36. *Home:* Charlotte, NC. *Quote:* "I find myself thinking nonstop about whether I'm heading in the direction I want to head for the rest of my life. This experience has re-newed my attention to that purpose."

MOLLY SCHUGEL: Seat 11E. *Age:* 32. *Home:* Charlotte, NC. *Quote:* "The prayer now starts out, 'Thank you so much for leaving me on this earth. I still want to stay longer. Leave me here until I'm old and wrinkly.'"

FRANK SCUDERE: Seat 24B. *Age:* 48. *Home:* Fort Mill, SC. *Quote:* "Once I got on top of the ferry, this woman came over to me with a fur coat on. She was dry and I don't even know who she was and she gave me her coat. She saw me shaking, and [I] couldn't stop shaking."

PAM SEAGLE: Seat 12A. *Age:* 42. *Home:* Weddington, NC. *Quote:* "There are those moments when I realize the hole I would have left, and the impact it would have had on my family."

JERRY SHANKO: Seat 18C. *Age:* 31. *Home:* Matthews, NC. *Quote:* "At every point where things could have gone wrong, God took care of it."

SCOTT SHARKEY: Seat 19C. *Age:* 33. *Home:* Waxhaw, NC. *Quote:* "The worst day now is not as bad as it was."

EILEEN SHLEFFAR: Seat 13D. *Age:* 56. *Home:* Charlotte, NC. *Quote:* "When I finally talked to my daughter, she was crying and she said, 'I'm so thankful, Mom.' Then when I flew home to Charlotte the only reason I could get on the plane was my eyes were on the prize—Samantha. I had to see her. I couldn't wait to see her."

ALECIA SHUFORD: Seat 4B. *Age:* 40. *Home:* Matthews, NC. *Quote:* "God is saying, 'It's time to take care of you.' I have permission to take care of myself."

BRIAN SIEGEL: Seat 8E. *Age:* 36. *Home:* Charlotte, NC. *Quote:* "The plane is stopped. We're intact, nothing bad has happened yet, but a lot of bad could still happen, so let's go."

LARRY SNODGRASS: Seat 15F. *Age:* 59. *Home:* Lake Wylie, SC. *Quote:* "It's very difficult to pray when it is going to be your last time on earth. I finally looked up to God and said, 'You know what I'm thinking, what kind of person I am,' and there's a calm that came over me."

DAVID SONTAG: Seat 23F. *Age:* 74. *Home:* Chapel Hill, NC. *Quote:* "Our society tries to make heroes. . . . Life is more complicated than that," he said in an interview with *Independent Weekly*.

DAMIAN SOSA: Seat 19E (lap child). *Age:* 9 months. *Home:* New York, NY.

MARTIN SOSA: Seat 23B. *Age:* 48. *Home:* New York, NY. *Quote:* "It's gotten a little better. Still not wrapped up. It's a preoccupation, a distraction on a daily basis. Clearly this brings out something within you that makes you feel you have a higher purpose and we've not yet found what that is. There's a need to try to give back. You're less tolerant about some things and a lot more tolerant about other things."

SOFIA SOSA: Seat 23A. *Age:* 4. *Home:* New York, NY. "The airplane turned into a boat."

TESS SOSA: Seat 19E. *Age:* 40. *Home:* New York, NY. *Quote:* "I made it through all of this and you think I'm going to throw my baby now? No."

KRISTY SPEARS: Seat 8A. *Age:* 40. *Home:* Tega Cay, SC. *Quote:* "Sometimes I feel like my husband and my friends are tired of hearing about it, but I'm not tired of talking about it. It is part of my life and who I am now."

VINCE SPERA: Seat 16C. *Age:* 39. *Home:* Waxhaw, NC. *Quote:* "I never thought I was going to die," he told the New York *Daily News*.

CHARLES SPIGGLE: Seat 4D. *Age:* 40. *Home:* Charlotte, NC. *Quote:* "I was thinking *You have to get off this plane. You can't die here. You have a wife and kids.* I've never really thought about not being there with them. I'm less scared about being in a plane crash now, but I'm much more fearful of something happening to me."

JIM STEFANIK: Seat 6A. *Age:* 30. *Home:* Chicopee, MA. *Quote:* "Granted we know the outcome, I would never wish this on anyone in a million years," he told a local newspaper, *The Republican*.

ERIC STEVENSON: Seat 12F. *Age:* 45. *Home:* Paris, France. *Quote:* "I don't want to waste this opportunity and I don't want to isolate it. Instead it can help me become a better person."

HIROKI TAKIGAWA: Seat 19D. *Age:* 43. *Home:* New York, NY. *Quote:* "Our pilot did a perfect job. I think that was 90 percent of why we're still here. And we also had the Hudson River. If we had departed from Dallas, Texas, or inland, we would have had no way to survive. So we had much good luck on that day and we still have it."

RICARDO VALERIANO: Seat 3F. *Age:* 38. *Home:* Charlotte, NC. *Quote:* "It was the smoothest descent and calmest glide in and one of the smoothest approaches that I've ever experienced. Unfortunately, there wasn't a runway."

DAN VINTON: Seat 15E. *Age:* 43. *Home:* Charlotte, NC. *Quote:* "As long as boats don't crash into the plane, I had a great feeling that we were all going to get out of this alive."

STEWART WALLACE: Seat 16D. *Age:* 46. *Home:* Charlotte, NC. *Quote:* "By and large, it was very quiet, the entire impact. People were on their own personal odyssey at that point."

VIC WARNEMENT: Seat 13E. *Age:* 50. *Home:* Charlotte, NC. *Quote:* "On the way to the airport I was laughing with Molly Schugel, who worked with me and was making the same flight. Joking because her middle name is Brown. I was kidding her about the unsinkable Molly Brown. She managed to fall in the water, too."

BEVERLY WATERS: Seat 21E. *Age:* 48. *Home:* Gastonia, NC. *Quote:* "The outpouring of love and friendship, it was overwhelming. At church a lady wanted to touch me. Total strangers just wanted to do that."

AMBER WELLS: Seat 20F. *Age:* 34. *Home:* Waxhaw, NC. *Quote:* "I'm not really questioning what the reason is. I'm just thankful for it."

IAN WELLS: Seat 25D. *Age:* 21. *Home:* Rye, NY. *Quote:* "People I haven't talked to in years reached out to me."

BRAD WENTZELL: Seat 21C. *Age:* 31. *Home:* Charlotte, NC. *Quote:* "It was the most helpless feeling I've ever had in my entire life. You're on something that's out of control, and little did I know there was someone who knew what they were doing who was controlling the uncontrollable. It's amazing."

JIM WHITAKER: Seat 19F. *Age:* 44. *Home:* Charlotte, NC. *Quote:* "The heroism part of the story certainly took a twist and became something special when we got to land. These first responders—it was not their first rodeo. These people were noble and special servants of their special person, one of us, and they were an incredible group. It was a fierce and highly capable and convicted group of people."

MICHAEL WHITESIDES: Seat 10B. *Age:* 37. *Home:* Dallas, NC. *Quote:* "It's given me three things: One, be ready every day; two, embrace every moment; and three, make a difference with your life."

WILLIAM WILEY: Seat 2F: *Age:* 52. *Home:* Johnson City, TN. *Quote:* "If Sullenberger had stalled out fifty feet above the water, everyone would have been killed. If he had been going much faster, everyone would have been killed. He had about ten miles per hour one way or the other to work with. It was truly beautiful."

BRAD WILLIAMS: Seat 1F. *Age:* 31. *Home:* Charlotte, NC. *Quote:* "Until it hit the water, it was a totally unremarkable experience."

REENEE WILLIAMS: Seat 24E. *Age:* 24. *Home:* Tallahassee, FL. *Quote:* "I saw the sunlight and said, 'Thank you, thank you so much. All I have to do is get out of this plane.'"

SUSAN WITTMANN: Seat 17C. *Age:* 57. *Home:* Charlotte, NC. *Quote:* "I don't like geese very much and never did, and like them less now."

BILL ZUHOWSKI: Seat 23E. *Age:* 23. *Home:* Mattituck, NY. *Quote:* "I've got a better outlook on life. I am in a better mood. I appreciate the smaller things more."

LAURA ZYCH: Seat 17D. *Age:* 30. *Home:* Charlotte, NC. *Quote:* "When I was rescued, I wasn't traumatized. I was more worried about people who were rescuing than I was about myself. When the ambulance crew was asking, 'Can you feel your fingers? Can you feel your toes?' I said, 'I'm okay, I'm used to this, I'm from Fargo.'"

Source Notes

The personal recollections of the passengers form the basis of this book. Among the 150 passengers on board, 118 candidly shared their most personal feelings and fears about the events on Flight 1549 in at least one detailed and often several follow-up interviews. The interviews were conducted between April and July of 2009 in Charlotte, New York, and Washington. These are the passengers who were interviewed.

Tracey Allen-Wolsko	Glenn Carlson	Wendell Fox
Derek Alter	Shae Childers	Nick Gamache
Keith Anthony	Remington Chin	Balaji Ganesan
Vicki Barnhardt	Brent Cimino	David Graham
Carl Bazarian	James Clark	Andrew Gray
Darren Beck	Chris Cobb	Linda Hahn
Alyson Bell	Vallie Collins	Joe Hall
Mary Berkwits	Laurie Crane	James Hanks, Jr.
Mike Berkwits	Kanau Deguchi	Tripp Harris
Fred Berretta	Michelle DePonte	Joe Hart
Craig Black	March Dolphin	Diane Higgins
Ben Bostic	Jennifer Doyle	Karin Hill
Maryann Bruce	Bill Elkin	Warren Holland
Billy Campbell	Lisa English	Mark Hood

Adelaide Horton

John Howell

Laurel Hubbard

Nico Iliev

Amy Jolly

Casey Jones

Donald Jones

Paul Jorgensen

Matt Kane

Heyam Kawas

Stephanie King

Mike Kollmansberger

Jeff Kolodjay

Theresa Leahy

Barry Leonard

Michael Leonard

Irina Levshina

Lori Lightner

Stephen Lis

Luther Lockhart

Denise Lockie

Alex Magness

Raymond Mandrell

James (Jay) McDonald

Beth McHugh

Gerry McNamara

Beverly Mills

Jorge Morgado

Brian Moss

Jenny Moulton

Freida Muscatell

Sheryl Nejman

Bill Nix

Don Norton

Michael Nunn

Steve O'Brien

Lucille Palmer

Josh Peltz

Clay Presley

Debbie Ramsey

Dick Richardson

Chris Rooney

Dave Sanderson

Robin Schoepf

Douglas Schrift

Molly Schugel

Frank Scudere

Pam Seagle

Jerry Shanko

Scott Sharkey

Eileen Shleffar

Alecia Shuford

Brian Siegel

Larry Snodgrass

Martin Sosa

Tess Sosa

Kristy Spears

Charles Spiggle

Eric Stevenson

Hiroki Takigawa

Ricardo Valeriano

Dan Vinton

Stewart Wallace

Victor Warnement

Beverly Waters

Amber Wells

Ian Wells

Brad Wentzell

Jim Whitaker

Michael Whitesides

Bill Wiley

Susan Wittmann

Bradley Williams

Reenee Williams

Bill Zuhowski

Laura Zych

The National Transportation Safety Board's investigation of Flight 1549 produced more than 3,500 pages of documents. In addition to investigative reports detailing the operation and behavior of the Airbus A320 involved in the accident, the files also contain:

• Air Traffic Control transcripts of radio calls between the pilots of Flight 1549 and air traffic controllers.

- The forty-seven-page cockpit voice recorder transcript of the pilots' conversations includes Capt. Chesley Sullenberger's PA announcement, "This is your captain. Brace for impact," as well as the flight attendants' safety briefing.
- Photographs of damage to the aircraft.
- A DVD of the Con Edison and coast guard videos of the impact and evacuation.
- Time line of the impact and evacuation.
- Official interviews of the flight crew and 143 of the 150 passengers on board, who are not identified by name.
- The Wildlife Factors Report, a study of geese populations near airports and a Smithsonian Institute DNA analysis of 69 bird fragments found on the accident aircraft or in its engines.
- The Meteorological Factual Report describing conditions on the Hudson River and weather on January 15, 2009.

The NTSB conducted a hearing about the accident on June 9, 10, and 11 in Washington. The investigation documents and transcripts of the hearing testimony are available on the NTSB website, www.ntsb.gov.

Seventy-five Tons over the Bronx

The first 9-1-1 call from the 9-1-1 transcript.

Air traffic controller Patrick Harten's instructions and thoughts from the air traffic control transcript and his testimony before U.S. House Transportation and Infrastructure Subcommitte on Aviation, February 24, 2009.

The government's immediate response, Al Baker, "Flight 1549—From New York to Norad, Testing a Response Network," *The New York Times*, February 8, 2009.

Crash of American Airlines Electra February 3, 1959, Morton M. Hunt, "A Reporter at Large: The Case of Flight 320," *The New Yorker*, April 30, 1960.

Economy and banking from widespread news reports in 2008–09.

Water landing of US Airways Flight 1549, National Transportation

Safety Board hearings June 9–11, 2009, and videos by Con Edison and the U.S. coast guard.

1 Come Fly with Me

The weather from the National Oceanic and Atmospheric Administration and local weather reports.

Delays at LaGuardia Airport from the NTSB hearing, ibid; Xinhua new agency, January 15, 2009; flight activity, John Toscano, "FAA to Keep Present Flight Activity Levels at LaGuardia," *Queens Gazette*, August 30, 2006.

The origins of LaGuardia Airport, H. John Jeffers, *The Napoleon of New York*, 2002, John Wiley and Sons (New York); other details, The Port Authority of New York and New Jersey.

Details about US Airways from "US Airways Files for Bankruptcy," *Consumer Affairs*, September 12, 2004.

Banking mergers and Charlotte economy, Peter Applebome, "Banking Lifts Charlotte, City on the Rise, to the Top," *The New York Times*, April 24, 1991; "Bank of America–Merrill Lynch: A $50 Billion Deal from Hell," *Wall Street Journal*, January 22, 2009; Kirsten Valle and Rick Rothaker, "Financial Crisis Has Battered Charlotte's Wealth, *Charlotte Observer*, February 2, 2009. Passenger interviews.

David Letterman Show, January 14, 2009, transcript.

US Airbus A320 N106US, 16,300th cycle from the NTSB Structures Group Chairman's Factual Report, May 12, 2009, pp. 2.

Boeing-Airbus rivalry, Peter Pae, "Airbus Stays No. 1 in Jet Sales, Edging out Boeing at Year-End," *Los Angeles Times*, January 18, 2006, and multiple articles about loss of Boeing dominance.

Eleventh in line for takeoff, the cockpit voice recorder and air traffic control transcripts.

Passenger travels from passenger interviews.

2 "One Thousand One, One Thousand Two, One Thousand Three"

The takeoff from the cockpit voice recorder transcript.

Rikers Island—Prison population, City of New York Department of

Corrections, 2008. Geese population, Glenn Collins, "Geese Pose Big Risk at Airports in Region," *The New York Times*, January 16, 2009.

Fear of flying figures, Gallup Poll, March 19, 2001.

Safety records and flights, Alan Levin, "Airlines go two years with no fatalities," *USA Today*, January 11, 2009.

Passenger Eric Stevenson's experience, "Crew Cuts Engines in Error, Sending Jetliner Toward Sea," *The New York Times*, July 2, 1987.

Xanax and Ambien as air passengers' companions, Alex Williams, "You are Cleared for Takeoff," *The New York Times*, September 07, 2006.

3 The Flight from Labrador

The Colgan Air crash, Matthew L. Wald and Liz Robbins, "50 Killed as Plane Hits House Near Buffalo," *The New York Times*, February 14, 2009; NTSB investigative reports.

Sullenberger and Skiles on seeing geese, from transcript of their interviews with NTSB investigators, January 17, 2009.

Speed, cockpit conversation from the cockpit voice recorder, testimony at NTSB hearing June 9–11, 2009.

General information on the number of aircraft collisions with birds, and the types of birds, from Orville Wright's collision in 1905, through 2008, can be found at Bird Strike Committee–USA and Bird Strike Committee International; www.birdstrike.org and www.int.birdstrike.org.

"Astronaut Dies in Trainer Crash," *The New York Times*, November 1, 1964.

Aircraft damage, NTSB hearings on US Airways Flight 1549, June 10–12, 2009.

"Ryanair jet makes emergency landing in Rome after birds sucked into engine," *The Guardian*, Nov. 10, 2008.

Vulnerability of A320 engines, NTSB hearings, June 8–10, 2009.

"Migratory Canada Geese Brought Down Flight 1549," June 8, 2009, Smithsonian.com.

Analysis that birds came originally from Labrador on a short midwinter flight and struck the plane laterally from "DNA Barcoding Suggests Migratory Canada Geese Caused Hudson River Crash," Birdstrike Control Program, June 8, 2009, birdstrike.control.com.

"Space shuttle hits vulture (2005)—Bye-bye, Birdies," June 30, 2006, www.space.com.

Migration habits of bar-headed geese over the Himalayas, "The High Life," *Audubon Magazine,* 2000.

The Chinese discovery of the H5N1 virus in bar-headed geese, "Avian flu: H5N1 virus outbreak in migratory waterfowl," *Nature,* July, 2005.

"Mortality of Geese as a Result of Collision with the Ground," *Journal of Wildlife Diseases,* 2005.

"The Next Big Natural Disaster," William Prochnau and Laura Parker, *Vanity Fair,* November, 2005, an article on avian flu, research including an interview with Professor Malik Pierus, a microbiologist at the Queen Mary Hospital at Hong Kong University, May 22, 2005.

"Runway Geese Called Cause of AWACS Crash," *Los Angeles Times,* January 12, 1996.

"Avian Flu Moves Among Wild Geese," BBC News, July 7, 2005.

4   The Bridge

Maneuvering of aircraft from testimony at the NTSB hearing, June 9–11, 2009.

Description of the George Washington Bridge from the Port Authority of New York and New Jersey: Bridges, www.panynj.gov.

The New York skyline and height of buildings from "New York's Tallest Buildings," www.discussny.com.

"This is your captain. Brace for impact" from the cockpit voice recorder transcript.

Passenger reactions from interviews with writers. Chris Rini's comment, Rick Minter, www.racintoday.com, April 22, 2009.

5   "Brace! Brace! Heads Down! Stay Down!"

"Brace! Brace! Heads down! Stay down!" from passenger interviews and flight attendants interviews with NTSB, January 16, 17, 2009, Survival Factors Report, pp. 5, 8, 10.

Silicon Valley of India, Sanjoy Hazarika, "In Southern India, a Glimpse of Asia's High-Tech Future," *The New York Times,* October 6, 1991.

Crash of Japan Air Lines Flight 123, Stanley Stewart, *Air Disasters,* Ian Allen Ltd (London), 1986. Ron Schleede, chief U.S. investigator at crash scene, interviews with authors, June 19, 2009, July 27, 2009; John W. Purvis, partner at Safety Services International and the Boeing Company's chief accident investigator at crash, interview with authors, September 7, 2009.

The crash of Ethiopian Airlines Flight 961, the 1996 FAA report, "Criminal Acts Against Civil Aviation," pp. 42–44; Interview, John W. Purvis. The tourist video of the ditching is available in various forms on YouTube and other websites.

Details of the 1982 Air Florida crash from the final NTSB report, August 10, 1982.

6 The Last Moments of Flight 1549

The Tupolev ditching, Matt Brown, "Last Safe Water Landing Was on Neva," *St. Petersburg Times,* January 20, 2009; "Tupolev 124 ditching in Neva River," NationMaster.com, March 2007. (Sources on the Neva landing are many but sketchy because of international relations at the time.)

The San Francisco Bay landing: Aircraft Accident Report, File No. A-0002, Japan Airlines, DC-8, San Francisco Bay, NTSB, December 31, 1969. (Captain Asoh's quick and colorful acceptance of blame became notable in many crisis-management books and studies, the best known being Jerry B. Harvey's semi-humorous *The Abilene Paradox and Other Meditations on Management,* 1988, Jossey-Bass (San Francisco).

The Northwest Airlines Flight 2 ditching, "33 Saved, Four Die in Plane Crash on Puget Sound," *The New York Times,* April 2, 1956.

The Pan American Flight 006 ditching, "All 31 Saved as Airliner Ditches in Pacific," *The New York Times,* Oct 17, 1956.

Footnote[1]—Videos by Con Edison and the U.S. Coast Guard; NTSB timing sequence analysis, "Survival Factors Report," p. 157.

Background on New York firefighter George DiPasquale, *Portraits: 9/11/01: The Collected "Portraits of Grief,"* from *The New York Times,* 2002, Times Books–Henry Holt (New York).

Eric Stevenson's experience on the 1987 Delta Airlines flight, ibid.

The cockpit computerized warning, *"Caution! Terrain!"* from the cockpit voice recorder, pp. 43–46.

7 A Crash in Weehawken, a Bow to New York

Details about the aircraft's impact from NTSB investigative reports.

The impact and moments afterward from passenger interviews. Passenger Chris Rini's description from www.racintoday.com.

Details about swimming in the Hudson from passenger interviews.

The timing from the NTSB analysis of the time stamp videos of the impact and evacuation, Survival Factors Report, p. 157.

The weight of the left engine, interview with Jamie Jewell, at CFM International, the engine manufacturer, July 23, 2009.

The Dec. 20, 2008, Continental Airlines accident in Denver, NTSB "Operations/Human Performance Factual Report," June 19, 2009.

8 Water, Water Everywhere

Details of passenger experiences from interviews and passenger Billy Campbell's NTSB hearing testimony June 9, 2009.

Flight attendant Doreen Welsh's instructions, "Turn around. . . . You have two minutes," multiple passenger interviews. Welsh's other descriptions from her January 17, 2009, statement to the NTSB.

The description of the impact on the river and the damage to the Airbus are from NTSB investigative documents, analyzed for the authors by Ron Schleede.

9 "Honey, I'm in the Hudson"

The evacuation from passenger interviews.

Details about life rafts, FAA regulations for extended over-water flights, and the 1962 ditching in Sitka Sound, Alaska, from the 1985 NTSB study, "Air Carrier Overwater Emergency Equipment and Procedures," NTSB Chairman Deborah A.P. Hersman to the authors on August 7, 2009.

A description of the rescue response and the comment by Philip Zelikow are contained in the "Flight 1549: From New York to Norad, Testing a Response Network," *The New York Times,* February 8, 2009.

The New York Police Department response, interview, retired NYPD Lt. Ken Solosky, September 1, 2009; interview in New York, rescue diver, Detective Michael Delaney, May 14, 2009.

The New York City Fire Department response from Michael Buckheit in "US Airways Flight 1549: New York Marine Operations," *Fire Engineering,* July 1, 2009; and professionalmariner.com, April, 2009. Chief John Peruggia response, Michael Wilson and Al Baker in "A Quick Rescue Kept Death Toll at Zero," *The New York Times* January 16, 2009. The commandeering of the Circle Line tour boat from Corey Kilgannon, "A Detour on the Circle Line Trip," *The New York Times,* January 16, 2009.

Con Edison's Chris Simeone video taping from Ty Chandler at ny1.com, January 23, 2009.

New Jersey Battalion Chief Michael Cranwell response, "US Airways Flight 1549: New Jersey Rescue Operations," *Fire Engineering*, July 1, 2009.

Information about New York Waterway from the company interviews between May and August, 2009; interviews with former ferry captain Michael Starr on May 8, July 22, and July 23, 2009. Deckhand Natale Binetti's reaction, Teri Thompson, Alison Gendar and Bill Hutchinson, "Ferry Changed Course to Save," the New York *Daily News*, January 16, 2009. Ferry captain Vince Lombardi response, Seafarers International Union LOG, February, 2009. Ferry captain Brittany Catanzaro's description of the Airbus looking like a bathtub toy, Ashley Kindergan, "Young captain reacts like 'seasoned pro,'" NorthJersey.com, January 16, 2009.

Tugboat CO salvage work, professionalmariner.com, April, 2009.

Scott Koen, interview in New York, May 13, 2009.

The U.S. Coast Guard rescue, interviews in New York with coast

guardsmen Jessica Wolchak, Ben Foster, Von Rankin, Ian Kennedy, and
Barbara Patton, May 14, 2009.

10 The Hudson Swim Team

Details of swim in the Hudson River from passenger interviews.

Description of the dents on the Airbus nose from NTSB photographs.

Details of the 1982 Air Florida crash, Structures Group Report, p. 3
NTSB final report, August 10, 1982.

Effects of cold shock response and hypothermia, interviews, author,
with Doctor Alan Steinman, a retired U.S. Coast Guard physician, June 3,
2009, July 17, 2009.

11 Wing Walkers

Descriptions of the experience on the wings from passenger interviews.

Fulmer Duckworth's observations, "What Happened on Flight 1549,
Inside and Out," *The New York Times,* January 15, 2009.

12 All Aboard

Details about the evacuation from passenger interviews.

The *Titanic* radio operator's testimony to Congress, "Thrilling Tales by
Titanic's Surviving Wireless Man," *The New York Times,* April 19, 1912,
and "In A Maze of Flashes Two Messages Were United to Make the Erro-
neous One," *The New York Times,* April 21, 1912.

The 1956 Northwest Airlines Flight 2 ditching, ibid.

The arrival times of the ferries from an NTSB time analysis, ibid.

The Twitter photo, www.twitpic.com, January 15, 2009; Lauren John-
ston and Matt Marrone, "Twitter user becomes a star in US Airways crash—
Janis Krums sets Internet abuzz with iPhone photo," The New York *Daily
News,* January 16, 2009.

Fire department chief Chief John Peruggia's reaction, Michael Wilson
and Al Baker in "A Quick Rescue Kept Death Toll at Zero," ibid.

13 Saving Shae

The rescue of Shae Childers, interviews with Childers, New York police diver Michael Delaney, and other passengers. Childers provided details from her medical records.

The sequencing of the ferries was calculated on the Con Edison video. The description of the ferries at the scene, interview with former ferry captain Michael Starr, July 23, 2009.

Heyam Kawas's rescue, from interviews with Kawas and Delaney.

14 "Throw the Baby"

The rescue of nine-month-old Damian Sosa, interviews with passenger, Scott Koen, and Michael Starr, whose ferry carried the Sosa family to Weehawken.

Details of the rescue of the last passengers, interviews with coast guardsmen Jessica Wolchak, Ben Foster, Von Rankin, Ian Kennedy, and Barbara Patton in New York, May 14, 2009.

15 Night in New York

Details of the scene in New York from passenger interviews.

New York Gov. David Paterson declared that the accident was "a miracle on the Hudson" at a live news conference at the New York Waterway ferry terminal in Manhattan on January 15, 2009.

The passenger injuries, passenger interviews and an NTSB injury chart.

Fame, Faith, and Fear of Flying

Passenger experiences from their interviews.

The salvage and inspection of the Airbus from the NTSB Structure Group Factual Report.

The Colgan Air crash details from NTSB transcripts of the hearing into the crash, held May 12–14, 2009; the NTSB "Operations Group Factual Report," April 22, 2009, and other investigative reports.

The June 1, 2009, Air France accident, Daniel Michaels and Max Colchester, "Air France Jet Hit Water Largely Intact, Investigators Say," *Wall Street Journal,* July 3, 2009: Donald G. McNeil, Jr., and Christine Negroni, "Search Is On for Wreckage of Missing Air France Jet," *The New York Times,* June 2, 2009.

The June 30, 2009 Yemenia Airlines crash, Xan Rice, "Yemenia plane crash: girl survives as jet carrying 153 plunged into ocean," the *Guardian,* June 30, 2009; Victoria Burnett, "Yemenia Crash Stirs Calls for Stronger Watchdogs," *The New York Times,* July 3, 2009.

The airline fatality toll was compiled by Flight International, a weekly aviation magazine published in Britain, and reported in multiple news accounts, including "Air disaster death toll worst in seven years," dailyrecord .com, July 22, 2009.

Details about the closure of Arthur's Landing, New York Waterway, the owner.

Coastal fires in South Carolina, the Associated Press, the *Winston-Salem Journal*, April 24, 2009.

The Miracle on the Hudson Survivors, LLC was formed to write this book and includes eighty-one members:

Tracey Allen-Wolsko	Vallie Collins	Adelaide Horton
Keith Anthony	Laurie Crane	John Howell
Carl Bazarian	Michelle DePonte	Laurel Hubbard
Alyson Bell	Jennifer Doyle	Nico Iliev
Mary Berkwits	Lisa English	Amy Jolly
Mike Berkwits	Wendell Fox	Casey Jones
Ben Bostic	Nick Gamache	Donald Jones
David Carlos	Balaji Ganesan	Paul Jorgensen
Shae Childers	Andrew Gray	Stephanie King
Remington Chin	Joe Hall	Jeff Kolodjay
James Clark	James Hanks, Jr.	Robert Kolodjay
Chris Cobb	Tripp Harris	Theresa Leahy

Michael Leonard

Irina Levshina

Stephen Lis

Denise Lockie

Alex Magness

Raymond Mandrell

James (Jay) McDonald

Beverly Mills

Jorge Morgado

Brian Moss

Freida Muscatell

Sheryl Nejman

Bill Nix

Michael Nunn

Steve O'Brien

Josh Peltz

Clay Presley

Robin Schoepf

Douglas Schrift

Molly Schugel

Frank Scudere

Pam Seagle

Scott Sharkey

Eileen Shleffar

Brian Siegel

Larry Snodgrass

Damian Sosa

Martin Sosa

Sofia Sosa

Tess Sosa

Kristy Spears

Charles Spiggle

Jim Stefanik

Eric Stevenson

Dan Vinton

Stewart Wallace

Victor Warnement

Beverly Waters

Ian Wells

Jim Whitaker

Bill Wiley

Bradley Williams

Reenee Williams

Susan Wittmann

Laura Zych

Acknowledgments

The passengers of Flight 1549 would like to offer our sincere and eternal gratitude to Captain Chesley 'Sully' Sullenberger and First Officer Jeffrey Skiles. Their bravery, quick decisions, and uncompromised skills have given us all a "miracle."

To flight attendants Sheila Dail, Donna Dent, and Doreen Welsh, thank you for your stoicism and calm demeanor in the moments before impact and your quick actions and level-headed thinking after. We are so grateful to have had you on board with us.

We are indebted to the first responders, including but not limited to: New York Waterway, Circle Line, Coast Guard, FDNY and NYPD, and New Jersey State Police and emergency workers, the local Red Cross, the individual citizens, and everyone who played a role in our rescue.

We would like to thank Jennifer Joel at ICM, who has been a wonderful support to us in the last few months, helping us navigate the publishing world. Her grace is unparalleled, as are her smarts.

Acknowledgments

Thank you to all the known and unknown people who prayed for us and kept us in their thoughts. Through your prayers we have found incredible encouragement.

Last, to all of our families, friends, and loved ones who anguished when first learning of our situation, who celebrated with us upon our rescue, and who live with the "new" us each and every day. We love you all and are so grateful to still be with you.

Author's Acknowledgments

First and foremost we want to thank the passengers of US Airways Flight 1549. Your time, your trust, and your understanding of the complexity of this undertaking, especially in its tight time frame, was beyond what we ever could have expected from a wonderfully diverse group. We talked with 118 of you, usually at great length and often several times. These conversations required painful recountings of an almost indescribable moment in your lives. We knew that. You were superb.

Among you we especially thank, warmly and with admiration, Pam Seagle and Casey Jones, who proved day after day to be persons of social and managerial talents nonpareil. Without you, this would not have happened.

Ron Schleede, our aviation guru and the most knowledgeable investigator of aviation accidents we have ever known, spent hours with us on details to keep us from committing technical blunders. If any errors slipped past, they are entirely ours.

At the National Transportation Safety Board, Ted Lopatkiewicz, Peter

Acknowledgments

Knudson, Jason Fedok, and Nora Marshall provided valuable assistance on innumerable technical details.

Our good friend and superb journalist, Lisa Zagaroli, put in long hours sifting through the interviews, and Alan Levin generously gave advice and counsel.

For all the interviewing and coordination required for this project we would be greatly remiss if we did not acknowledge the help of Shelby Blackmore, Jennifer Peterson, Hughon Haye, Kseniia Shteinburg, and David Callihan in Charlotte.

Writers can't survive without thoughtful and patient editors of creative skill and a nose for a passive verb. We were unusually fortunate in having at our side, Luke Dempsey, editorial director for nonfiction, and Ryan Doherty at Ballantine Books. We also thank Shona McCarthy, the production editor at Random House Publishing Group, for unusual patience and all her hard work.

At our talent agency, International Creative Management in New York, thanks go to Laura Neely, Nicki Castle, and Joan Weist for valuable assistance of many kinds with the New York interviews. Within the agency, special thanks go to agents we often pressed to the limit on deadlines. Liz Farrell is one.

As always, we can find no way to sing higher praises about our lifelong friend and world-class personal agent at ICM, Kris Dahl. Thanks.

Finally, we give special and loving thanks to those who give the greatest sustenance and sometimes pay the highest price for having writers as kin.

So thank you: to all of the Parker and Prochnau family members who lost our annual get-together and hoedown at Lopez Island in the San Juans for the first time in twenty years and especially to Jesse, Melissa, and Sarah for missing a tradition they have known their entire lives. To Bruce Parker, Shirley Parker, Monica Bradley, Anna Prochnau, and Jenny McMaster for opportunities we missed. To Natasha Prochnau for understanding.

William Prochnau
Laura Parker
Washington, D.C.
August, 2009

About the Authors

WILLIAM PROCHNAU and LAURA PARKER write collaborative articles for *Vanity Fair,* where Prochnau is a contributing editor. Prochnau, a former national correspondent for *The Washington Post,* has written three acclaimed books including *Once Upon A Distant War.* Parker covered aviation for *The Washington Post,* and later spent ten years as a national correspondent at *USA Today.* She has been awarded the Patterson and Nieman fellowships.